A Lifetime of Genesis

A Lifetime of Genesis

An Exploration of and Personal Journey Through the Covenant of Abraham in Genesis

Henry A. Zoob

WIPF & STOCK · Eugene, Oregon

A LIFETIME OF GENESIS
An Exploration of and Personal Journey Through the Covenant
of Abraham in Genesis

Copyright © 2016 Henry A. Zoob. All rights reserved. Except for brief quotations in critical publications or reviews, no part of this book may be reproduced in any manner without prior written permission from the publisher. Write: Permissions, Wipf and Stock Publishers, 199 W. 8th Ave., Suite 3, Eugene, OR 97401.

Wipf & Stock
An Imprint of Wipf and Stock Publishers
199 W. 8th Ave., Suite 3
Eugene, OR 97401

www.wipfandstock.com

PAPERBACK ISBN: 978-1-4982-9505-5
HARDCOVER ISBN: 978-1-4982-9507-9
EBOOK ISBN: 978-1-4982-9506-2

Manufactured in the U.S.A.

To Barbara

Thanks for over five decades
of love and support

Contents

Acknowledgments | ix
Introductory Notes | xi
Notes on Hebrew Transliteration | xiii
Introduction | xv

Chapter 1: Genesis and The Purpose of Creation | 1
Chapter 2: The Purpose of Our Lives | 8
Chapter 3: God's Call to Abraham Initiates the Covenant | 19
Chapter 4: My Call to the Rabbinate | 32
Chapter 5: Abraham's Journey from Doubt to Faith | 40
Chapter 6: Our Difficult Journey to Parenthood | 50
Chapter 7: The Covenant Between the Pieces and the Covenant of Circumcision | 58
Chapter 8: Our Son's Inspirational Bris | 69
Chapter 9: The Testing of Abraham | 77
Chapter 10: The Test of Leaving My Father's House | 88
Chapter 11: Isaac Puts Down Roots in the Land of Canaan | 94
Chapter 12: How I Came to Love Israel and Its People | 102
Chapter 13: Jacob Stays the Course | 111
Chapter 14: Wrestling with My Brother and Depression | 130
Chapter 15: The Matriarchs and the Covenant | 141

CONTENTS

Chapter 16: My Mother the Matriarch | 157
Chapter 17: Joseph, The Saving Covenantal Link | 165
Chapter 18: My Commitment to Jewish Messianism | 173

Addendum 1: Divine Covenants in the Bible | 181
Addendum 2: Sh'mini Atzeret—Simchat Torah in Reform Judaism | 184
Addendum 3: The Documentary Hypothesis | 187

Bibliography | 189

Acknowledgments

I RETIRED FROM THE pulpit in 2006. One of many things I wanted to do in retirement was to write a book. Ten years later, I am ready to remove this task from my bucket list. As expected, I got sidetracked over the decade on other projects, including a lengthy article entitled "A Positive Perspective on the Three Embarrassing Wife-Sister Stories in Genesis," published in the 2014 fall edition of the CCAR Quarterly Journal. I have also been tutoring homeless children in the Brockton and Randolph schools for SOWMA, Schools On Wheels Massachusetts. Perhaps the most joyful and fun activity in retirement has been playing and reading with our grandchildren, Lexi, age three and a half, and Jordan, age one. Lexi loves me to read *Knuffle Bunny Too* again and again. Jordan has yet to settle on a favorite book to read with his Saba.

So, now the book is finally finished. I have learned a tremendous amount about Genesis, which I consider the greatest book ever written. My book, *A Lifetime of Genesis: An Exploration of and Personal Journey Through the Covenant of Abraham in the Book of Genesis*, has been a difficult challenge. For thirty-six years I wrote a monthly bulletin article for my temple. It usually took me an hour to write my "From the Rabbi's Study" article. Why would a book be that much more difficult? Well it was, in too many ways for me to write about.

There were a number of people who helped tighten up my writing as well as provide guidance in regard to the content. I'd like to thank them.

First of all, I want to thank my Beth David congregants. In our two year adult education study of Genesis, time and again we discovered that the Covenant of Abraham provides the unifying focus for our discussion

Acknowledgments

of Genesis. Indeed, there were many occasions when we were in search of understanding that we came to the conclusion, "It's the covenant, stupid!"

Secondly, many thanks to Judith Robbins, a Harvard/Radcliffe '61 classmate, a long time teacher of English at the Winsor School in Boston, the daughter of Jewish pioneers in Westwood, Dr. Alexander and Mrs. Yetta Fisher, and most importantly a good friend. During the last two years, Judith helped me smooth out my writing and improve my argument.

Others who have helped by making suggestions or by reading my manuscript in various stages are Rabbis Deanna Douglas, Joseph Meszler and Donald Splansky. Dr. Jonathan Imber, a congregant, friend, and professor of Sociology at Wellesley College offered advice on my manuscript, and Betsy Wice, a veteran teacher in the public schools of Philadelphia and the wife of my classmate and friend David Wice, also offered her counsel. My thanks to Anita Diamant who offered some helpful advice and to my friend Richard Reich for taking a promotional photo of me for the book. An additional word of appreciation to two rabbinic colleagues—Larry Kushner, who suggested my title *A Lifetime of Genesis*, and Ken Roseman who directed me to my wonderful publishers, Wipf and Stock.

Most importantly, my wife Barbara offered many excellent suggestions as to what to include and what to remove. She has an uncanny ability to help weed out that which is extraneous. It's somewhat difficult for a spouse to provide dispassionate criticism, but she did it in style.

Finally, I pray that *A Lifetime of Genesis* may help you, the reader, find a greater appreciation of the significance of the Covenant of Abraham and the lives of our covenanted Patriarchs and Matriarchs for your own life.

Henry A. Zoob
Westwood, MA
June 30, 2016
24 Sivan, 5776

Introductory Notes

Translations of Biblical Text

For the most part, I use the translation of Genesis from *Tanakh, The Holy Scriptures* (Jewish Publication Society: Philadelphia, 1985) which I identify as NJPS—the New Jewish Pubication Society translation. If no citation is listed for a biblical translation, I have used the NJPS. Please note that when the word "Lord" appears in the NJPS translation, I have used the tetragramaton YHVH, the four letter name for the God of Israel from the original Hebrew text. On occasion, I use the euphemism that the Rabbis ascribed to YHVH—*Adonai*. When other translations are used, such as Everett Fox's *The Five Books of Moses* published by Schocken in 1995, or my own translation, I indicate as such in a footnote.

The Usage of the Names Abraham and Sarah

In Genesis 17, God changes the names of the first patriarch and matriarch from Abram to Abraham and from Sarai to Sarah. To avoid confusion, I employ the names Abraham and Sarah throughout this book. But when passages from Genesis that precede Genesis 17 are quoted, I retain the names Abram and Sarai, as they occur in the text.

The Use of Gender Neutral Language

Except for a few biblical quotations, I have tried to use gender neutral language in reference to God throughout this book.

Introductory Notes

Abbreviations

ANET	Ancient Near Eastern Texts
BCE	Before the Common Era, before 0 AD
CE	The Common Era, after 0 AD
BT	Babylonian Talmud
HUC-JIR	Hebrew Union College-Jewish Institute of Religion
JPS	Jewish Publication Society.
NJPS	New Jewish Publication Society translation of the Hebrew Bible.
UAHC	Union of American Hebrew Congregations
URJ	Union for Reform Judaism
z"l	*zichrono/zichronah livrachah* "May his/her memory be for a blessing"

Notes on Hebrew Transliteration

WHEREVER I HAVE TRANSLITERED Hebrew in my book, I have put the transliteration in italics. My transliterations are according to the table of consonants below. I developed this system with the objective of helping the reader to best understand the pronounciation of the word according to the Sephardic tradition while maintaining a fairly accurate record of the Hebrew spelling. (My system does not include a method of indicating the two silent letters, *aleph* and *ayin*.) All Hebrew names that are not in italics follow the spelling of the NJPS translation of the Bible, e.g., Terah, Rebekah, Noah, etc. The spelling of some Hebrew words have become so common in the Jewish world that in certain instances I do not follow the table below. Examples are words like *tz'dakah* (righteousness or charitable giving) rather than *tz'daqah* and *tikkun olam* (repair of the world) rather than *tiqqun olam*.

Transliterated Consonants

א	no sign	ט	t	פ	p
בּ	b	י	y	פ	ph
ב	v	כ	k	צ	tz
ג	g	כ	ch	ק	q
ד	d	ל	l	ר	r
ה	h	מ	m	שׁ	sh
ו	v	נ	n	שׂ	s
ז	z	ס	s	ת	t
ח	ch	ע	no sign		

Introduction

OF ALL THE BOOKS in the Hebrew Bible, the first book, Genesis, is the most well known. Its universal appeal stems from its compelling narrative, its importance to Jews and Christians concerning the origins of their faith, and its relevance to the basic questions of human existence.

In the last two years of my thirty-six-year rabbinate at Temple Beth David of Westwood, MA, I taught an adult education course on Genesis. As my students and I examined the ancient stories of our beginnings, it became clear to us that the Covenant of Abraham, the contract that God initiates with the first patriarch and renews with Isaac and Jacob, is the primary focus of the book of Genesis. To my knowledge, none of the contemporary Jewish studies of Genesis sufficiently highlight the thematic centrality of the Covenant of Abraham in Genesis. This observation led to *the first of my two major objectives in writing this book—the explication of the structure, content, and significance of the Covenant of Abraham in Genesis,* an objective that calls for a close analysis of the lives of the Patriarchs and their covenantal relationship with God. I also include studies of the Matriarchs and Joseph, because even though God does not establish specific covenants with them, they make signficant contributions to the continuity of the Covenant of Abraham. A rewarding byproduct of my analysis of the Covenant of Abraham is a thorough portrayal of the character and personality of each patriarch and matriarch, as well as Joseph.

Beginning with chapter 1 and continuing with *the odd-numbered chapters* up to chapter 17, I concentrate on my initial objective, the explication of the Covenant of Abraham in Genesis. Aided by teachings from Jewish medieval commentary and modern biblical scholarship, these chapters

Introduction

retell and analyze the life stories of the protagonists of Genesis as they relate to the covenant.

My second major objective is an exploration of the lives of the Patriarchs, Matriarchs, and Joseph, as a source of understanding and inspiration for my own struggles and joys, failures and achievements. By sharing connections between my life and the lives of my biblical ancestors who lived in covenant with God, I hope to encourage the reader to look for a similar experience of self-discovery in his/her encounter with the covenantal heroes and heroines of Genesis.

Relevant to my second objective, it is important to note that all of the protagonists of Genesis are portrayed as real human beings with their weaknesses alongside their more attractive features. The Rabbis in the Midrash (Midrash refers to Rabbinic collections of legal and homiletical interpretations of the biblical text from 300 BCE to 1500 CE) evince some discomfort with the realistic depiction of our ancestors in the Bible. A clear example is their understanding of Jacob, the third patriarch, who is most often portrayed in the Midrash as totally righteous, while his brother Esau is described as the inveterate wicked twin.[1] This one-sided Rabbinic characterization is not in accord with the text of the Tanach[2] where we find that Jacob's actions seem at times dubious, such as when he manipulates Esau

---

1. An example of the Rabbinic stereotyping of Jacob and Esau occurs in a famous midrash which seeks to explain why, in Gen. 25:22, the twins struggle within the womb of their mother Rebekah. According to *Genesis Rabbah* 63:6, when Rebekah passes by a synagogue or school, the pious Jacob tries to get out, but when she goes by a pagan temple, the idolatrous Esau struggles to emerge. The Rabbis often refer to Esau as "the wicked Esau" (e.g., *Genesis Rabbah* 65:15). Esau is further demonized by identifying him with the oppressive Romans, as in the Rabbinic interpretation of Jacob's exclamation in Gen. 27:22 "the voice is the voice of Jacob, but the hands are the hands of Esau." A paraphrase of their interpretation from *Genesis Rabbah* 65:21 follows: Rabbi Yohannan said that "the voice of Jacob" refers to the slaughtered Judeans, who were *crying out* at their suffering at "the hands of Esau," the accursed Hadrian and his troops, who slew eighty thousand at Bethar (a reference to the Roman slaughter of Jews in the Bar Kochba rebellion at the conclusive battle of Bethar in 135 CE). Rabbinic prejudice against Esau may also arise from his identification as the ancestor of the cruel Amalekites (Gen. 36:12) who attacked the rear of the Israelites in the wilderness where the weakest members of the group marched (Dt. 25:17–18). The Rabbis, however, are not totally blind to Jacob's faults. For example, they take him to task for delaying his return home from Haran (twenty years) to fulfill the vow he made to establish an abode for God at Bethel and to tithe all the wealth that he accrued in Haran (*Tanchuma* 8.22).

2. Tanach is an acronym for the three sections of the Hebrew Bible: *Torah, N'vi-im, K'tuvim*—Torah, Prophets, and Writings.

INTRODUCTION

into selling his birthright for a bowl of lentil stew,[3] and later, when with the help of his mother, he deceives his father, Isaac, in order to steal the blessing of the first born.[4] Conversely, Esau, the so-called wicked son, displays a generous spirit when, after a twenty-year separation, he runs to embrace Jacob and then encourages Jacob and his entire household to visit him in his home territory of Seir.[5]

In contrast with the Rabbis, I appreciate the candid biblical portrayal of our ancestors in Genesis and believe that the balanced biblical outlook on the founders of our people has contributed to making Genesis one of the most significant writings in Western civilization. If our biblical ancestors in Genesis had been described as perfect, we would not be drawn to their life stories, nor could we learn from their experiences. We are vitally interested in them, not only because like all people, we yearn to connect with our roots, but because their lives in many respects are similar to our own. In addition, when we observe the determination, faith, and courage of the Patriarchs and Matriarchs, as they strive to overcome their human weaknesses to meet the challenge of maintaining the covenant, we can be inspired to live meaningful Jewish lives which contribute to the continuity of our ancient pact with God.

All of the nine *even-numbered chapters* in *A Lifetime of Genesis,* starting with chapter 2 and continuing up to chapter 18, are devoted to my second objective, the task of relating the challenges, attitudes, experiences, and achievements of the leading personalities in Genesis to my own life. Each of these even-numbered chapters contains an autobiographical essay which, in the manner of midrash, draws on an inspirational aspect of the life of the biblical personality highlighted in the preceding chapter.

Peter Pitzelle's work *Our Fathers' Wells* and Rabbi Norman Cohen's two books, *Self, Struggle and Change* and *Voices from Genesis* have already provided relevant perspectives on the protagonists in Genesis that can help us discover meaning in our relationships with God, our family members, and others. I have had a number of opportunities to study with Rabbi Cohen in my synagogue and at rabbinic retreats, and it is clear to me that by encouraging me to look at the lives of the heroes and heroines of Genesis as a source of personal insight, his teachings became a catalyst for the writing of this book. Ultimately, my hope is that *A Lifetime of Genesis* adds

3. Gen. 25:29–34
4. Gen. 27.
5. Gen. 33:4, 12–16.

to Cohen and Pitzelle's endeavors of looking to our founding Fathers and Mothers as a source of personal inspiration and self-discovery.

A final introductory note: my understanding of how Genesis came to be is that our ancestors who authored the Torah included sagas based on oral legends about God and their forefathers and foremothers in order to provide inspirational connections with their past and moral guidance for themselves and their descendants. I also firmly believe that their writings are infused with the spirit of God. Despite our inability to confirm the historicity of the events of Genesis, I would argue that much of what is described could have actually happened, because the description of the customs and happenings are consistent with the traditions of the ancient Near East during the second millennium BCE, an era which coincides with the Patriarchal period.[6] In addition, I and many other Jews who grew up hearing stories about Abraham and Sarah and their immediate successors, experience the protagonists of Genesis as real people. I have therefore written about the events of their lives as if they actually took place, because from my perspective they did. Indeed, Abraham, Isaac, and Jacob, Sarah, Rebekah, Rachel and Leah are very real to me. I feel that they are part of the historical and genetic legacy that helped make me what I am today.

---

6. See Speiser, *The Anchor Bible Genesis,* and Sarna, *Understanding Genesis,* where both scholars often cite Mesopotamian traditions from the second millennium BCE as fundamental for understanding the events in the lives of the Patriarchs and Matriarchs.

CHAPTER 1

Genesis and the Purpose of Creation

God Creates Humanity In Order to Witness Righteousness

According to the Rabbis, God agonized over the decision to create human beings. The Holy One thought, "If I create humanity, their descendants will be wicked; but if I do not create humanity, how are the righteous to be born?" What did the Holy One do? God disregarded the wicked who were to come and called on [God's] attribute of Mercy, "Let us (God and God's Mercy) fashion a human being . . ." (Gen. 1:26).[1] And so, God created humanity because the Eternal's hope for *human righteousness* prevailed over God's foreknowledge that humans would turn to wrongdoing.

Following Creation, God Looks for Righteousness but Encounters Evil

The midrash cited above, in which God deliberates over the pros and cons of creating humanity, is the Rabbis' response to the central theme of the first eleven chapters of Genesis—the persistence of human evil. Following

---

1. *Genesis Rabbah* 8:4. In the very next midrash, *Genesis Rabbah* 8:5, the Rabbis imagine that the angels argue over whether humans should be created. In the midst of the debate, God casts the Angel of Truth, who is opposed to creating human beings, to the ground, so that the Eternal can momentarily overlook humanity's shortcomings to allow for the creation of human beings and the possibility for the righteous to come into existence.

Creation, the four major introductory stories covering the era of primordial human history[2]—Adam and Eve, Cain and Abel, Noah and the Flood, and the Tower of Babel—comprise an account of human beings who continually frustrate God's desire for righteousness and obedience to the divine will. In the initial story, God grants Adam and Eve the opportunity to live in the Garden of Eden provided they refrain from eating the fruit of a single tree, the Tree of Knowledge. By eating from it, they break the only divine command they were given and are expelled from Eden. In the second story, Cain murders his brother Abel and indicts himself before God with the rhetorical question, "Am I my brother's keeper?"[3] He too is exiled from his home and sent off to be a wanderer. In Noah's generation, the whole earth becomes so corrupt that God is moved to destroy "all flesh"[4] and to start anew with Noah and his family.

The exact nature of the rebellion against God in the fourth major primordial story, the Tower of Babel, is not clearly stated. The legend involves settlers from the east who come upon a valley in the land of Shinar. They decide to build "a city and a tower with its top in the sky."[5] Since one of their explicit goals is to "make a name"[6] for themselves, perhaps building a skyscraper is an act of hubris, an attempt to achieve fame by breaching God's heavenly abode. Benno Jacob (1862–1945), a German rabbi and biblical commentator, offers a different rationale. He identifies the transgression of the builders of Babel as pitting themselves against God's directive to the first man and woman at Creation: "Be fertile and increase, *umilu et ha-aretz* fill the earth and master it."[7] Following the Flood, when God re-creates the world,[8]

---

2. From the biblical perspective, the primordial era begins with Creation and comes to an end with the birth of Abraham.

3. Gen. 4:9.

4. Gen. 6:13.

5. Gen. 11:4.

6. Gen. 11:4.

7. Gen. 1:28. Jacob, *First Book of the Bible, Genesis*, 78–79 (hereafter cited as Jacob, *Genesis*).

8. In Genesis 9, immediately following the Flood, we encounter words and phrases drawn from the Creation story in Genesis 1, suggesting that God is initiating a second Creation. For example, Gen. 1:28 "And God blessed them (the first man and woman) and God said to them *p'ru ur'vu umilu et ha-aretz* 'Be fruitful and multiply, fill the earth'..." is mirrored in Gen. 9:1 "And God blessed Noah and his sons saying to them, 'Be fruitful and multiply and fill the earth.'" The phrase *kol chayyat ha-aretz* "every land animal" from Gen. 1:30 also occurs in Gen. 9:2, 10, and the root *shin-reish-tzadi* which describes the swarming or abounding of creatures in the water on the fifth day of Creation—*yishr'tzu*

Genesis and the Purpose of Creation

we find almost the exact same words in God's charge to Noah, "Be fertile and increase, *umilu et ha-aretz* fill the earth."[9] But the succeeding generation, the builders of Babel, reject God's standing command to "*fill the earth*." Instead, they decide to construct a "city and a tower" in the hope that the concentrating effect of their new urban structures will hold them together.

> Come, let us build a city and a tower with its top in the sky,
> to make a name for ourselves
> *else we shall be scattered over all the world.*
>
> Genesis 11:4

God's response to their rebellious attempt to resist being "scattered" is to do just what the builders feared—disperse them over the face of the earth and mix up their languages so that they remain scattered.[10] The Hebrew root *nun-pei-tzadi* "to scatter" occurs in three separate verses in this nine verse story. The frequency of this verbal root supports Benno Jacob's contention that the central issue is the tension between God's intent on *scattering* the rebels so that they "fill the earth" (Gen. 11:8, 9) as opposed to the builders' desire to resist being *scattered* (Gen. 11:4). A divine preference for rural over urban life seems to lie beneath this tension, which leads to the supposition that the semi-nomadic existence of the Hebrews is to be preferred over life in the capital city of Babylon.

There is also a brief reference to another story of human misconduct in the first eleven chapters of Genesis, the tale of the overly vengeful Lamech who brags about slaying "a man for wounding me, and a lad for bruising me."[11] Lamech goes on to boast "if Cain is avenged sevenfold, then Lamech seventy-sevenfold."[12] Lamech's excessive vengeance echoes the pattern of the four major episodes outlined above—human beings behaving badly.

---

and *sheretz nephesh* in Gen. 1:20, and *shar'tzu* in Gen. 1:21—reappears in Gen. 9:7 when God commands Noah *shirtzu va-aretz* "abound on the earth."

9. Gen. 9:1.

10. Gen. 11:8–9. The Babylonians understood the name of their sacred city *Bab-ilim* to mean the "gate of the god" with its great *ziggurat* (cultic tower) as the nexus to heaven. The bibical Tower of Babel story, in addition to providing another example of primoridal human rebellion against God, is an Israelite jab at the famous city of Babylon and its great tower. Thus, the story in Genesis concludes with the word play that the name of the city is *Bavel* because there God *balal* "mixed up or confounded" their speech, making it a city of babbling confusion.

11. Gen. 4:23.

12. Gen. 4:24.

The Decline In Primordial Human Longevity Reflects God's Displeasure

The first ten generations of biblical progenitors, from Adam to Noah, are described as remarkably long-lived. Seven of these antediluvians (those who lived prior to the Flood)—Adam, Seth, Enosh, Kenan, Jared, Methuselah, and Noah—live longer than 900 years, the oldest being Methuselah who dies at the age of 969. The three who live less than 900 years are Mehalalel, who lives for 895 years, Lamech, who dies after 777 years, and Enoch, who is "taken by God" at the age of 365.[13] These exceptionally long life spans are in accord with the "folkloristic notion that associates ancient heroes with extraordinary longevity."[14]

After Noah is born in the tenth generation, we read of the strange mythic incident in which "divine beings" (angels) marry and cohabit with the "daughters of men," a trespass which leads to God's shortening of the human life span.

> Now as people began to multiply on the earth,
> daughters were born to them.
> And when the divine beings (angels) saw
> how fair were the human women
> they took wives for themselves, as they chose.
> Then the Eternal One said, "My spirit will not forever endure the humans,
> as they are but fallible flesh—their lifespan shall be [only] 120 years."
> The Nephilim were on earth in those days; and afterward, too,
> When the divine beings mated with the human women,
> They bore for them those heroes
> who from old enjoyed great renown.[15]
>
> Genesis 6:1–4

At the outset, we should note that this mysterious partial story is another example of the prevailing theme of negative behavior that we encountered in the four major stories about primordial humanity, except here, it is misconduct on the part of the angels. Nahum Sarna of Brandeis (1923–2005) makes

---

13. See Genesis 5 for the listing of all these ages except for that of Noah, whose life span in Gen. 9:28 is recorded as 950 years which includes 350 years of life after the Flood.

14. Sarna, *JPS Commentary on Genesis* (hereafter referred to as *JPS Genesis*), 41. Sarna also comments that in a history of Creation to Alexander written by Berossus, a third century BCE Babylonian priest of Marduk, there is a list of ten antediluvian kings who are recorded as having lived a total of 432,000 years.

15. The translation is that of Chaim Stern (Plaut and Stein, *Torah*, 32).

the pointed comment that "even the celestial host is corrupted!"[16] He posits that the unions between the divine beings and human women are contrary to the natural order of God's Creation.[17] Strangely enough, God does not punish the offending angels. God's response to the inappropriate congress between humans and angels is to limit human life to 120 years, a boundary which apparently does not go into effect until the time of Moses.[18] Perhaps by setting a ceiling on human life of 120 years, God seeks to make a more pronounced separation between mortal human beings and the immortal angels, a barrier which might deter future unions.

The motif of the divine curtailment of human longevity resurfaces five chapters later in Genesis 11:10–17 where we learn about the life spans of the ten postdiluvian generations of humanity from Noah[19] to Abraham. Human life in the postdiluvian genealogical list (excluding Noah) never comes close to the 900 year plateau of seven of the ten antediluvian ancestors; instead, it varies from a high of 500 years, in the case of Shem, to a low of 119 years for Nahor, Abraham's grandfather. Although the biblical text does not provide an explanation for the rather striking diminishment of longevity between the leaders before and after the Flood, the marked difference is surely an indication of God's growing distress at the persistence of human iniquity. By diminishing human longevity in the postdiluvian generations, God is giving expression to divine disappointment in human behavior which adds to the sense of God's dismay regarding the entire primordial period.

---

16. Sarna, *JPS Genesis*, 45.

17. Ibid., 46.

18. Following the stories about the unions between the angels and human women and the Flood, all of the leaders of the ten postdiluvian generations live longer than 120 years (Gen. 11:10–26). Furthermore, most of the life spans of the Patriarchs and Matriarchs, who lived after the primordial era, exceed the limit of 120 years. Thus, the ceiling of 120 years for human life which God declares in this brief myth (Gen. 6:3) does not appear to take effect until the time of Moses who dies at the age of 120 (Dt. 34:7). Aaron, however, dies at the age of 123 (Num. 33:39), so it seems that the boundary of 120 years imposed by God is only an approximate limitation on human life.

19. Since Noah lived before and after the Flood, he is both the last of the ten antediluvian leaders and the first of the ten postdiluvian leaders.

The Covenant of Noah, A Moment of Hope in the Midst of Darkness

While there are a few isolated examples of primordial human beings reaching out to God, such as the generation of Enosh who "began to invoke YHVH by name,"[20] and Enoch, who walked with God so that God took him,[21] the recurring acts of human sin and rebellion convey the unequivocal message that following Creation, human iniquity is on the rise. It is, therefore, not surprising that immediately before the Flood, God saw "how great was man's wickedness on earth, and how every plan devised by his mind was nothing but evil all the time!"[22]

In the wake of the Flood, however, God has a change of heart. God is so appalled by the wholesale destruction of life at the Eternal's own bidding that the Holy One decides to treat humanity, despite its proclivity toward evil, with a resigned sense of toleration. Thus, following Noah's sweet smelling sacrifice, God makes this covenantal pledge:

> Never again will I bring doom upon the world
> on account of what people do,
> though the human mind inclines to evil from youth onward;
> never again will I destroy all living beings as I have [just] done.
> As long as the world exists, planting and harvesting, cold and heat,
> summer and winter, day and night will never end.[23]
>
> Genesis 8:21–22

The Covenant of Noah is not a mutual pact between two parties but an unconditional unilateral divine promise not to destroy all flesh, a pledge God makes to Noah and every living survivor of the Flood. The rainbow which God sets in the sky is a sign to the Eternal and to humanity, that the Holy One has no intention of giving up on humanity by ever again destroying almost every living being on earth.

Amidst the bleak background of primordial humanity, the Covenant of Noah sounds the only major note for a more promising future. Because of his righteousness,[24] God selects Noah for survival and offers him a

---

20. Gen. 4:26.
21. Gen. 5:22–24.
22. Gen. 6:5.
23. The translation is that of Chaim Stern, (Plaut and Stein, *Torah*, 63).
24. Gen. 6:9 "This is the line of Noah—Noah was a righteous man; he was blameless in his age; Noah walked with God."

covenant, but after the Flood, the pattern of human wrongdoing begins anew with Noah's drunkenness, the disrespectful act of Ham towards his father, Noah,[25] and the rebellious project of the builders of the city and tower of Babel. This sets the stage for God's dramatic decision in Genesis 12 to take an entirely new approach to the divine quest for goodness by inviting Abraham to join the Eternal in a covenantal relationship.

The Purpose of Human Existence According to Genesis 1–11

In the first eleven chapters of Genesis, the Narrator[26] sought to address the most important questions of human existence—why were human beings created, and what is the purpose of our lives? These questions naturally come to mind when we contemplate our mortality. If we are here for only a brief moment in the great expanse of time, in a tiny corner of the vast universe, what is the significance of what we do or say during our fleeting days on earth? Religion is a response to this existential question. Some religions propose that the divine gift of life is an opportunity to overcome our finitude, to conquer death, so that by right belief and/or right action, we can attain eternal life with the One who gave us life. I do not think that the Narrator of Genesis had this in mind. Rather, the Narrator believed that the Eternal created man and woman in the hope that they would choose to follow the path of goodness, so that the world that God created would become a place of justice and peace. We have seen that in the four major Genesis accounts of human life in primordial times—Adam and Eve, Cain and Abel, Noah, and the Tower of Babel—humanity consistently fails to fulfill God's hope for righteousness. And even though in our own time, we too have not come close to attaining God's hope for universal justice, God perseveres, as God did in the aftermath of the Flood, by maintaining within us the awareness that *when we strive for goodness, we fulfill God's purpose for creating us*. In this way, even if we do not live forever, the way we live, can have enduring significance.

---

25. Gen. 9:20–27.

26. I use the term "Narrator" to refer to the individual who wove the different strands of Genesis into a unified narrative with a particular point of view. I prefer this to the term Editor or Redactor which can be understood as someone who stiches different parts of the text together with no specific perspective in mind.

CHAPTER 2

The Purpose of Our Lives

ARISTOTLE LABELED US *HOMO sapiens* "a knowing or wise human," because he thought that our ability to think rationally and accumulate empirical wisdom made us uniquely human. In our day, Victor Frankl posited that we humans are set apart by our inherent need to seek meaning.[1] Before the modern era, the quest for meaning was not of great concern. By and large, to work and live in the manner of one's parents was meaningful in and of itself. In the modern world, however, and particularly in Europe and America, with so many choices in regard to education, work, familial life style, etc., the search for meaning has taken on tremendous importance.

I cannot pinpoint the exact moment when I first wrestled with the question of the meaning of my life, but I sense that even in my high school years, I was concerned with the challenge of how to live purposefully. Over the years, I have come to the same conclusion that arises from the stories of Creation and primordial history in Genesis—that despite our inclination to commit evil, God has faith that we human beings can live meaningful lives by responding to *qol d'mamah daqqah* "the still small voice"[2] of the Eternal that calls us to do the good. In this chapter, I would like to share my efforts to hear and respond to that "voice" in my quest for meaning.

---

1. See Viktor E. Frankl, *Man's Search for Meaning*. Frankl's book was initially published in German in 1946 following his survival at Theresienstat, Auschwitz, and Dachau. Soon afterwards, it appeared in an English translation under the title *From Death Camp to Existentialism*. Later, the English translation was published as *Man's Search for Meaning*.

2. I Kings 19:12. This is an allusion to the prophet Elijah who flees from Queen Jezebel after besting the prophets of Baal at Mt. Carmel. God commands the prophet to go to Mt. Horeb (Sinai). There, Elijah is confronted by a great wind, an earthquake, and fire, but God is not in any of them. Finally, God appears to Elijah in *qol d'mamah daqqah* "a still small voice" and helps Elijah refocus his prophetic mission.

The Purpose of Our Lives

I had the good fortune to spend my last three years of high school (1954–57) at Friends' Central School, a Quaker preparatory school, located on the city line of Philadelphia and the suburban community of Wynnewood. In the summer after my junior year, on behalf of my school, I attended a Quaker international summer work camp where I joined other volunteers from around the world in refurbishing a community center in Featherstone, England, a small coal mining town in the Midlands. Germantown Friends School sponsored the American contingent and made up the majority of our group of about ten American students who were assigned to different international Quaker summer work projects throughout Great Britain. In preparation for our overseas experience, we were required to attend a Quaker weekend work camp in South Philadelphia.

On a Friday evening in April, we gathered at the Quaker settlement house on South St., located in the midst of a poor, predominantly black area of the city. After dinner, the neighborhood community workers in charge of the settlement house spoke with us about the issues of inner city poverty. The next morning we were split into teams of two and given an address where we were to help paint a room with the family or individual who lived in the house. Marilyn, my partner from Germantown Friends, and I were assigned to paint the living room of an elderly African American woman. We arrived early Saturday morning with paint brushes, a can of blue paint, and a bag lunch. Although it was the beginning of April, it was very cold. We were greeted at the door by a slight woman with short wavy silver hair who was wearing several sweaters. She introduced herself as Mrs. Moore[3] and shared with us the announcement that the boiler was not functioning and there would be no heat. Marilyn and I entered her chilly apartment and along with our hostess began painting the walls of her spare living room. As the three of us painted, we warmed up a bit and got to know each other. Prompted by our questions, Mrs. Moore told us about her childhood and her life as a young woman in the South. Her stories were tinged with nostalgia about the warmth and support of family life which she had experienced in the small town of her youth. By comparison, even though she lived in the midst of a densely populated area of South Philadelphia, her current situation seemed isolated. Although she didn't complain, I kept wondering how does she stand being so cold? Does she get enough to eat? Does she have support from friends and neighbors? I knew that our task was to paint

---

3. This is the name I remember, but considering that sixty years have passed between today and then, my memory is pobably incorrect.

her living room, but I could not help feeling concerned about the many challenges she had to confront every day. While my mind was full of anxiety for Mrs. Moore, the three of us continued to work side by side. At one point, she began humming "Swing Low, Sweet Chariot" and other spirituals; Marilyn and I joined in whenever we could. At noon, Mrs. Moore made us some hot Campbell's tomato soup to go with our sandwiches. By the end of the day, we had painted her living room a lovely light blue, but more importantly, we had established a friendly connection and learned a little about her very different life.

On our way back to the Quaker settlement house, Marilyn and I stopped by a local florist to order a corsage for Mrs. Moore, who had invited us to join her for church on Sunday, which happened to be Easter. After dinner and a few hours of sleep at the settlement house, we were awakened while it was still dark, loaded on to an old white van, and driven out to a hill in Fairmount Park overlooking the city for a Quaker sunrise service.[4] As we sat shivering in silence, the outline of the city's skyline rose to meet us. After the service, we were taken to Sunday morning magistrate's court in South Philadelphia where we observed the sad array of arrests from the previous night—prostitutes (the first I had ever seen), drunks, and thieves. It was very disheartening, a sharp contrast to the quiet beauty of our sunrise service in the park.

Following magistrate's court, Marilyn and I picked up the corsage from the florist and returned to Mrs. Moore's home where we helped pin our flowers to her shimmering brown dress. She seemed genuinely pleased. She then donned a generous white hat decorated with large silk flowers and declared that she was ready to "step out" in her Easter finery. Her church was just around the corner, and as we entered, everyone greeted her. Mrs. Moore introduced us as her new friends. I sensed she was proud to have us as her guests. The service included lots of joyous communal singing and a fiery sermon accompanied by many rousing "amens." I recall that the minister chided the congregation because he felt they were lacking in "spirit." Despite the minister's reproof, I found the worship exhilarating. It

---

4. There is no liturgy at a Quaker meeting (service). Attendees pray in silence, but if moved to speak, hopefully by God's spirit, individuals may stand and share their thoughts and prayers with the congregation. At Friends' Central there was a Quaker meeting once a week. I found them to be meaningful. The service comes to an end when the group leader stands and shakes hands with another person.

was certainly different from the solemn prayer service I was used to at my Classical Reform[5] temple in center city.

Reflecting on this sixty-year-old memory, I recall being filled with joy as I reached out to help and to learn about another human being who was very different from myself. The simple experience of joining Mrs. Moore to paint her living room and the pleasure of attending worship with her in her church suggested to this naïve fifteen year old that the plagues of poverty and racism in America might be healed with heartfelt effort. Since then, I have learned that societal problems are much more complex and challenging than I had thought, but I still look back upon that weekend in South Philadelphia as an experience that encouraged me to participate in *Tikkun Olam* "Repair of the World" even by the smallest of deeds.

As I think back over my rabbinate, I am somewhat disappointed that I have not been involved in more hands-on acts of social action such as I did that weekend in South Philadelphia and the following summer when I worked on the refurbishment of the community center in Featherstone, England. I have, however, had the opportunity to facilitate and encourage members of my synagogue to engage in person to person social action mitzvahs such as tutoring underprivileged children, supporting a half-way shelter for single mothers and their children, helping to establish an ongoing collection and distribution of basic food staples to poor Jews in the Boston area, mentoring inmates at a local prison in pursuit of a college degree, and helping refugee families from Laos and Belarus to settle in our community.

In retirement, I have been tutoring students from homeless families in nearby Brockton and Randolph. The sponsoring organization is SOWMA, Schools On Wheels Massachusetts. I have helped tutor a bright fifth grader of Cape Verdian extraction as well as a charming but mischevious first grader from the same background. I found it challenging because I had never thought about how a child learns to read or what is the best way to acquire basic math skills. Nonetheless, I sense that my tutees appreciated my attention, and I feel that we made some progress. I especially enjoyed reading with my students and helping them comprehend and appreciate a Dr. Seuss book or one of my childhood favorites such as *Stuart Little*. Of

---

5. Classical Reform is a term that is applied to the main stream of the Reform movement for approximately the first seventy years of the twentieth century. It was characterized by an emphasis on ethics, social action, and decorum in worship, and a de-emphasis of traditional ritual and the use of Hebrew. Today, Reform Judaism has a more balanced outlook in which both Jewish ritual and social action are viewed as important.

course, when I reflect on my day to day experience as a rabbi, I realize that I was involved in mulitple deeds of lovingkindness every single day from visiting the sick and comforting the bereaved to trying to bring peace and healing to troubled individuals and families. I now know that this is a major reason why I found the rabbinate so rewarding.

From the pulpit, in public, and in the halls of government, I've also spoken out and lobbied for causes in which I believed. Among them were the cause of justice and peace during the Vietnam War, the struggle for gay and lesbian rights, the plight of Russian Jewry, and the fight against capital punishment.

I think the single most meaningful community service that I have done in my life was to initiate the founding of the Rashi School. In 1982, along with a few other Boston area rabbis and some dedicated lay people, I plunged into the project of establishing a Boston Area Reform Jewish Day School.[6] I was the first president of the Rashi School, and three years into our preparatory work, we hired Rabbi Rim Meirowitz to serve as our first Headmaster. Rim, by means of his hard work, charisma, and leadership, was instrumental in helping give birth to the Rashi School in the fall of 1986 with a first and second grade that was housed at Temple Shalom in Newton.

The most pressing goal in those early days, which is part of every startup, was to raise money. I had no idea how to do it. On a number of occasions, I would be in the presence of potential donors, tell them about my dream of a Reform Jewish day school in the Boston area and expect that having heard my story, they would automatically be moved to invest in the school. It took me a long time to learn that I had to make the "ask"—a clear request for a specific amount of money!

We also had to overcome a major idealogical issue. Reform Jews in the twentieth century were ardent supporters of public education as an expression of their belief in the ideal of a diverse and integrated America. Public schools were also in the forefront of educating several generations of American Jews in preparation for their remarkable academic success at the nation's top colleges. To advocate a Reform Jewish day school, even in

---

6. The initial clergy who worked with me on founding the Rashi School were Rabbi Dov Taylor from Temple Ohabei Shalom, Rabbi David Katz from Temple Israel, and Cantor Jodi Sufrin from Temple Beth Elohim in Wellesley. The first lay volunteers were Burt and Betty Goldfarb from Temple Beth Avodah (Burt succeeded me as President) and Larry and Muriel Gillick, Nancy Kaplan, and Paul Harmatz, all from Temple Ohabei Shalom.

the 1980s, was seen by some as turning our backs on the public school, the very institution that had played such an important role in the success of American Jewry. Critics also argued that establishing a Jewish day school was "a return to the ghetto," a form of isolationism, a turning away from the American ideal of diversity. While I certainly recognized the contribution of public education to the successful integration of generations of Jewish immigrants and to the academic and professional achievements of the American Jewish community, I felt there was a need for a school where Reform Jewish children could learn to be literate in the great Hebrew texts of our tradition and at the same time be inspired to engage in social action, to fulfill the ideals of "Prophetic Judaism," the byword of Reform Judaism in the twentieth century.[7]

Fortunately, there were a number of Reform rabbis and lay leaders in the Boston area who joined our initial group by contributing their knowledge, leadership, and financial resources, to the founding of the the school.[8] Today, thirty years and five temporary locations after we first opened our doors, the Rashi School has an enrollment of 320 students from kindergarten through eighth grade and has celebrated the building of its first permanent home in Dedham, a colonial town on the southwest border of Boston, on an intergenerational campus that we share with Newbridge on the Charles, a beautiful senior housing facility sponsored by Hebrew Senior Life. Up to this year (2016), there have been five devoted headmasters of Rashi: Rabbi Rim Meirowitz, Jennifer Miller *z"l*, Rabbi Joseph Eiduson, Matt King, and now, having completed her first year, Mallory Rome. Each

---

7. For approximately the first seventy years of the twentieth century, Reform Judaism enthusiastically embraced the label "Prophetic Judaism," meaning that Reform Jews held as our highest values the ideals of social justice emanating from the ancient prophets of Israel.

8. Other Boston area rabbis who supported our early efforts were Paul Menitoff (New England Regional Director of the UAHC), Robert Miller, Bernard Mehlman, Donald Splansky, David Mersky, Herman Blumberg, Ronne Friedman, Murray Rothman *z"l* and Sandy Seltzer. Cantor Roy Einhorn also joined his wife Jodi Sufrin in supporting us in the early days. The cantors were especially helpful by sponsoring cantorial concerts which raised much needed funds for Rashi. Additional lay people who participated in the founding of the Rashi School include Emily Lipof (later ordained as a rabbi), Yitz Magence, Emily Mehlman *z"l*, Jane Taubenfeld Cohen (soon afterwards the Head of the South Shore Solomon Schechter Day School), Esther Karten (from the BJE), Joan Kaye, Nancy Kaplan (our fourth president), Mitchell and Carol Kur, Lewis *z"l* and Bonnie Millender, Merrill Hassenfeld and Paula Brody, Carol Mersky, Michael Rukin *z"l* and Jerry and Sheridan Kassirer (our third president). I'm sure there were others, and I sincerely apologize to those individuals I failed to mention.

one has made a significant contribution to our growth and educational excellence. In addition, the joint efforts of faculty, students, parents, and community volunteers, have helped build a school which, in the words of our founding mission statement, encourages our students to become knowledgeable Jews with "critical minds and compassionate hearts."

What I appreciate most about the Rashi School is that it is a community that enables its students and their families to make the world a better place. To witness Rashi students, under the guidance of Social Justice Coordinator, Stephanie Rotsky,[9] work with the underprivileged and the elderly, advocate for just legislation, raise money for worthy causes, and strive to create a school community built on the Jewish values of *kavod*—respect, *limud*—learning, *kehilah*—community, *tzedek*—justice, and *ruach Elohim*—the spirit of God,[10] brings me more joy than anything I can imagine. The success of the Rashi School has clearly demonstrated that Jews can participate in intensive Jewish education and at the same time be involved in the issues of the greater community; Rashi students help create a better America through the realization of their Jewish values.

Over the years I have come to understand that the quest for meaning can also take place in our own families. In that regard, I feel blessed to be the beneficiary of a continuing gift of loving support from my wife Barbara.

Barbara and I met during the summer of my first year of rabbinic school in Cincinnati. I was assigned the task of asking a number of Cincinnati girls from the Jewish community to meet a group of first year HUC-JIR students who were studying beginning biblical Hebrew over the summer in preparation for our first year. Barbara thought I was asking her for a date, so she was rather surprised when she discovered that I had invited a whole group of girls to the same event. It didn't take me long to appreciate her

---

9. In 1999, Michael and Linda Frieze of Newton helped establish the Social Justice Coordinator position at the Rashi School which Stephanie now holds. Stephanie subsequently won a Covenant Foundation award in 2005 for her excellent work in the field of Jewish education, especially for helping the entire community of Rashi students and parents actualize the Jewish pursuit of justice and righteousness.

10. These core values were the fruit of a three year (1996–99) extensive group project known as Jewish Day Schools for the 21st Century under the leadership of Michael Zeldin from the HUC-JIR Rhea Hirsch School of Education in Los Angeles. At Rashi, the effort was chaired by Alison Kur and Lesley Litman with the participation of faculty, current and alumni parents, and community leaders. Beginning with text study, the group steadfastly worked to discover the core values of the Rashi community. One of the strengths of Rashi has been that the core values that the 21st Century group identified grew to become part of the daily conversations and conscious ideology of the school.

lovely smile, her winning personality, and her incisive intelligence. At the time, Barbara was a student at the University of Cincinnati studying to be a teacher of the deaf. After a two and a half year courtship, we were married at the apartment of Barbara's cousin, Irene Lowenthal, on December 22, 1963. Now, over fifty years later, we are still married and still in love.

Despite a successful academic record at HUC-JIR, by the time I began my first rabbinical position in 1967 as an assistant rabbi at Temple Emanuel in Worcester, MA, I was not very self-assured. I was twenty-eight years old and beneath my daily veneer of greeting everyone in an upbeat, cheerful manner, lurked a somewhat nervous, hesitant, young rabbi. In learning how to preach, teach, be an effective leader, visit the sick, and comfort the bereaved, I often felt that I was barely up to the task. One of the most important sources of support in helping me attain a measure of confidence was Barbara's love and encouragement. She believed in me from the very beginning, and when I became fretful, discouraged, or afraid, no matter what the challenge, whether I was delivering a eulogy for a young person who had committed suicide or serving as the dean at a teenage retreat of over a hundred and fifty youth groupers, Barbara would reassure me by reminding me that I had the capacity and talent to do a good job. I certainly know that when I was feeling down about a challenge or crisis at the temple, I was not much fun to live with. I would withdraw and beat myself up until my inner self was black and blue. At those times, I didn't have much to give Barbara in the way of love and attention. Thank God she had the patience to put up with my periodic lows and stick with me, for her love and support were crucial in helping pull me through those crises.

Barbara was also an invaluable partner when I became the rabbi of Temple Beth David of Westwood in 1970. Barbara is blessed with a tremendous capacity to make strangers as well as long time temple members feel at home in the synagogue. Whenever newcomers entered our doors, Barbara greeted them with a winning smile and warm words of welcome. She attended every Bar/Bat Mitzvah and was an avid participant in adult education and Sisterhood. I owe much of my success as the Rabbi of Temple Beth David over a thirty-six year period to her positive involvement in the congregation. The warm and welcoming atmosphere at Beth David is in part a reflection of her positive and vivacious personality.

We have also found meaning in our marriage of fifty-two years. By jointly enduring and overcoming the challenge of infertility, by learning how to tolerate each other's likes and dislikes, by working diligently to understand each other as we changed as individuals, by raising a son whom we love and admire, by sharing a deep appreciation of art, music, literature, and theater, by delighting in travel to Israel, New Zealand, Ireland, Alaska, and other wonderful sites, and most of all, by maintaining our love through disagreements and trials, our marriage has brought meaning to our lives.

Parenting children is perhaps the most demanding challenge in life and certainly one of the most meaningful. No one gets it perfect, but loving, nurturing, guiding, supporting, disciplining, and giving one's children the space to grow and become independent self-sufficient members of society and contributors to others as well as their own families is a most meaningful aspect of life.

I also see friendship as an important source of meaning. Throughout my life, I have appreciated my friends and have worked at maintaining my friendships. I have beloved friends from high school and college with whom I regularly correspond as well as treasured rabbinic colleagues. I have also tried to nurture friendships in my congregation and among my many contacts in Boston.

And so, from Barbara's continuing support for me and my rabbinate, from our marriage, from my positive experience as a rabbi, a son, brother, parent, grandparent, and friend, and from other meaningful experiences such as the memorable weekend I spent as a teenager in a poverty ridden area of South Philadelphia, and the summer of volunteer work in a poor English community, I have come to embrace the basic lesson of the introductory chapters of Genesis, that despite humanity's propensity for evil, God created us to partner with the Eternal in making the world a better place by living righteous lives and by giving to others. This personal conviction has been reinforced time and again in my life by a feeling of joy every time I am involved in an act of kindness or righteousness. I believe that this sense of joy is God's way of affirming, "Yes. This is why I created you!"

Some acts of righteousness such as Rabbi Abraham Heschel's marching arm and arm with Dr. Martin Luther King through an angry menacing crowd in Selma, Alabama, require great courage. Others, like caring for an elderly parent or a handicapped child, lending support to a terminally ill friend, raising funds for a worthy cause, or being a supportive marriage partner to a spouse in crisis, do not demand the same kind of public bravery. They do, however, call for tremendous effort, empathy, and patience. I also believe meaning can be found in life experiences which are not dominated by compelling needs. If one can truly love another human being, be it a child, a marital partner, a friend, or a parent, and demonstrate that love by real giving, a sense of meaning naturally ensues. In addition, I would contend that every job has within it the opportunity for service to others. Whether one is a clerk in a department store, a doctor, an artist, or a venture capitalist, work can take on meaning when we approach it with the understanding that what we do is of benefit to others.

I am well aware, however, that there are millions of people in the world who only know a life of suffering. How can a child working as a slave laborer in Africa or Asia, or an individual whose entire life is a series of illnesses find meaning? For a possible answer to this difficult question, I turn again to Viktor Frankl, a psychiatrist who survived imprisonment for a number of years at three different Nazi concentration camps. I was fortunate to hear him speak at HUC-JIR in Cincinnati when I was a rabbinic student. In his book *Man's Search for Meaning*, Frankl affirms that one can find meaning in times of suffering by confronting that suffering with human dignity and holding on to moral and spiritual values even when there is little or no hope for physical survival.[11] In Auschwitz, Frankl was occasionally permitted to resume his role as a doctor. On one occasion, he had an encounter with a young woman in the typhus block who was aware that she would die in a few days. She confessed that in her former life, she did not take spiritual accomplishments seriously. Frankl's recollection of his conversation with her follows:

> Pointing through the window of the hut, she said, "This tree is the only friend I have in my loneliness." Through that window she could see just one branch of a chestnut tree, and on the branch were two blossoms. "I often talk to this tree," she said to me. I was startled and didn't quite know how to take her words. Was she delirious? Did she have occasional hallucinations? Anxiously, I asked her if the tree replied. "Yes." What did it say to her? "It said to me, I am here—I am here—I am life, eternal life."[12]

This woman's spiritual response to her suffering in Auschwitz is an example of a human being who found meaning even in the darkest of times, because she aspired to an ideal that was above and beyond her personal trial. In this spirit, Frankl writes that those prisoners who held on to some future goal beyond mere survival, such as the hope of being reunited with a loved one, or the dream of completing a significant project, often did not succumb to

---

11. Frankl, *Man's Search*, 66–68.
12. Ibid., 69.

total despair that might lead to suicide in the camps.[13] Survivors have also testified that those who continued to perform small deeds of kindness such as helping a weakened fellow inmate walk to a munitions factory so that he would not be killed outright, or sharing a bit of food with another prisoner who seemed especially frail, enhanced their chance of survival because they were fortified by the bonds of human kindness and friendship. While there is nothing in the biblical stories of Creation and primoridal times that specifically speaks to the problem of finding meaning in the midst of suffering, the overall theme of the first eleven chapters of Genesis—that regardless of our life situation, God expects us to aspire to do what is good, kind, and holy—is still relevant for all who have to endure tremendous hardships.

Ultimately, whether one strives to better the lives of others in the world, labors for the conservation of our planet, provides a continuous source of love and support to a family member or friend, or responds with dignity and courage in the face of personal suffering, we human beings can find meaning in our lives. And once we have found our own particular path to meaning, we won't have to ask why God created us. We will know.

---

13. Ibid., 72–75.

CHAPTER 3

God's Call to Abraham Initiates the Covenant

L*ech* l'*cha*, God's Call to Abraham to "go forth" signals the opening bell for the Holy One's covenant with Abraham, a covenant that has endured for 4,000 years to this day. Despite its importance, the Torah does not prepare us for that historic moment. All we learn from Genesis is that Terah, Abraham's father, leaves Ur with Abraham, Sarah,[1] his daughter-in-law, and Lot, his grandson, on a migration to Canaan. They stop halfway at Haran. And then, seemingly out of nowhere, God calls Abraham to "go forth." We yearn to understand how Abraham came to know God and why God chose Abraham for this special mission, but the Torah is silent.

How Abraham Comes to Believe in God and Why God Choses Abraham

When God selects Noah for a covenant, there is a self-evident reason for the choice—"Noah found favor in the eyes of YHVH . . . Noah was a righteous man, he was blameless in his generation; Noah walked with God."[2] By contrast, the choice of Abraham is not as clear. The Rabbis respond to this difficulty with a legend about Abraham's birth and growing up in Ur.

---

1. In the Introductory Notes, we informed the reader that in Genesis 17, God changes the names of the first patriarch and matriarch from Abram to Abraham and from Sarai to Sarah. Except in direct quotations from the biblical text, I use the names Abraham and Sarah throughout to avoid any possible confusion.
2. Gen. 6:8–9.

Nimrod, the ruler of the world, reads in the stars that a child is about to be born who will challenge his pagan religion. And so, the apprehensive king issues an edict to kill all male infants at birth. To escape this decree, Abraham's pregnant mother hides in a cave where she gives birth to a son. Later, Abraham emerges from the cave and begins to look for God. Initially, he thinks that the stars are the gods, but when dawn arrives, and the stars disappear, he realizes that the stars are not gods. He then ascribes divinity to the sun, but the sun sets. And when in turn the moon rises and disappears, he realizes that the moon is also not a god. Abraham then arrives at the realization that there must be one power who sets all the heavenly bodies in motion, and that one is God.[3] Armed with this significant insight, Abraham begins to publicly proclaim his belief in the one God and to challenge Nimrod's pagan idolatry among the citizens of Ur.[4] From the Rabbis' perspective, because Abraham comes to the realization that the universe is sustained and ordered by the one God, and because he has the courage to promulgate this belief, he is the clear choice to serve as God's partner in a covenant. This Rabbinic legend may aproximate reality.

Rabbi Nehemia Polen, in a class at Hebrew College, suggested that Abraham demonstrates his suitability for a covenantal partnership with God when he generously takes Lot, the son of Abraham's deceased brother Haran, under his wing.[5] Jon Levenson proposes that God's choice of Abraham is simply a matter of divine grace.[6] I disagree. At certain points in the life of each patriarch, the Torah tells us that God becomes aware of their innermost thoughts and concerns, even though the patriarch does not give voice to them. For example, when Abraham becomes anxious about God's fulfillment of the covenantal promise of children, God senses his anxiety and says to him, *al tira* "Fear not, Abram, I am a shield to you; Your reward shall be very great."[7] Hence, even though it is not explicitly stated in the text, I believe that God is aware of Abraham's righteous character, his leadership potential, and his nascent faith, as key factors in singling him out as a covenant partner.

3. Ginzberg, *Legends of the Jews*, 1:186–189. Ginzberg cites the *Apocalypse of Abraham* as an early source of this legend (Ginzberg, *Legends*, 5:210 note 16).

4. Ibid., 1:193–198, includes a summary of the midrashic legends about Abraham's public battle against Nimrod's idolatry.

5. Gen. 11:28 records that Lot's father "Haran died in the lifetime of his father Terah, in his native land."

6. Jon D. Levenson, Commentary on Genesis in *The Jewish Study Bible*. (Oxford: Oxford University Press, 2004), 30.

7. Gen. 15:1.

Why Does Terah Discontinue His Journey at Haran?

As noted above, just before God's Call to Abraham, we learn that Terah, Abraham's father, sets out with his family from Ur,[8] a major center of Sumerian and Babylonian civilization located near the Persian Gulf, on a journey to the land of Canaan. Terah halts his migration in Haran, a city at the top of the Fertile Crescent, and settles there.[9] The name Haran means "route, journey, caravan, or crossroads"[10] all of which suggest that it was a center of trade.[11] We are left to wonder why Terah stops at Haran, rather than continuing on to his stated destination, the land of Canaan. Perhaps he is attracted by economic opportunities in this northern trade center, or it might be, as Sarna suggests, that Terah, who is identified as an idolator in Joshua 24:2, decides to settle in Haran because the worship of the moon god Sin among the denizens of Haran reminds him of the central role of that deity in his native Ur.[12] It is from Terah's new homeland in Haran that his son, Abraham, is called by God to set out on his historic pilgrimage to Canaan.

---

8. In Gen. 11:31, Terah's starting place is identified as "Ur of the Chaldeans." The term Chaldean is an anachronism since it refers to the people who ruled Babylonia in the 6th and 7th centuries BCE, anywhere from six hundred to a thousand years after the Patriarchal period.

9. Gen. 11:31.

10. Sarna understands the name of the city to mean "route, journey, caravan" (Sarna, *JPS Genesis*, 87), while Fox suggests "crossroads" (Fox, *Five Books of Moses*, 50).

11. In addition to Haran, Genesis identifies Abraham's second homeland as Paddan-aram (Gen. 25:20, 28:2), Aram-naharaim (Gen. 24:10), and the city of Nahor (Gen. 24:10), all of which refer to the same general locale northeast of Canaan at the top of the Fertile Crescent. Nahor is the name of Abraham's grandfather (Gen. 11:24), as well as the name of Abraham's brother (Gen. 11:27). Nahor's name is not included in the family group who migrate north with Terah and Abraham. Later, we learn that Bethuel, Nahor's son, and Rebekah and Laban, Nahor's grandchildren, dwell in this area during the lifetimes of Abraham and Isaac (Gen. 24). So how did Nahor's family get to Haran? Nahor, Abraham's brother, probably made the migration from Ur to Haran after Terah's journey, perhaps with the express purpose of joining the rest of his family. Note that Haran, Abraham's other brother who died in Ur, lends his name to the most frequently mentioned city in this new homeland for the family of Terah. Thus, each of the three sons of Terah—Abraham, Nahor, and Haran—is connected by name or by deed to this area at the top of the Fertile Crescent.

12. Sarna, *JPS Genesis*, 87–88.

God's Call to Abraham Initiates the Covenant

God's failed initiatives with primordial humanity at the beginning of Genesis set the stage for a new divine strategy to attain human righteousness—a call to Abraham to be a partner in a covenant.

> *Lech l'cha* Go forth
> *Mei-artz'cha umimmoladt'cha umibbeit avicha*
> from your land, from your kindred,[13] from your father's house
> to the land which I will show you.
> I will make you a great nation,
> and I will bless you,
> and I will make your name great.
> *Vehyei b'rachah* Be a blessing![14]
> And I will bless those who bless you,
> and I will curse anyone who curses you.
> Through you, all the families of the earth shall be blessed.[15]
>
> Genesis 12:1–3

I identify this famous divine challenge of *lech l'cha* "Go forth" in Genesis 12 as God's initial offer to Abraham of a covenantal partnership.

---

13. NJPS translates *mei-artz'cha umimmoladt'cha* as a hendiadys (adjacent words connected by a copulative "and" expressing a single idea) "from your *native land.*" And in Gen. 24:4, Abraham sends his servant to *moladti* "the *land of my birth*" (NJPS) to obtain a wife for Isaac. These two NJPS translations imply that *Haran is Abraham's birthplace*. If that is the case, the references in Genesis to Abraham migrating from Ur to Haran (Gen. 11:31; 15:7) must be false interpolations, possibly intended to add luster to Abraham's origins. In support of the belief that Abraham was born in Ur and was called to "go forth" after he migrated to Haran, I prefer Fox's understanding of *umimmoldt'cha* in Gen. 12:1 that God is asking Abraham to go forth "from *your kindred.*" A clear meaning of "kindred" or "family" for this word occurs in Gen. 43:7 where Judah says to Jacob, his father, that the vizier (Joseph) whom they (the brothers) encountered in Egypt, "kept asking about us *ul'moladteynu* and our family."

14. According to the norms of parallelism in biblical poetry, following the initial phrase expressed in the future *va-agadd'lah sh'mecha* "I will make your name great" (Gen. 12:2), one would expect the subsequent parallel phrase to be in the same tense, but instead, we encounter an *imperative* of the root *hey-yod-hey* "to be"—*vehyei b'rachah* "Be a blessing!" Later in Gen. 17:1, we hear an echo of this divine charge when God uses the same command form in addressing Abraham, "Walk before me *vehyei tamim* and be whole!" Here in Genesis 12, I follow Fox who understands *vehyei b'rachah* as an imperative, a challenge to Abraham—"Be a blessing!" NJPS and others translate it as if it were an imperfect (future) "and you shall be a blessing," which suggests that *vehyei b'rachah* may be understood as a divine oracle or as a goal for the future.

15. The translation is mine.

God's Call to Abraham Initiates the Covenant

In the Tanach,[16] a human covenant is a pact between two or more leaders representing themselves or their constituent groups. In Genesis, the word *b'rit* "covenant" is used in connection with three *human covenants* which mark the resolution of three separate conflicts: the agreement between Abraham and King Abimelech (Gen. 21:27); a subsequent treaty between Isaac and King Abimelech (Gen. 26:28); and a compact between Jacob and his father-in-law Laban (Gen. 31:44).[17]

The Tanach also features divine covenants—agreements or declarations affecting God's relationships with an individual, a group, or all humanity.[18] Because the word for covenant—*b'rit*, does not occur in Genesis 12, and there is no accompanying covenantal ritual, some biblical scholars claim that the covenant between God and Abraham does not come into being until Genesis 15, where the word *b'rit* appears for the first time in connection with the Covenant of Abraham,[19] and where there is a covenant ceremony in which God, in a theophany of smoke and fire, passes between bisected pieces of animals.[20] I do not believe, however, that the word *b'rit* or a covenantal ceremony must be present for a covenant to take place. Indeed, as we shall delineate under the next heading (The Content of God's Covenant with Abraham), despite the absence of the word *b'rit* in the Call to Abraham in Genesis 12 and the lack of a covenantal rite, the three major components of the Covenant of Abraham—God's promises, Abraham's responsibilities, and the covenantal goal—are all present! Furthermore, when God seeks to renew the Covenant of Abraham with Abraham's successors, Isaac and Jacob, there too, *the word b'rit does not appear!*[21]

---

16. In the Introduction note 2, we mentioned that the word Tanach is an acronym for Torah, N'vi-im, and K'tuvim, the three sections of the Hebrew Bible—Torah, Prophets, and Writings.

17. The word *b'rit* also appears in Genesis in reference to a group of kings identified as *ba-aley y'rit avram* "Abram's covenanted allies" who took up arms against five invading kings.

18. See addendum 1 for a brief discussion of divine covenants in the Tanach.

19. Gen. 15:18.

20. Gen. 15:17. We will discuss this ritual at length in chapter 7.

21. The word *b'rit* does not appear when God seeks to renew the Covenant of Abraham with Isaac in Gen. 26:2–5, or with Jacob in Gen. 28:13–15 and Gen. 35:9–12. A covenantal ceremony, however, does take place when Jacob sets up a stone pillar at Bethel and annoints it with oil (Gen. 28:18) and when he returns to Bethel after a twenty year hiatus and pours both wine and oil on a second pillar (Gen. 35:14). When God establishes the covenant with Isaac in Gen. 26 there is no ritual at all. The two major covenantal ceremonies between God and Abraham, the Covenant Between the Pieces in

At Sinai, the Israelites accept God's offer of a covenant with the words *na-aseh v'nishmah* "we will faithfully hearken."[22] This is followed by a covenantal ceremony in which Moses dashes sacrificial blood upon the people.[23] By contrast, Abraham accepts God's invitation to enter into a covenant solely by his actions, i.e., going forth with his family, his household, and his possessions, from Haran to the land of Canaan. And even though no ceremony takes place at the time of God's Call in Genesis 12, once Abraham embarks on his mission, the covenant is surely in force. We see confirmation of this when *prior* to the ritual of the Covenant Between the Pieces in Genesis 15, Abraham questions God as to why the covenantal promises of progeny and land have not been fulfilled.[24]

The Content of God's Covenant with Abraham

In God's Call to Abraham, the Eternal states that Abraham is to go to "the land that I will show you,"[25] an intimation that God intends to assign a particular land to Abraham and his descendants. In order for God to officially confirm this intimation, Abraham must actually walk upon the land. This takes place a few verses later, when Abraham takes his first steps in Canaan and passes through the land as far as Shechem, prompting God's explicit pledge, "I will give this land to your offspring."[26] The second charge God gives to Abraham is "Be a blessing," a model of righteousness. In return for Abraham's carrying out God's two covenantal tasks—departing from his father's home for the land of Canaan, and striving to be a blessing—God promises Abraham that his descendants will become a great nation. The Eternal also pledges to bless Abraham, his progeny, and his allies, while calling forth destruction to his enemies. The Holy One's covenantal objective is identical to the divine goal we encountered in the first eleven

---

Genesis 15 and the Covenant of Circumcision in Genesis 17 *confirm* rather than establish the covenant (See chapter 7), because the Covenant of Abraham is already in effect from Genesis 12 on.

22. Ex. 24:7. NJPS translates *na-aseh v'nishma* as a hendiadys, adjacent words connected by a copulative "and" (we will do and we will hear) that express a single idea "we will faithfully do." I prefer "we will faithfully hearken" since hearken encompasses both doing and hearing.

23. Ex. 24:8.
24. Gen. 15:2–3, 8.
25. Gen. 12:1.
26. Gen. 12:7.

chapters of Genesis—a just world. God hopes that such a world can come into existence when Abraham and his descendants have successfully modeled righteousness for all the families of the earth to follow.

Below I have arranged this first declaration of God's covenant with Abraham from Genesis 12 in outline form in order to clarify its structure and terms.

I. **God's twofold covenantal charge to Abraham**
   1. "Go forth . . . from your father's house" (verse 1)
   2. "Be a blessing" (v. 2)

II. **God's seven covenantal promises to Abraham**
   1. An intimation of a gift of land—"Go forth . . . to the land I will show you" (v. 1)

      (Three verses later in Gen. 12:7, the intimation becomes an explicit promise when Abraham sets foot on the land of Canaan.)

   2. National existence—"I will make you a great *nation*" (v. 2)
   3. Numerous progeny—"I will make you a *goy gadol* great (populous) nation" (v. 2)
   4. Divine favor—"I will bless you" (v. 2)
   5. Fame—"I will make your name great" (v. 2)
   6. Allies will be favored—"I will bless those who bless you" (v. 3)
   7. Enemies will be condemned to destruction—"I will curse anyone who curses you" (v. 3)

III. **God's covenantal objective**
   1. "Through you all the families of the earth shall be blessed" (v. 3)

God's First Covenantal Challenge to Abraham: "Go Forth From Your Homeland, Your Kindred, and Your Father's House"

In regard to God's initial charge to Abraham—*lech l'cha* "Go forth!" Rashi (Rabbi Sh'lomo ben Yitzchak, 1040-1105 CE, French biblical and talmudic commentator) proposes that the unusual presence of the preposition and personal object *l'cha* (literally "to or for yourself") following the imperative *lech* "go," should be understood as "Go for your own benefit," that is, so as to merit the divine blessings of progeny, land, nationhood, etc. I would add that "Go forth for yourself" has the effect of making God's Call to Abraham a challenge for personal growth—Abraham is being offered an opportunity to find his life's purpose by commencing a covenantal mission for God. The Zohar also understands *lech l'cha* as a journey of self-discovery—"Get thee forth so as to know thyself and prepare thyself."[27] Note that the same expression *lech l'cha* is used by God when challenging Abraham to sacrifice Isaac.[28] The journey to Moriah is also for Abraham's benefit, since the reward for Abraham's passing this ultimate divine test is God's firm commitment to the covenantal promises made to Abraham and his descendants.[29]

Abraham's challenge in carrying out God's Call to leave his home in Haran is heightened by a series of three noun phrases—he is asked to separate himself "from your land, from your kindred, and from your father's house."[30] The focus of this triplet narrows from the wider sphere of homeland to Abraham's relatives, and finally, to the most intimate circle of his father's household. To leave what is familiar and dear to undertake a lifelong mission on behalf of God is indeed a major act of faith.

Terah, Abraham's father, is still alive when Abraham departs from Haran. This may come as a surprise to the reader, because in Genesis 11:32, just before God's Call to Abraham, the text states that Terah dies in Haran at the age of 205. Although the Rabbis issue a general caveat that "there is no before or after in the Torah,"[31] (a warning that one should be wary of formulating a definitive chrononlogy based on different times and ages in the Torah), if we examine the biblical clues in regard to Terah's age at certain milestones in his life and the life of Abraham, we discover that Terah's death occurs sixty years after Abraham leaves Haran.[32] That his father is still

---

27. *Zohar*, translated by Harry Sperling and Maurice Simon. (London: Soncino, 1956), 1:264.

28. Gen. 22:2.

29. Gen. 22:16–17. "By myself I swear, the Lord declares: Because you have done this and have not withheld your son, your favored one, I will bestow my blessing upon you and make your descendants as numerous as the stars of the heaven and the sand on the seashore; and your descendants shall seize the gates of their foes. All the nations of the earth shall bless themselves by your descendants, because you have obeyed my command."

30. Gen. 12:1.

31. BT *Pesachim* 6b.

32. Gen. 11:26 states that "when Terah had lived seventy years, he begot Abram

alive in Haran when Abraham hears God's Call, renders God's challenge to Abraham to go forth from his "father's house" especially significant.[33] It means that Abraham's departure from Terah is a psychological separation, a rite of passage from being under his father's authority to independence and self-sufficiency. It also signifies a breaking away from the paganism of his father's house, so that Abraham might bear witness to the one God.

What is Meant by "The Land God Will Show You"

Most commentators understand God's charge to Abraham to go to *ha-aretz asher arekka* "the land I will show you"[34] to mean that God is offering to guide Abraham to an unknown destination. While we might want to credit Abraham with setting out for a place he does not know, an act which indicates blind faith in God, it is unlikely that God actually *shows* Abraham the way to Canaan, since immediately after the divine order to "go forth," the text states that Abraham and his household "set out for the land of Canaan."[35] This suggests that Abraham is fully aware of his final destination from the very beginning of his journey. We should also keep in mind that Terah, Abraham's father, departed from Ur with the land of Canaan as his final destination.[36] Surely, Abraham, an adult married member of Terah's family was acquainted with his father's itinerary. In part, then, Abraham's journey to Canaan represents the completion of his father's unfinished objective. For all of the above reasons, I prefer Benno Jacob's understanding that God's promise to "show" the land to Abraham means that once Abraham arrives in Canaan, God will reveal the extent of his inheritance by *showing* it to him.[37] Accordingly, Abraham's divinely guided "show tour" of

---

(Abraham), Nahor and Haran." I take this to mean that at the age of seventy, Terah began to have children, and since Abraham was the first born, Terah was seventy at the time of Abraham's birth. Abraham leaves Haran for Canaan when the patriarch is seventy-five (Gen. 12:4). Thus, at the time of Abraham's departure from Haran, Terah is 145 years old and has sixty more years of life before he dies at the age of 205 as stated in Gen. 11:32.

33. The Rabbis are concerned about Abraham leaving his father's home at this time because it implies that he is willing to abandon his father in Terah's old age. They propose that God specifically excuses Abraham from the obligation of caring for his aging father (*Genesis Rabbah* 39:7).

34. Gen. 12:1.

35. Gen. 12:5.

36. Gen. 11:31.

37. Jacob, *Genesis*, 85.

the land of Canaan takes place in the very next chapter, Genesis 13, when God says to Abraham "Raise your eyes and look out from where you are, to the north and south, to the east and west, for I give all the land that you see to your offspring forever . . . Up, walk about the land, through its length and its breadth, for I give it to you."[38]

The Pragmatic Challenges to Abraham's Journey

The site of the ancient city of Haran lies on the Balikh River, a tributary of the Euphrates in what is present day southern Turkey, ten miles north of the Syrian border.[39] Abraham's journey from Haran to Canaan is a distance of approximately five hundred miles.[40] Such a trip with his entire household and all his possessions and flocks, poses problems of safety and sustenance. In addition, the Torah makes a point of reminding us that the Canaanites occupy the land.[41] Thus, Abraham cannot take immediate possession of the land that God has promised him nor can he dwell wherever he chooses; he must first find a way to help his family and servants survive amidst the settled Canaanite majority. In Gerar, Abraham reports to King Abimelech that Abimelech's servants have siezed a well of water that Abraham had excavated.[42] Apparently, then as now, there was intense competition in the land for water. Later on, by the time Sarah dies, even though Abraham does not as yet own any land in Canaan, he has gained the respect of his Canaanite neighbors who say to him, *n'si Elohim atah b'tocheynu* "you are a mighty prince in our midst."[43] Abraham's journey from Haran to Canaan, then, is difficult, not only because it requires separation from family and the familiarity of home, but also because it poses many practical obstacles which Abraham must overcome.

---

38. Gen. 13:14–15, 17.

39. Sarna, *JPS Genesis*, 87.

40. On a contemporary map of the Mid-East, I estimated the distance between Haran and Canaan to be approximately 500 miles.

41. Gen. 12:6.

42. Gen. 21:25.

43. Gen. 23:6. Chaim Stern translates *n'si Elohim* "a mighty prince" (Plaut and Stein, *Torah*, 154) rather than "the elect of God" (NJPS). I believe that Stern's understanding comes from the linguistic feature that when the word *Elohim* follows a noun, it can have the effect of intensification. For example, Chaim Potok notes that some scholars understand *ru-ach Elohim* in Gen. 1:2 as "a mighty wind" rather than "the spirit of God" (Lieber, *Etz Hayim*, 4).

God's Call to Abraham Initiates the Covenant

The Significance of Abraham's Migration from Ur and Haran to Canaan

Abraham's migration from east to west across the Fertile Crescent, beginning in the great Babylonian city of Ur on the Euphrates River in the south, continuing to Haran, a trading center in the north, and concluding in the pastoral hill country of Canaan in the west, signifies a transition from a major urban setting to a semi-nomadic frontier. The Rabbis expound extensively on the difficulty Abraham has in Ur as a budding monotheist in the midst of an entrenched polytheistic population. They portray Abraham as an iconoclast in rebellion against his father's idolatry and that of King Nimrod, who sentences Abraham to a fiery death for publicly broadcasting his belief in the one God. With God's help, Abraham survives the fire, which gives rise to the midrashic interpretation of Genesis 15:7 in which God brings Abraham *mei-ur ka<u>s</u>dim*—instead of "out of Ur of the Chaldeans," read "out of the *fire* of the Chaldeans."[44] Both E. A. Speiser (1902–1965), a biblical scholar at the University of Pennsylvania, and Nahum Sarna posit that the Ur-Haran-Canaan migration may signify that the covenantal relationship between Abraham and the one God could only begin to take root in a predominantly semi-nomadic setting, because the prevalence of pagan idolatry in the urban centers of Ur and Haran might suffocate Abraham's attempt to launch a new faith.[45] This calls to mind the examples of later religious pioneers such as the sectarians of Qumran who fled to the barren shores of the Dead Sea, the Pilgrims who crossed the Atlantic to settle in the wilderness of New England, and the Mormons who trekked out to the deserts of Utah. Each group sought isolated or sparsely inhabited locales in order to find room for the growth and survival of their fledgling religious communities. Although Canaan was not an uninhabited wilderness, its semi-nomadic setting provided Abraham with sufficient room to give birth to Judaism and the Jewish people.

---

44. *Genesis Rabbah* 38:13. See also BT *Pesachim* 118a; *Pirkey de Rabbi Eliezer* 26. In the Hebrew of the Torah where the vowels are not indicated, the word for the city, Ur, in Gen. 15:7, is spelled the same as the word for fire—*aleph-vav-reish*. When vocalized (vowels are introduced), they are pronounced differently—"*ur*" refers to the city while "*or*" means fire. This is an example of a homograph, two words that are spelled the same but pronounced differently.

45. Speiser, *Anchor Bible Genesis*, xlvii; Sarna, *Understanding Genesis*, 101.

God's Second Covenantal Charge to Abraham—"Be A Blessing"

While Abraham carries out his first task of going forth from his father's house in a relatively short period of time, the challenge to fulfill God's charge of being a blessing continues throughout his life and the lives of his son Isaac, his grandson Jacob, and beyond. In Genesis 18, the divine call to "be a blessing" is given more weight and specificity when God decides to consult with Abraham, the Eternal's new covenant partner, about the troublesome situation in Sodom:

> Now YHVH said, "Shall I hide from Abraham what I am about to do,
> since Abraham is to become a great and populous nation
> and all the nations of the earth are to bless themselves by him?
> For I have singled him out, so that he may instruct his children
> and his posterity to keep the way of YHVH
> by doing *tz'daqah umishpat* what is right and just
> in order that YHVH may bring about for Abraham
> what He has promised him."
>
> Genesis 18:17-19

God's deliberation reveals that Abraham's role in the covenant is to be more than just a beneficiary of God's promises of land and progeny. God needs Abraham to achieve the raison d'être of the covenant—the realization of the day when "all the nations of the earth shall be blessed"[46] because they will have followed the example of Abraham and his descendants by building a world based on *tz'daqah umishpat* "righteousness and justice." This is precisely the kind of community that God had sought without success in the primordial era following Creation.

The Call to Abraham is also a call to us, the Jews of the twenty-first century. When, during our lifetime, we engage in acts of goodness and righteousness, we become active participants in the covenant which God first made with *Avraham Avinu* "Abraham Our Father," when God called out to him, "Go forth!" and "Be a blessing!"

I cannot leave God's covenantal Call to Abraham without commenting on the uniqueness in the ancient Near East of a covenant between a god and a human being. This relationship probably did not occur to the Sumerians, Babylonians, Assyrians, or Egyptians, because the vast majority of their gods were capricious, subject to changing their minds and moods

---

46. Gen. 18:18.

God's Call to Abraham Initiates the Covenant

in an instant.[47] Why enter into a covenant with an unreliable diety? The God of Israel, however, was a god one could trust; the covenantal promises of the Eternal One endured and could be relied upon. The idea of a covenantal partnership between God and Abraham bespeaks the unique religious creativity of our Israelite ancestors who were the first to maintain the belief in a single *trustworthy* God.

---

47. An exception might be the Babylonian god Shamash, the god of the sun, who ruled the world in justice and imparted to the Babylonian king Hammurabi an extensive code of laws.

CHAPTER 4

My Call to the Rabbinate

AT THE AGE OF twenty-one, I had a *lech l'cha* moment. In the summer after my junior year in college, in a span of about ten minutes, I decided I wanted to become a rabbi. Up to that moment, I had never consciously thought about choosing the rabbinate as a profession. In retrospect, I can now see that there were many life experiences which laid the foundation for what at the time seemed to me like a sudden impulsive decision.

My unknowing path to the rabbinate began at a very young age. For the first nine years of my life, my family lived in Trenton, New Jersey. We belonged to Har Sinai, a Reform synagogue not far from our home on Overbrook Avenue. Attending religious school and services awakened within me a positive feeling about being Jewish. Among my earliest Jewish recollections are gazing intently at the beautiful stained glass windows in the sanctuary, reciting by memory the 23rd Psalm in English for a religious school assignment, and receiving a nifty board game for finding the afikomen at a temple seder.

In 1948, we moved to Merion, PA, a suburb just west of Philadelphia. Since most of my parents' friends were part of the Trenton Jewish community, they decided that my brother Mike's bar mitzvah, which was scheduled for the fall of that year, would be held at Har Sinai in Trenton. I recall the tense car ride that day as Mike practiced his demanding Torah and Haftarah portions all the way from Philadelphia to Trenton. Shortly after we returned home, I urged my parents to join a synagogue. I don't know whether I was motivated by the special connection I felt at that young age to my Jewish heritage, or if I just wanted to make sure that I would have a bar mitzvah like my brother.

My Call to the Rabbinate

My mother, Eleanor Lowenstein Zoob, had the strongest familial influence on my love of Judaism. She was blessed with an ardent Jewish heart which she inherited from her parents. My mother's childhood home was observant, and its influence on her showed in her being visibly moved by Jewish rituals such as *bentshen licht* "kindling Sabbath candles" and participating in the seder. Unlike her two brothers, Aaron and Bob, who were tutored privately in preparation for bar mitzvah, my mother and her three sisters, Ida, Evelyn, and Jean, received no formal Jewish education. In those days it was the norm in many Orthodox Jewish families that sons were given a perfunctory Jewish education in order to prepare for bar mitzvah, while daughters were left to absorb as much *Yiddishkeit* as they could at home.

I was given the Jewish name *Chayyim* "Life" in memory of my mother's father, Heiman Lowenstein, who was a jeweler. He helped found a synagogue in Newark, New Jersey. I treasure a silver cup that was awarded to him by his synagogue with the somewhat awkwardly phrased inscription:

PRESENTED TO

HI LOWENSTEIN

BY CONG

RABBI MEYER ISSERMAN[1]

11 15 1927

I feel spiritually connected to my grandfather, for he was obviously a devoted synagogue Jew. I often imagine how proud he would have been to have a grandson who became a rabbi. He died in August, 1938, one year before I was born. My brother Mike, who was three at the time, remembers Grandpa Lowenstein blessing him from his hospital bed, an image which evokes the blessing Jacob bestowed upon his sons at his death bed. My mother often spoke of her father's final words as he lay dying in pain with colon cancer, "*Gott, nemt meine n'shamah!* God, take my soul!"

Grandma Helen Lowenstein survived her husband by thirty-three years and lived to attend my ordination at Hebrew Union College–Jewish Institute of Religion in Cincinnati in 1967. She observed *kashrut* throughout her life and was a loyal supporter of Israel. When she visited

---

1. When I first saw this inscription, I thought it included the name of the rabbi of the congregation, but left out the name of the congregation. To my surprise, I learned from a 1930 list of synagogues in Newark that the synagogue was named "The Congregation of Rabbi Meyer Isserman." It was the only synagogue of twenty-eight that was named for its rabbi.

our non-kosher home, her observance of the Jewish dietary laws helped me understand that *kashrut* was not some strange antiquated rite. Her outspoken love of Israel also had a positive influence on me.

My father, David Beresin Zoob, was not as connected to Jewish life as my mother. He was born and raised in the industrial towns south of Cleveland—Akron, Canton, and Massillon. His parents, Morris and Lena Zoob, were not particularly observant Jews, but he remembered being confirmed at the Reform synagogue in Akron by Rabbi Abraham Cronbach, a pacifist and non-conformist, who later volunteered to serve as the rabbi for Julius and Esther Rosenberg during their famous trial and execution in the fifties for spying for the Russians. The generational cycle of teaching and learning came full circle, because near the end of Rabbi Cronbach's life, I came to know him at the Hebrew Union College. When I asked Dr. Cronbach if he remembered my father as a confirmation student in Akron, he responded in his high pitched, croaky voice, "Ah yes, Zoob!" Rabbi Cronbach was known for having a remarkable memory[2] so I would like to think that he did indeed retain a half-century-old recollection of my dad.

The only other story that my father shared with me about his Jewish life was that after he graduated from the University of Pennsylvania Law School near the top of his class and went on to earn a post-graduate law degree there, he was turned away from a prestigious Philadelphia law firm when one of the partners said to him, "Zoob, you have an outstanding academic record, but you're Jewish. Unfortunately, you can't come to work at our firm."

When we moved to Merion, the first community on the Main Line[3] in the western suburbs of Philadelphia, there were no Reform synagogues in the area, but since my father had several relatives who belonged to Rodeph Shalom,[4] a Classical Reform congregation in downtown Philadelphia, we looked into membership there. I remember the first time I set foot in Rodeph

---

2. Although I never witnessed it, I was told that at NFTY (National Federation of Temple Youth) worship services, Dr. Cronbach would collect personal prayers written by the teenagers a day prior to a worship service, memorize them, and then include all of them in an ad-lib creative prayer during the service.

3. This area is called the Main Line because in the 19th Century the Pennsylvania Railroad train line ran through it connecting Philadelphia with important cities to the west such as Harrisburg (the state capital), Pittsburgh, and Chicago.

4. Congregation Rodeph Shalom in Philadelphia, incorporated in 1795, is the oldest Ashkenazic synagogue in the Western Hemisphere. It became a Reform synagogue in 1873 as a charter member of the Union of American Hebrew Congregations.

My Call to the Rabbinate

Shalom at the age of nine. Rabbi David H. Wice was conducting a model seder for the children of the religious school from the old grey Union Haggadah.[5] I had participated in seders at home but found it especially exciting to witness a hundred or more Jewish children learning about Pesach together. After the model seder, Rabbi Wice came over to my father and me, smiled, and introduced himself with a slight southern drawl. (I later learned he grew up in Petersburg, Virginia.) I was hooked! We joined Rodeph Shalom, and from that initial friendly greeting and many other personal contacts with Rabbi Wice, I came to understand the impact a rabbi can have on a child's experience of Judaism. In a short time, my family developed a close friendship with Rabbi Wice and his family. He always greeted me in the halls of the synagogue with a breezy salutation—"Mr. Zoob." I came to admire his knowledge of Jewish history and his outspoken support of Israel, as well as his clear stance on behalf of civil rights for African Americans and other minorities. Later, his son David H. Wice Jr., and I became roommates at college; Barbara and I have been lifelong friends with David and his wife Betsy. David became a lawyer, my father's profession, while I followed his father into the rabbinate.

Rabbi Martin Katzenstein, the Assistant Rabbi at Rodeph Shalom when I was a teenager, was also a very important rabbinic role model for me. He too was very outgoing and personable. When I attended Harvard, I sometimes worshipped at Temple Emanu-el, a congregation that Rabbi Katzenstein came to serve in Marblehead, MA, following his tenure in Philadelphia. And when I decided to enter the rabbinate after my junior year at Harvard, I drove up to Marblehead every other week to begin my study of biblical Hebrew with him. Rabbi Katzenstein attended my ordination in Cincinnati in 1967, and the following fall, he installed me in my first position as Assistant Rabbi at Temple Emanuel in Worcester.

My parents became active members at Rodeph Shalom, and we attended services regularly even though the synagogue was a thirty minute drive from our home in Merion. My father served on the temple board, and being an accomplished pianist, he was a longstanding member of the music committee. My mother was an active member of Sisterhood. I celebrated my bar mitzvah on October 11, 1952, which happened to fall on Sh'mini Atzeret–Simchat Torah, the festival marking the conclusion and beginning of the annual cycle

---

5. *The Union Haggadah* was edited and published by the Central Conference of American Rabbis in 1923. Generations of Reform Jews used the *Union Haggadah* at Pesach. It was succeeded by *A Passover Haggadah, The New Union Haggadah* published in 1974 by the CCAR.

of Torah reading.[6] As a bar mitzvah, I was thrilled to have the honor of reading the last words from *D'varim* (Deuteronomy) and the first lines of *B'reishit* (Genesis). I recall being extremely nervous as I stood before the open Torah in the cavernous sanctuary of Rodeph Shalom. I could feel my legs shake! I distinctly remember the steadying hand of Rabbi Katzenstein on my shoulder which was meant to calm me. Nonetheless, nerves contributed to my mixing up the order of the Torah blessings, so that I chanted the blessing that follows the Torah reading when I should have recited the blessing that precedes it. In preparing my bar/bat mitzvah students at Beth David in Westwood, I often shared my slight slip-up to help relieve any pressure they might have been feeling to perform perfectly.

In addition to my positive synagogue experience at Rodeph Shalom, the love of learning that permeated my home was an important factor in my decision to become a rabbi. Both of my parents were avid readers. Our home was filled with books, and my mother and father read at least a book a week. They were content to sit for hours in our den, my father in a reclining easy chair, my mother in her reading chair with her feet on a soft rose-colored footstool, each absorbed in a book or magazine article. When they came across something of particular interest, they would share it with each other. And so as a child, I was exposed to the joys of reading and learning, activities that are essential to the rabbinic role.

My parents were liberals. Although they were not political activists, they believed strongly in the ideals of integrity, justice, and freedom, in the private and public spheres of life, ideals that permeate the sacred texts of Judaism. Rabbis Wice and Katzenstein also preached these values from the pulpit, so that I came to see the life of a rabbi as a life devoted to the teaching and modeling of liberal values.

In the fall of 1957, when I was a college freshman, I thought I might want to become a psychiatrist. I'm not sure why I thought of psychiatry, other than my mother's strong interest in Freud and her enduring faith in psychotherapy, and my father's service on the local board of the Mental Health Association of Southeastern Pennsylvania. I also had some personal issues that I yearned to understand and thought that psychiatry might be a path to self-knowledge. Through the Phillips Brooks House[7] on campus I

---

6. See addendum 2 for an explanation of the one day observance of Sh'mini Atzeret-Simchat Torah in the Reform movement versus the two day observance in Orthodox and Conservative congregations.

7. The Phillips Brooks House is the name of the organization at Harvard which administers volunteer social action programs. It is named in memory of the great Episcopal

volunteered to work with mental patients at the Metropolitan State Hospital in Waltham, MA. My volunteer work on the locked mental wards at Met State focused on forming positive social relationships with the residents. I think the intent of the program was the hope that we college students might bring some normalizing socialization to the psychotic patients on the locked wards of the hospital. I found the experience sad and scary. Even though I was able to establish casual ties with some of the patients by playing cards and chatting, I found their sudden shrieks and compulsive bobbing back and forth unnerving. On one visit, we were invited to witness the administration of shock therapy. The violent twitching of the patient's limbs when the electricity coursed through his body made me tremble with fright and concern. Looking back, I see that my volunteering at Met State was perhaps the worst possible way to explore psychiatry as a career, but at the age of seventeen, I did not know any better way.

In the summer of 1960, as I headed into my last year at college on a pre-med course of study, I obtained a coveted job as a "hut boy" in the White Mountains of New Hampshire. The AMC (Appalachian Mountain Club) sponsors a series of eight huts in the White Mountains which provide hospitality enabling hikers to go from hut to hut along the summits without packing their own food or sleeping bags. It was my responsibility along with my fellow Zealand Falls hut boys to carry food up the mountain, prepare meals for the hikers, and maintain the hut, which had sleeping quarters for about fifty. As a camper for six years at Camp Milbrook in Bridgton, Maine, I had been introduced to hiking in the White Mountains and absolutely loved it. I loved being surrounded by nature, in particular, traversing the different strata of vegetation as one ascended a mountain, and the exhilarating feeling of standing on a summit and being able to see nothing but sky, clouds, trees, forests, lakes, and neighboring mountain peaks. Although I have slowed down quite a bit, my friend Arthur Glasgow and I still tackle two or three New England peaks each summer. Climbing a mountain continues to give me a physical and spiritual high.

The AMC Zealand Falls Hut is situated next to a beautiful waterfall. One sunlit afternoon, as I sat alone next to the falls, it suddenly occurred to me that I wanted to be a rabbi. Did God speak to me? I don't recall hearing any voices. My revelation, however, seemed perfectly clear. If asked to describe what happened, I would say that at that moment I came

---

minister, Phillips Brooks, who served Trinity Church in Copley Square in Boston at the close of the nineteenth century.

to believe that by becoming a rabbi, I could best fulfill my life in the world that God had created. No doubt the natural surroundings—the rushing waterfall, the massive granite boulders glistening with silvery streams of water, and the lush green vegetation splashed with sunlight—helped bring me close to God. Another Abraham, Rabbi Abraham Joshua Heschel, the great twentieth century scholar, religious poet, mystic, and Jewish leader, writes of "radical amazement," the feeling we experience when we sense the presence of God in the wonders of nature.[8] On that summer day, I came to understand Heschel's concept through my apprehension of God's presence in nature at a crucial moment in my life. I emerged from that moment full of joy and thanksgiving.

Looking back, I think my "call" to the rabbinate had two elements in common with Abraham's. Abraham understood his call as an appeal to "go forth" to serve God and others, but it was also a call to serve himself, a view expressed by the *Zohar* in its interpretation of *le<u>ch</u> l'<u>ch</u>a*—"Get thee forth so as to know thyself and prepare thyself." My experience on that beautiful summer day in New Hampshire encompassed the same two dimensions—I felt called to serve God, my people, and all humanity; but I also believed that by doing so, I would be serving myself, because I sensed that the rabbinate would bring great meaning and satisfaction to my life.

I confess to another personal revelation at that moment. Although I had always thought I was comfortable with my Jewish identity, upon reflection, I admit to having had an occasional feeling of discomfort by living my life with one foot in the Jewish world and one in the gentile world. When I made the decision to become a rabbi, I suddenly felt relieved that I could stop straddling the two worlds. My decision was a declaration that I wanted to immerse myself in Jewish life, that I wanted to live Jewishly twenty-four hours a day, three hundred and sixty-five days a year. Amazingly enough, that is what happened. From that summer day to this very day, I have felt a sense of Jewish wholeness in the way I live my life.

The integration of my Jewish identity, however, did not mean that by becoming a rabbi, I sought to isolate myself from the non-Jewish world. On the contrary, throughout my rabbinate, I have continued to maintain strong community contacts with Christian and Muslim clergy and laity. How could I look to fulfill Abraham's call to be a blessing to others unless I was concerned and involved in the world of my neighbors? While serving my Westwood,

---

8. See Abraham Joshua Heschel, *God in Search of Man*. (New York: Ferrar, Straus and Giroux, 1981), 45–48.

My Call to the Rabbinate

MA congregation, along with my friend and colleague, Rev. Ted Fritsch of the First Parish Church, I worked to help found the Westwood Interfaith Council, an organization devoted to interfaith education, worship, and community service, which has been a blessing to our town since its founding thirty-four years ago in 1982. This organization and my ties to it were crucial in laying the groundwork for the remarkable community support for our synagogue when we suffered a devastating arson fire in 1987 that destroyed our synagogue building.[9] On the Tuesday evening after the fire, which had been set late at night on *Erev Shabbat*, the Westwood Interfaith Council sponsored a service of support at the Westwood High School. There were probably over 700 individuals at the service, some of whom had to stand at the back of the auditorium. They came from our small town in Massachusetts to show us that they cared. In the wake of the fire we had to make use of the worship and meeting facilities of all the churches in the town for two years while we built a new synagogue on a different site in Westwood.[10] Our Christian neighbors were unfailingly hospitable and supportive. I am convinced that the strength of my Jewish identity helped facilitate the communitywide support that we received and continued to contribute to the effectiveness of my interfaith work in the community throughout the thirty-six years of my rabbinate in Westwood. Abraham was identified by his Canaanite neighbors as a "mighty prince in our midst." Like Abraham, I felt acceptance and respect from the clergy and laity in the town of Westwood.

As I have described above, many influences led to my becoming a rabbi—the spiritual connection to my Jewish heritage that I felt from the time I was a very young child; the *Yiddishkeit* I inherited from my mother, my grandmother Helen, and my grandfather Heiman; the positive rabbinic models of Rabbi Wice and Rabbi Katzenstein; and the love of learning and liberal idealism of my parents. All of these came together as I sat next to a beautiful waterfall in the White Mountains in the summer of 1960, so at that special moment I, like Abraham, felt "called" by God and made one of the most important decisions of my life—to become a rabbi—a decision in which I have rejoiced from the moment I made it to this day.

---

9. The perpetrator was a young resident of the town in his twenties who had experienced a great deal of trouble as an adolescent. He was tried, convicted, and jailed for several years.

10. Daniel Strier and Dr. Gary Rosenberg donated land in Westwood where a beautiful new Temple Beth David was built and dedicated in 1989. Rabbi Alexander Schindler, who as Regional Director of the UAHC had helped found our synagogue in 1960, returned as the President of the UAHC to honor us by delivering the dedicatory message.

CHAPTER 5

Abraham's Journey From Doubt to Faith

From the Call of Abraham in Haran to the deaths of Jacob and Joseph in Egypt at the conclusion of Genesis, an aura of suspense surrounds the covenant: Will God fulfill the covenantal promises? Will the Patriarchs uphold their end of the partnership? Which son will inherit the leadership position? Will famine in Canaan, or a sojourn in a foreign kingdom threaten the continuity of the covenant? The tension between God and Abraham is particularly suspenseful—Abraham expresses doubts and even questions God as to whether the Eternal will fulfill the covenantal promises of progeny and land (the focus of this chapter), while the Holy One tests Abraham again and again to determine whether he is a worthy covenantal partner (the subject of chapter 9).

Abraham Voices His Concern About the Promise of Offspring

After Abraham's arrival in Canaan, and a series of events including Abraham and Sarah's flight from famine to Egypt, their return to Canaan, Abraham's separation from Lot, and Abraham's divinely guided visual survey of the land, there are no signs of the promised heir, and Abraham remains landless in the promised land. God senses the patriarch's anxiety about the situation and speaks to him in a vision, "Be not afraid, Abram. I am a delivering-shield to you, your reward is exceedingly great."[1] Despite God's assurance, Abraham openly questions his divine partner.

1. Gen. 15:1b. Translation by Fox, *Five Books*, 65.

Adonai YHVH (*Elohim*), what can you give me,[2] seeing that I shall die childless, and the one in charge of my household is Dammesek Eliezer!"[3] Abram said further, "Since You have granted me no offspring, my steward will be my heir."

Genesis 15:2–3

And so Abraham complains that without an heir, family leadership and his considerable wealth[4] will pass on to Eliezer, his steward. God's prompt response speaks to the heart of Abraham's concern, "That one shall not be your heir; none but your own issue shall be your heir."[5] God then directs Abraham to go outside and count the stars, "So shall your offspring be."[6] After visualizing the myriad of promised descendants, Abraham "puts his trust in YHVH."[7]

Abraham Expresses His Concern About the Promise of Land

Strangely enough, immediately after "Abraham puts his trust in YHVH" regarding the divine pledge of progeny, the patriarch's doubts about the promise of land come to the surface. Just as God became aware of Abraham's concern about the promise of children, the Eternal now senses Abraham's anxiety about the land. And so, once again, God tries to reassure the patriarch, "I am YHVH who brought you out of Ur of the Chaldeans to give you this land as a possession."[8] Not content with the reiteration of God's

---

2. Benno Jacob suggests that Abraham's statement "What can you give me?" is a rhetorical expression meaning "What more do I need?" (Jacob, *Genesis*, 99). The point is that Abraham has all the material wealth he needs (See note 4 below), but he lacks the heir God has promised

3. The exact meaning of this phrase *uven mesheq beiti hu dameseq eli-ezer*, which features consonance in the repetition of the letter *qof*, is obscure. The most common understanding is that Eliezer is Abraham's chief steward. W. F. Albright suggests that Eliezer is Abraham's creditor (Albright, *Yahweh and the Gods of Canaan*, 57–58). In any event, this expression indicates that Eliezer, whether steward or creditor, is currently in line to inherit Abraham's wealth.

4. Gen. 12:16 recounts the many flocks and slaves Abraham obtained in Egypt; Gen. 13:2 states that in Canaan, Abraham was rich "in cattle, silver, and gold."

5. Gen. 15:4.
6. Gen. 15:5.
7. Gen. 15:6.
8. Gen. 15:7.

promise, Abraham asks for a clear sign of God's commitment—"*Adonai YHVH* (*Elohim*), by what shall I know that I am to possess it?"[9] God's response to Abraham's second direct challenge is to confirm the promise of land in a dream oracle in which the Eternal declares to Abraham that his descendants will experience oppressive slavery in a foreign land for four hundred years. Their enslavement will come to an end with divine judgment against their oppressors. They will then leave with great wealth and return to Canaan.[10] Following this oracle, the divine presence in the form of "a smoking oven and a flaming torch"[11] passes between bisected animal pieces[12] that Abraham had prepared. This theophany confirms God's covenantal pledge to grant Abraham and his descendants their promised land.

> On that day YHVH made a covenant with Abram, saying,
> "To your descendants I give this land from the river of Egypt
> to the great river, the river Euphrates, . . ."
>
> Genesis 15:18

In the wake of this vivid demonstration of God's commitment to the covenant, Abraham should have been reassured about God's intentions, but because the inheritance of the land has been postponed for four hundred years, and Abraham has no idea when the promise of children will be realized, he probably retains some doubts.

Sarah's Surrogate Strategy and the Birth of Ishmael

Ten years pass from the time Abraham and Sarah first enter the land of Canaan, and still, there is no child.[13] Sarah's frustration turns to anger as

---

9. Gen. 15:8.

10. Gen. 15:13–16. This oracle is an obvious allusion to the future enslavement and redemption of Israel from Egypt.

11. The images of a "smoking oven and a flaming torch" are certainly strange. Robert Alter writes that it seems "unwise to 'translate' the images into any neat symbolism" because the disembodied oven and torch "are wonderfully peculiar to this scene" (Alter, *Genesis*, 66).

12. Gen. 15:17.

13. In Gen. 16:3 we learn that ten years of infertility have gone by since they entered the land: "So Sarai, Abraham's wife, took her maid, Hagar the Egyptian—after Abram had dwelt in the land of Canaan *ten years*—and gave her to her husband Abram as a concubine."

she complains to Abraham "YHVH has kept me from bearing [a son]!"[14] She then takes matters into her own hands when she says to her husband, "Come into my maid; perhaps I may be built-up-with-sons through her."[15] By directing Abraham to have relations with Hagar, Sarah is offering her Egyptian slave as a secondary wife.[16] She hopes that Hagar will have a son whom she can adopt as her own. Because God has not expressly indicated that Sarah will be a mother, Abraham may think that Sarah's proposal is an appropriate option to help realize the divine promise of progeny. Sarah's plan seems to work, for Hagar becomes pregnant. Hagar, however, lords her pregnancy over her barren mistress so that Sarah complains to Abraham, who leaves the matter in Sarah's hands. Sarah treats Hagar so harshly that the Egyptian handmaiden flees into the wilderness.[17] Marooned in the wilderness, an "angel of YHVH"[18] encourages Hagar, with promises of her child's future greatness, to return, and names her yet-to-be-born son *Yishma-eil* "God hears," since God *shama* "has hearkened" to her suffering.[19] Hagar returns, and when the child is born, Abraham confirms the divinely ordained name *Yishma-eil*,[20] a name that also holds special meaning for the patriarch, since God has finally *heard* his prayers for a son.

---

14. Gen. 16:2.

15. Gen. 16:2. Fox's translation of *ibbaneh* "I-will-be-built-up-with-sons" artfully gives voice to the Hebrew word play on the noun *bein* "son" and the root *beit-nun-hey* "to build" (Fox, *Five Books*, 68).

16. The text in Gen. 16:3 says that Sarah gave Hagar to Abraham *l'ishah* "as a wife." The Hebrew word for concubine *pilegesh*, which is not used here, can also refer to a secondary wife. Keturah, for example, in Gen. 25:1, is identified as Abraham's wife. Five verses later in Gen. 25:6, she is designated as one of Abraham's *pilagshim* "concubines." Once Sarah gives Hagar to Abraham as a wife, she is no longer just Sarah's handmaid, she is also Abraham's wife. That being the case, Sarah must ask permission from Abraham to deal with Hagar's impudence (Gen. 16:5). Just as Hagar becomes Abraham's wife, Bilah and Zilpah, the handmaidens of Rachel and Leah, become Jacob's third and fourth wives.

17. Nachmanides (Rabbi Moses ben Nachman, Spanish biblical commentator, kabbalist, and philosopher, 1194–1270) is critical of Sarah's cruelty and Abraham's laissez faire attitude towards Hagar.

18. Angels of God are extensions of the Eternal, so that their actions and words can be considered as if God is doing the action or saying the words.

19. Gen. 16:11.

20. Gen. 16:15. The Hebrew root *shin-mem-ayin* "to hear" is used in several forms in the story of *Yishma-eil* "may God hear" as a leitmotif. In Gen. 16:11, God *shama* "hearkened" to Hagar's affliction. In Gen. 17:20, we read, "I (God) *sh'maticha* hearkened to you (Abraham)" in regard to your concerns about Ishmael's future, and in Gen. 21:17 "God *vayishma* heard" Ishmael crying after the boy and his mother had been banished to the desert.

Abraham Laughs in Disbelief at God's Announcement that Sarah will Conceive

The Torah does not tell us about Ishmael's childhood, but we know from the announcement of Isaac's birth just prior to Ishmael's circumcision at the age of thirteen, that for thirteen years Ishmael was an only child. During that period, based on Abraham's intense concern about Ishmael's role in the family after learning from God that he will have a second son, we can assume that the patriarch developed a close relationship with his first born son and that he held the expectation that Ishmael would succeed him as the bearer of the covenant. Suddenly, God hints at a different course of covenantal succession by returning to the promise of progeny.

> I am El Shaddai
> Walk before me and be whole
> And I will set My covenant between us
> and multiply you exceedingly.[21]
>
> Genesis 17:1–2

Why does God reiterate the promise of children when Abraham already has a son? The theme of increased progeny, however, continues, as the Eternal changes the patriarch's name from *Avram* "exalted father" to *Avraham*, which is interpreted in the text as *av hamon goyey* "the father of a multitude of nations."[22] Then, to the patriarch's astonishment, God announces that he and Sarah will have a son.[23] Abraham *vayyitzchaq* "laughs"[24] in disbelief

---

21. The translation is mine.

22. Gen. 17:5. David Stein suggests that "the father of a multitude of nations" may derive from a word play on the name *Avraham* as in *av-rav-am* "father of a multitude of people" (Plaut and Stein, *Torah*, 101). Sarna comments that the other nations who look upon Abraham as their genealogical father are the Ishmaelites, the Edomites (the descendants of Esau), and the Midianites—the seed of Midian from Keturah, Abraham's concubine (Sarna, *JPS Genesis*, 124).

23. Gen. 17:16.

24. Gen. 17:17. The Hebrew root *tzadi-chet-qof* "to laugh" appears as a leitmotif in the narratives about *Yitzchaq* "Isaac." Here in Gen. 17:17, it refers to Abraham's laugh of disbelief. In Gen. 17:19, God names the son of Abraham and Sarah *Yitzchaq* "he laughs." In Gen. 18:12, upon hearing that she will have a son, *vattitzchaq* Sarah "laughs" a laugh of incredulity, but when Isaac is born, Sarah exclaims "God has brought me *tz'choq* laughter, all who hear me *yitzchaq li* will laugh (in the sense of rejoice) with me" (Gen. 21:6). Three verses later, in Gen. 21:9, Sarah sees Ishmael *m'tzacheiq* "taunting" or "making fun of" Isaac. In Gen. 26:8, Abimelech observes Isaac *m'tzacheiq* "laughing-and-loving with Rivka his wife" (Fox, *Five Books*, 119).

and says to himself, "Can a child be born to a man a hundred years old, or can Sarah bear a child at ninety!"[25]

Abraham Resists God's Plan to Elevate Isaac Over Ishmael, but Ultimately Puts His Faith in God

Abraham's sudden laugh of incredulity appears to be a reflexive response, for after a moment, the patriarch realizes that God can indeed bring a son to him and Sarah regardless of their age. This realization causes Abraham to be concerned that Sarah's son will displace his beloved first born Ishmael, and so he cries out to God, "O that Ishmael might live by your favor."[26] Abraham's spontaneous entreaty is a plea to the Eternal to allow Ishmael to be Abraham's successor rather than Sarah's child.[27] The Eternal, however, urges Abraham to accept that Ishmael will not succeed him, and that Sarah's son will be the next bearer of the covenant.

> God said, "Nevertheless, Sarah your wife is to bear you a son,
> you shall call his name *Yitzchaq*/He Laughs,[28]
> and I will establish My covenant with him
> as an *everlasting covenant*,[29] for his seed after him."
>
> Genesis 17:19

---

25. Gen. 17:17. In the next chapter, we learn that Sarah had ceased having her period (Gen. 18:11).

26. Gen. 17:18.

27. Robert Alter writes that Abraham's plea indicates that "he would be content ... to have Ishmael carry on his line with God's blessing" (Alter, *Genesis*, 75). *Genesis Rabbah* 47:4 uses a parable to comment on this situation by likening it to a king who wishes to double his friend's allowance. The friend responds, "Do not fill me with a false hope. Pray only that you do not withhold my present allowance!" In applying this parable to the oracle foretelling the birth of Isaac, it suggests that Abraham is telling God that he is very thankful for his first son, Ishmael, and that he would be content if God blessed Ishmael with a long, healthy, and successful life, rather than give Abraham hope that he will have a second son.

28. This part of the verse is according to Fox, *Five Books*, 73; the rest of the verse is my translation.

29. If the Covenant of Abraham is "everlasting" can we assume that God's covenantal promises of progeny, land, nationhood, and universal blessing, are divinely guaranteed, to be realized at a time of God's choosing, regardless of what the Patriarchs and their descendents do? I do not think that the Torah has this in mind. God's covenantal promises are "everlasting" because God will never rescind them, but there is no guarantee that they will be fulfilled without Israel's cooperation and compliance with God's covenantal

The Holy One goes on to assure the distressed Abraham that God will also bless Ishmael and make him fertile, and that Ishmael will become a great nation, a father of twelve chieftains.[30] Still sensing Abraham's resistance to Ishmael's displacement, God tells the patriarch for the second time that Sarah's son is the one who will carry forth the covenant into the next generation, "My covenant I will establish with Yitzchak, whom Sarah will bear to you *at this set-time, another year hence.*"[31] Finally, upon hearing this unequivocal divine announcement of a specific time for the birth of Isaac, Abraham's resistance dissolves, freeing him to accept God's will and have faith in God's intent to fulfill the covenantal promise of progeny through Sarah.

Abraham Demonstrates his Faith Through the Covenant of Circumcision

In the same chapter (17), just prior to God's announcement of the birth of Isaac the Eternal issues the commandment to Abraham that he and his descendents should observe the rite of circumcision as a sign of the covenant throughout the generations.[32] And so, with Abraham's newfound trust in God's promise of a son by Sarah, the ninety-nine year old patriarch

---

expectations. This concept is explicitly articulated in Genesis 18:19 in God's deliberation before Sodom and Gomorrah concerning Abraham's role as God's covenant partner when God says, "I have singled him out that he may instruct his children and his posterity to keep the way of YHVH by doing what is just and right *l'ma-an* in order that YHVH may bring about for Abraham what He has promised him." Thus, Abraham's descendants must model righteousness for the nations *in order for* God to bring about the blessings of progeny and land as well as the covenantal goal of a just world. This means that the Covenant of Abraham for Abraham and his descendants is conditional, since its fulfillment depends upon their actions.

30. Gen. 17:20. The twelve chieftains descended from Ishmael are Nebaioth, Kedar, Adbeel, Mibsam, Mishma, Duma, Massa, Hadad, Tema, Jetur, Naphish, and Kedmah (Gen. 25:12–16).

31. Gen. 17:21 (Fox, *Five Books,* 73). Later, in Gen. 21:10, when Sarah asks Abraham to banish Ishmael so as to provide room for Isaac to mature and assume his rightful role as the second patriarch, the Torah states "the matter distressed Abraham greatly for it concerned a son of his." God comforts Abraham by reminding him that Ishmael will also become a great nation (Gen. 21:11–13).

32. Gen. 17:9–14.

demonstrates that trust by hastening to fulfill the divine commandment of circumcision on himself and his entire household.[33]

Sarna comments that in the Tanach "a change of name is of major significance symbolizing the transformation of character and destiny."[34] I would suggest that at this pivotal point in Genesis such a transformation takes place in the patriarch—from *Avram,* who has doubts about God's intent to fulfill the covenantal promises, to *Avraham,* who displays complete trust in the word of the Eternal. Abraham's self-circumcision is the initial sign of his newfound faith in God's word. Let us now turn to additional indications of Abraham's transformation.

Abraham's Faith and the *Aqeidah*, the Binding of Isaac

Following the Eternal's declaration in Genesis 17 of Isaac's birth within a year, Abraham never again expresses any doubts about God's covenantal promises. Even during his most difficult test, when God asks him to sacrifice Isaac, he does not voice a single objection.[35] A midrash suggests that Abraham was on the verge of challenging God's command to sacrifice Isaac, but he restrained himself.[36] If he had given voice to his anguish, I think he might have said, "O God, Sarah and I have waited so long for a promised son, and now that You have given us Isaac, and declared him to be the one who will carry forth the covenant, You ask me to offer him up as a burnt offering!" Furthermore, if Abraham could contend with God about the injustice of the death sentence for all the citizens of the sinful city of Sodom,[37] why can't he raise his voice at Moriah on behalf of his innocent son? But we hear nothing. His silence signifies that the once doubting Abraham is now God's faithful servant.

I do not believe, however, that Abraham, with Isaac in tow, marches up the mountain with a sense of equanimity. Upon hearing God's frightful command, and no doubt during the three day's journey, Abraham is filled

---

33. The commandment of circumcision is given in Gen. 17:9–14. Abraham's fulfillment of this commandment comes ten verses later in Gen. 17:24–27, immediately following God's announcement of Isaac's birth.

34. Sarna, *JPS Torah,* 124.

35. Gen. 22.

36. In *Tanchuma, Vayeira* 23, the Rabbis suggest that after God halts the sacrifice of Isaac, Abraham reveals to God that when God had asked him to sacrifice Isaac, Abraham restrained his urge to challenge God concerning God's promise that the covenant would go through Isaac.

37. See Gen. 18.

with dread for himself and for Isaac. Nevertheless, I believe he is able to raise a knife over his son, not only because he wants to be faithful to God's command, but also because he trusts that God, in some unforeseen way, will fulfill the divine promise that Isaac will carry forth the covenant in the next generation. Thus, when it comes to the *Aqeidah*, that most difficult of biblical conundrums, we need to make room for a *mysterious paradox* in which Abraham's desire to be faithful to God's command to sacrifice Isaac, and his trust in God's promise that Isaac would continue the covenant, co-exist, even though they appear to preclude each other.

Eli Wiesel envisons a similar paradox. He writes that the *Aqeidah* is a "double edged-test. God subjected Abraham to it, yet at the same time Abraham forced it on God. As though Abraham had said: I defy you, Lord. I shall submit to Your will, but let us see whether You shall go to the end, whether You shall remain passive and remain silent when the life of my son—who is also Your son—is at stake!" Here the tension is between Abraham's desire to obey God's word and his faith in the Eternal as the God of life.[38]

Abraham Trusts God to Help Find a Wife for Isaac

After the *Aqeidah* and Sarah's death, when Abraham's thoughts turn to finding a wife for Isaac, he again demonstrates his complete trust in God. In pursuit of his objective, Abraham orders his servant to go to Haran to select a wife for Isaac from among Abraham's relatives. Abraham reassures him that "YHVH, the God of heaven," who took the patriarch from his father's house in Haran and promised to give him the land of Canaan can be trusted to help the servant obtain a wife for Abraham's son in the land of Abraham's kinsmen.[39] We see here the same Abraham we saw at the *Aqeidah*, a family leader who trusts in God and God's covenantal plan for the future.

Summary of Abraham's Journey from Doubt to Faith

In this chapter, we have traced a narrative in Genesis concerning Abraham's journey from doubt to faith. This suspenseful narrative has four stages: 1) Abraham expresses doubts concerning God's intent to fulfill the covenantal promises of progeny and land; 2) God attempts to overcome Abraham's

---

38 Wiesel, *Messengers of God*, 91.[13]

39. Gen. 24:7.

misgivings by likening the myriads of stars to Abraham's descendents and by affirming the promise of land in a covenantal ritual of smoke and fire; 3) Abraham laughs at God's announcement that he and Sarah will have a son, but then, after coming to the realization that God can indeed bring a child to him and Sarah, the patriarch tries to resist God's plan to displace Ishmael with Isaac; 4) won over by God's repeated declaration that Sarah will give birth to Isaac within a year and that Isaac will carry on the covenant, Abraham demonstrates his faith in God by his self-circumcision and the circumcision of his sons and his entire male household, by his willingness to sacrifice Isaac on the mountain in the land of Moriah, and by his conviction that God will guide Abraham's servant to find a suitable wife for Isaac. The suspense created by Abraham's initial doubts engages us in his plight; his eventual attainment of unshakable trust in God brings us to appreciate his trying journey from doubt to faith.

Why the Torah Speaks of Abraham as Doubting God

When we observe Abraham's doubts about God, we are moved to ask, "How can it be that Abraham, the first patriarch, whom Jewish tradition views as God's faithful servant, is portrayed in the Torah as having misgivings about God's intent to fulfill the divine promises?" I believe we learn from Abraham's uncertainty, that faith in God, even for a patriarch, is neither automatic nor constant. Abraham is a biblical hero, but still a human hero, who experiences crises of faith as he grows into God's trusting and trusted covenantal partner. The biblical author shares Abraham's concerns and doubts with us because he understands that in order for us, Abraham's descendants, to identify with our heroic ancestor, the narrative of Genesis has to portray him as a real human being. An Abraham who never experiences doubts about God's involvement in Abraham's world is not a credible Abraham.

CHAPTER 6

Our Difficult Journey to Parenthood

THE TORAH RECALLS THAT when Terah and his son, Abraham, depart from Ur, Sarah, Abraham's wife, is *aqarah* "barren."[1] This isolated comment about Sarah's lack of a child seems like an insignificant detail, but it turns out to be an ominous indication of what is to come. Once Abraham and Sarah enter Canaan, even though God has promised to make Abraham into "a great nation,"[2] he and Sarah struggle with infertility. They endure ten years without a child until Sarah rails against God for witholding a child from her.[3] She then turns to using her handmaiden Hagar as a surrogate, but when the pregnant Hagar acts superior to her barren mistress, Sarah becomes infuriated and does not carry through with her plan to adopt Hagar's child. Finally, after a quarter-century of infertility in Canaan, God informs Abraham and Sarah that within a year they will have a son whose name will be Isaac.[4] Like the first Jewish parents, Barbara and I tasted the bitterness of infertility, but after an extended journey that tried our spirits to the utmost, we too attained the blessing of parenthood.

Two years before Barbara and I arrived in Worcester, MA, for my first rabbinical post as an assistant rabbi at Temple Emanuel, we had stopped using contraceptives in the hope that we would have a child "whenever."

---

1. Gen. 11:30.

2. Gen. 12:2.

3. Gen. 16:2.

4. Abraham was seventy-five when he left Haran to go to Canaan; he was one hundred when Isaac was born.

Our Difficult Journey to Parenthood

For the three enjoyable but intensely busy years that we spent in Worcester, "whenever" never came. Little did we know that we were part of the large but rather invisible group of married couples who struggle with the problem of infertility.[5] I use the word "invisible" because even now in the twenty-first century, infertility is not something that sufferers discuss easily in public. Infertile couples often feel that they are to blame for the situation, a feeling which can engender guilt and shame. Friends and family are prone to tell them that if they would "just relax," it would happen, but problems with conception do not stem from an inability to relax; they can almost always be traced to specific physiological causes in either one or both marriage partners.[6] During our period of infertility, when a friend or family member would say "You really should get started on having a family," to spare myself the embarrassment and difficulty of going into a protracted explanation, I pretended that I did not hear them, or in a moment of pique, I might cut the discussion short by saying, "Yes, that sounds like a good idea," while thinking to myself, "We're trying like hell to have a child. You don't know the half of it!"

In 1970, when we left Worcester and moved to Watertown, and I began graduate studies at Brandeis while working as a part-time rabbi in Westwood, we sought medical help for our infertility. Over the next six years, we went to three different doctors in the Boston area who specialized in infertility. Barbara underwent numerous tests, and she was put on hormonal medications to regulate ovulation. Since a rise in temperature signals ovulation, like many infertile couples our marital relations were often scheduled by the thermometer.

In the Bible, and I sense for most of human history, if a couple was infertile, it was usually assumed that the problem resided with the wife. Today, we know that causes of infertility can also be found in the husband. I remember visiting a urologist who let me look at my sperm under a microscope. There was not much going on! The sperm count was low and there was very little motility. Fertility specialists have theorized that excessive heat is not good for the production of sperm. That may explain why the testicles, where sperm are generated, are not within the body cavity.

---

5. Dr. Mark Hornstein, a member of my congregation who is the Clinical Director of the Division of Reproductive Medicine at Brigham and Women's Hospital in Boston, in a presentation at our synagogue, remarked that 15% of married Americans experience infertility at some time in their marriage.

6. Gold, *and Hannah wept: Infertility, Adoption and the Jewish Couple*, 67.

In order to minimize heat in that sensitive area, I was instructed to wear boxer shorts rather than jockeys and told to apply ice on a daily basis—not a fun experience! In the meantime, we continued to explore other factors that might be hindering conception. One doctor suggested that there was an immune problem in that Barbara was allergic to my sperm. I assume he based his diagnosis on reliable research, but in retrospect, I tend to think this was his diagnosis du jour. We subsequently went to a third team of fertility specialists who discovered that I had a varicocele in my scrotum, a concentration of veins that could increase the temperature in the scrotum and thereby affect sperm production. I underwent surgery to correct this and soon afterward Barbara became pregnant. And so in the thirteenth year of our marriage after eleven years of trying to conceive, our son, Samuel Micah was born. We knew that medical assistance was an important factor in our success story, but our feeling was similar to that of Abraham and Sarah—God had finally blessed us with a child! While I do not believe that God intervened directly to help us, I do believe that God is the source of life and knowledge that enabled us to become parents. Our contribution was prayer and perseverance.

Our eventual success helped dull the pain of more than a decade of trying to have a child, but it still felt like a long time. A passage from the Mishnah, based on Abraham and Sarah's first ten years of infertility in the land of Canaan says that when a husband and wife are without children for a decade, the husband should take another wife.[7] The importance for the husband to have children is driven by the Rabbis' opinion that the husband alone is commanded to "be fruitful and multiply."[8] In taking a second wife for the purpose of fullfilling the commandment to procreate, a husband was allowed to create a polygamous marriage as Abraham did when Sarah gave her slave Hagar to Abraham at the ten year mark. Although permitted, polygamy was looked upon with disfavor by the Rabbis; not one of the

---

7. Mishnah *Yevamot* 6:6.

8. Gen. 1:28. Even though *adam* "humanity" is created male and female in Gen. 1:27, and the command *p'ru ur'vu* "be fruitful and multiply" is in the plural, the Rabbis understand that the commandment to reproduce is directed to the husband alone. In the Talmudic discussion on this subject in BT *Yevamot* 65b, the Rabbis cite as a proof text for their position Gen. 35:11, where Jacob is told by God *p'reih ur'veih* (in the singular) "be fruitful and multiply." There is a minority opinion in Mishnah *Yevamot* 6:6, attributed to Rabbi Yochanan ben Berucha, that women are included in the commandment to have children. This teaching is much more to my liking.

2,000 sages in the Talmud had a second wife![9] And even though marriage to a second wife was an option, rabbinic authorities did not insist upon it because they understood that marriage is not solely for the purpose of reproduction. Loving companionship is also an important goal of marriage, and if a childless husband and wife have found loving companionship in their marriage, *halachah* (Jewish law) does not force a husband to divorce his wife, even if it appears unlikely that he will be able to fulfill the commandment to have children.[10]

In the early seventies, the time we were trying to have a child, in vitro fertilization (fertilization of an egg by a sperm outside the womb) had not been achieved. In England, in July of 1978, Dr. Patrick Steptoe and Dr. Robert Edwards were the first doctors to facilitate a successful in vitro fertilization birth. Had "in vitro" been available when Barbara and I were trying to conceive, I think we would have had a child much earlier. There were, of course, other options open to us such as artificial insemination by a donor or adoption. We reached an understanding, however, that if we were to have children, we both wanted to be the biological parents.

Although our childlessness was difficult, because we were still in our thirties and had some hope that medicine was on the right track in helping us conceive, I don't think we experienced the depth of anguished feelings that are often engendered by infertility. I remember hearing about a couple whom we had met who were also dealing with infertility. A friend told me that when the wife heard that Barbara had become pregnant she burst into tears; her jealous frustration just overwhelmed her. I also recall a similar reaction during a Shabbat evening service at our synagogue. We were studying the Hallel, Psalms 113-118, which are recited on the festivals. When we reached Psalm 113:9, "God sets the childless woman among her household as a happy mother of children," a young wife who had been struggling with infertility, suddenly stood up and ran out of the sanctuary; this verse was just too difficult for her to hear at that moment.

Motivated by infertility in his marrige, Rabbi Michael Gold wrote a book, *and Hannah wept: Infertility, Adoption and the Jewish Couple*, about the halachic, psychological, and practical issues of infertility. In addition to jealousy, anger, and embarrassment, Rabbi Gold comments that some infertile couples experience grief, the sense of loss that a husband or wife feels when faced with the knowledge that they might never have a child; it

---

9. Gold, *and Hannah wept*, 45.
10. Ibid., 48.

is almost like suffering the death of a loved one. Infertile couples can also experience a threat to their sense of sexuality, problems in their marriage, loneliness, guilt, and the feeling of losing control. Rabbi Gold notes that while the synagogue community has rites and rituals to support the individual who has experienced the death of a loved one or those who are ill, there is nothing to comfort the infertile couple.[11]

Fortunately, there is an excellent organization, The National Fertility Association known as RESOLVE, which provides counseling, support groups, and medical advice, to assist couples of all faiths who are undergoing the often painful and lonely experience of infertility. For those in search of support with the trial of infertility, I heartily recommend contacting this organization.

I loved and still love being a father. I enjoyed playing sports with Sam and watching him compete in high school football, wrestling, and lacrosse. I loved introducing him to my favorite activity of hiking in the White Mountains. Every summer, Sam and I visited a different hut[12] in the White Mountains. We have many wonderful memories from those father-son hikes. I was filled with pride at his bar mitzvah, and have taken pleasure in his growth and maturity. I have, of course, conveniently repressed my memories of the times when I was angry, fearful, frustrated, worried, or totally exhausted in my role as a parent. Ultimately, what is most gratifying to me as Sam's father is that he is a son whom I love and like, and that he has become a person who has good values and cares about others.

If we had never had Sam, we might have eventually been moved, as Rabbi Gold and his wife were, to adopt. But I also wonder how I would have felt if we had not chosen to adopt, and I had never had a child to parent. I know I would have missed being a father, but looking back over the forty years of my rabbinate, I realize that in the course of teaching and mentoring children, I have had many rewarding experiences which were similar to parenting. I know that at every bar and bat mitzvah, I helped each child (I estimate around 500 during my rabinate) make the transition from Jewish childhood to the status of Jewish adulthood. The Rabbis understood the

---

11. Gold, *and Hanah wept*, 56-65.

12. In chapter 4, I refer to the Zealand Falls hut, the hostel where I worked in the summer after my junior year at college. There are eight such huts in the White Mountains. Sam and I managed to stay at each one over an eight year period.

role of a teacher as parental; they said that when a person teaches Torah to the child of a friend it as though he too was that child's father.[13]

I am especially gratified that some of my students have chosen to enter the rabbinate or are on their way to becoming rabbis. I was very close with Rabbi Danny Freelander, current President of the World Union for Progressive Judaism, who was a leader in the youth group when I was an assistant rabbi at Temple Emanuel in Worcester. Richard Rudnick, who was the president of the youth group for one of my three years in Worcester, after a successful career as a doctor, was recently ordained at the Hebrew College in Newton, MA. And Kenneth Brickman, who went on to HUC-JIR, was also a youth group leader during my tenure at Emanuel. Four young people from my congregation in Westwood who have become rabbis are Rabbi Eric Siroka, who most recently served as the rabbi of Temple Beth El in South Bend, Indiana; Rabbi Alison Kobey, the rabbi of Congregation Or Chadash in Damascus, Maryland; Rabbi Eli Freedman, who is an assistant rabbi at the congregation where I grew up, Congregation Rodeph Shalom, in Philadelphia; and Rabbi Elizabeth Piper-Goldberg Hirsch who has just been ordained at HUC-JIR in New York, and is serving as the Assistant Director of the URJ Eisner Camp in Great Barrington where she attended camp for many years. Waiting in the wings is Allison Poirier, a third year rabbinical student at the Hebrew College in Newton. I consider these young people who began their Jewish education at Temple Beth David and have entered the rabbinate or are on the way to ordination my spiritual children, and I take a great deal of satisfaction in their devotion to Judaism and the Jewish people.

I also believe if Barbara and I had not had a child, I might have spent more time with my two nieces, Jessica and Rachel, my brother's daughters. They are wonderful women, and I always enjoy their company. Jessica is married and living in New York with her husband, Rob, and two daughters, Gwendolyn and Evelyn Rose. Rachel lives in nearby Newton, MA with her husband, Doug, and their two sons, Theodore and Nathaniel. Rachel's proximity allows us to enjoy the Jewish holidays with her and her family and to join them on special outings. Her relationship with me and Barbara is somewhat reminiscent of the special bond I had with my Aunt Evelyn and Uncle Mel, who lived in Gloucester, MA. Their home was a haven for me and my brother when we were growing up and even when we became adults. We were always met with a warm embrace and more delicious food

---

13. BT *Sanhedrin*, 19b.

than one can imagine, including Aunt Ev's specialties—chopped liver, egg salad, New England fish chowder, and fresh strawberry shortcake. So although parenthood is unique and precious, there are also nieces and nephews and other familial loved ones who can become, in some sense, one's children.

I had always hoped for a daughter as well as a son, but we were blessed with only one child. In November 2009, Sam married a wonderful young woman by the name of Dina Filosi. I delight in being Dina's father-in-law, and with the birth of Alexis Eleanor Zoob on November 6, 2012, a baby girl joined our family circle. Barbara and I are thrilled to be Lexi's grandparents, and we are now doubly blessed by the birth of a grandson, Jordan Samuel Zoob, on Mother's Day, May 9, 2015. Who could ask for anything more!

I have always loved children. I used to enjoy standing with the children of our religious school outside of the temple building, sharing friendly banter with them as they waited for their parents to pick them up. Nowadays, I get a big kick out of getting on the floor and playing with my grandchildren. It is an opportunity to get really silly and no one is going to utter a discouraging word.

No doubt, one reason that children and grandchildren are so important is that they represent an aspect of our immortality. They carry our genetic heritage, but even more significantly, if we are successful and lucky in our parenting and grandparenting (*mazal* "good luck" plays an important role in everyone's life), they carry our values and the values of Judaism that we hold precious. As we believe we are part of the covenant that God made with Abraham four thousand years ago, we fervently hope that our children and grandchildren will feel the same. In that way the covenantal dream that God imparted to Abraham, namely, that through him and his descendants "all the families of the earth will be blessed," provides meaning to Jewish life that is transmitted from parents to children and on to grandchildren, from generation to generation.

At our son's bris, we gave him the name *Sh'mu-eil* "borrowed from God." [14] This Hebrew name is in accord with my belief that our children

---

14. This interpretation of the name *Sh'mu-eil* is based on understanding the name as *sha-ul mey-Eil* "asked or borrowed from God." A famous story in the Midrash that expresses the concept that our children are on loan from God is the tragic account of the death of the two sons of Rabbi Meir and his wife Beruriah. The boys died suddenly on the same day. Beruriah placed their bodies in a bedroom and covered them with a sheet. When her husband came home, she told him that a man left a precious deposit with her and now he has come to ask for its return. What should she do? Rabbi Meir told her that of course she

are on loan to us from God. After we have raised and nurtured them to adulthood, we are obliged to send them forth into the world to serve their Creator by serving humanity. Dr. Eugene Mihaly, my Midrash professor at Hebrew Union College, offered the following midrashic reading of Genesis 1:26 that speaks to this point. When God was about to create human beings, the Holy One said, "Let *us* make human beings in our image after our likeness." The immediate question that arises is who is the "us?" Weren't we created by just one God? Some commentators have suggested that the "us" is a royal "we," but most biblical scholars posit that "us" refers to the heavenly angels, God's cabinet, if you will. Dr. Mihaly offered another interpretation: the "us" is Adam and Eve and all future husbands and wives whom God invites to join in the act of co-creation—"Come join with Me, as together we try to fashion children in the divine image and likeness." In this spirit, Barbara and I have tried to raise our son to be godly so that he might participate in the covenant which calls on us to work in partnership with God for *Tikkun Olam* the "Repair of the World."

As Barbara and I, like Abraham and Sarah, were blessed with a child following a long and difficult journey of infertility, I pray that the hopes and prayers of infertile couples throughout the world may be realized in a way that brings joy and blessing to them and all humanity.

---

must return the deposit. She then led him to the bedroom and showed him their two sons and repeated to her grief-stricken husband the words from Job 1:21, "*Adonai* gave, *Adonai* has taken away, blessed be the name of *Adonai*" (*Midrash Proverbs* 31:10).

CHAPTER 7

The Covenant Between the Pieces and the Covenant of Circumcision

THE COVENANT OF ABRAHAM is confirmed[1] in Genesis by *two distinct sacrifical* rituals; the first is carried out by God, the second by Abraham. In Genesis 15, God, in a theophany of smoke and fire, confirms the divine covenantal promise of land by passing between bisected animals that Abraham had prepared. The Rabbinic name for this ritual is *B'rit Bein Habb'tarim*[2] the "Covenant Between the Pieces." The second ritual occurs two chapters later, in Genesis 17, when God commands Abraham to confirm the covenant by circumcising himself, his son Ishmael, and all the male members of his household, a ritual which the Rabbis call *B'rit Milah* the "Covenant of Circumcision."[3] God goes on to declare that "at the age of eight days, every male among you throughout the generations, shall be circumcised . . ."[4] The *sacrificial* dimension of *b'rit milah* is that a father, instead of sacrificing his new born son to the Creator, redeems him by means of the symbolic offering of circumcision. In Akkadian, the oldest Semitic language of Mesopotamia[5] and the lingua franca of that area from about 2,500 to 800 BCE,

---

1. I use the word "confirmed" because I believe the covenant is first established in Gen. 12. See chapter 3.
2. *Numbers Rabbah*, 14:11 features an example of this term.
3. BT *M'nachot*, 53b has an example of this term.
4. Gen.17:12.
5. Sumerian is older than Akkadian, but it is not a Semitic language. Sumerian

"to make a covenant" is expressed by the idiom *hayaram qatalum* "to kill a donkey."[6] This suggests that the *sacrificial nature* of both covenant rituals in Genesis derives from earlier ancient Near Eastern models.[7] One can also infer the sacrificial origins of covenant ceremonies in the Tanach from the fact that the most common *biblical expression* for making a covenant is *karat b'rit* "he *cut* a covenant."[8]

In this chapter, we will examine in greater detail the two sacrificial covenant rituals under discussion—the Covenant between the Pieces and the Covenant of Circumcison.

B'rit Bein Habb'tarim, the Covenant Between the Pieces (Genesis 15)

God's response to Abraham's challenge "*Adonai* YHVH (*Elohim*) how shall I know that I am to possess it (the land)?"[9] is to ask Abraham to bring a calf, a she-goat, and a ram, and two birds (a turtledove and a young bird). Apparently, Abraham is familiar with the ritual God has in mind, for without additional instructions, he slaughters the animals and the birds, bisecting the three animals but leaving the two birds whole.[10] He then places the animal halves and the two whole birds opposite each other so that there is a single aisle (on each side of the aisle there are three animal halves and one bird). Vultures descend upon the carcasses, but Abraham drives them off. As the sun is about to set, Abraham goes into a deep trance-like sleep.[11] In a dream

---

has no known linguistic relatives. The Sumerians invented cuneiform writing which the Akkadians borrowed.

6. See Held, "Philological Notes on Mari Covenant Rituals," 32-40. For additional discussion about the sacrificial dimension of the Covenant of Circumcision in Jewish tradition, see chapter 8 in this book.

7. Note that the Covenant at Sinai is established by the people's verbal assent, *na-aseh v'nishma* "we will faithfully hearken," along with the *dashing of sacrificial blood* by Moses on the people (Ex. 24:7–8).

8. The expression "to cut a covenant" appears in both divine and human covenants. In Gen. 15:18 it is applied to God's participation in the Covenant Between the Pieces— *karat YHVH et Avram b'rit* "YHVH made (cut) a covenant with Abram." An example of its usage in a human context is the pact between Abraham and Abimelech in Gen. 21:32, *vayyichr'tu vrit b'veir shava* "they made (cut) a covenant in Beer-sheba."

9. Gen. 15:8.

10. The practice of sacrificing a whole bird is specified in Lev. 1:17 where we read that a sacrificial bird should not be severed.

11. These preparatory acts are described in Gen. 15:9–11.

oracle, God reveals to Abraham that his descendants will experience oppressive slavery in a foreign land, followed by divine judgment against their oppressors and an eventual return to Canaan. After the dream, darkness descends and "a smoking oven and a flaming torch," manifestations of the divine presence,[12] course between the pieces in a dramatic demonstration of God's commitment to the covenant. At the conclusion of the ceremony, we encounter the first usage of the word *b'rit* "covenant" in connection with the covenant between God and Abraham—"On that day YHVH *karat b'rit* cut a covenant with Abram saying, 'To your offspring I assign this land, from the river of Egypt[13] to the great river, the river Euphrates.' "[14]

In Jeremiah 34, there is another biblical example of a Covenant Between the Pieces. Unlike the *divine* covenant in Genesis 15 which God makes with Abraham, the ritual in Jeremiah is a *human* covenant between King Zedekiah, the last King of Judah, and the nobles of Judah and Jerusalem. It takes place many centuries after the days of Abraham, when Jerusalem is under siege by the Babylonians (587 BCE). The Judean nobles have broken the Sinaitic Covenant by keeping their Hebrew slaves beyond the six year period enjoined in Deuteronomy.[15] King Zedekiah views the Babylonian army encamped outside the walls of Jerusalem as the instrument by which God intends to punish the city because of the nobles' transgression. In an attempt to avert God's wrath, Zedekiah has the nobles pass between the halves of a slaughtered calf as he executes a covenant with them to proclaim a *d'ror*, a "release" for their male and female Hebrew slaves.[16] Since the ceremony takes place at the Temple, God is a witness.[17] Suddenly, an Egyptian army approaches from the south causing the Babylonian forces

---

12. Gen. 15:17. Sarna observes that the identification of fire with the presence of God appears in many biblical settings such as the burning bush (Ex. 3:2), the revelation to Moses on Mt. Sinai (Ex. 19:18), and the pillar of fire by night in the wilderness (Ex. 13:21) (Sarna, *Understanding Genesis*, 126, 135 note 22). Smoke is another element in biblical theophany. At Sinai it appears in connection with an *eshen hakkivshan* the "smoke of a kiln" (Ex. 19:18).

13. Sarna comments that the "the river of Egypt" is not the Nile which is called *Ye'or* in the Bible (Gen. 41:1; Ex. 2:3–5), but its "most easterly arm, which empties into Lake Sirbonis near Pelusium, not far from Port Said" (Sarna, *JPS Genesis*, 117).

14. Gen. 15:18. The translation is mine.

15. Dt. 15:12. "If a fellow Hebrew, man or woman, is sold to you, he shall serve you six years, and in the seventh year you shall set him free."

16. Jer. 34:15.

17. Jer. 34:15.

to withdraw from the siege of Jerusalem.[18] The nobles see this as an opportunity to renounce the covenant they made with Zedekiah and recapture their Hebrew slaves,[19] an act viewed by God as a profanation of the divine name.[20] The Eternal's response is to declare a divine *d'ror* "a release . . . to the sword, to pestilence and famine,"[21] in which God "will make the men who violated My covenant[22] . . . *[like] the calf which they cut in two*"[23] so that "the officers of Judah and Jerusalem, the officials, the priests, and all the [wealthy] people of the land who had passed between the halves of the calf shall be handed over to their enemies who seek to kill them. Their carcasses shall become food for the birds of the sky and the beasts of the field."[24] The Eternal's devastating judgment comes to pass when the Babylonians, after turning away the Egyptian threat, return to destroy Jerusalem, burn the Temple, and slaughter many of the nobility.[25]

On the basis of similar rituals from other ancient Near Eastern cultures, the ceremony of the Covenant Between the Pieces most likely stems from rites confirming a treaty between a king and his vassal in which the vassal walks between the halves of an animal, priming a *magical curse* that if the vassal violates the terms of the treaty, he will be torn apart like the halved animal. Although an inscription detailing such a ceremony has yet to be unearthed, texts outlining similar treaty ceremonies which incorporate the use of sympathetic magic have been discovered. For example, in an 8th century BCE treaty between Ashurnairari V of Assyria and his vassal, Mati'ilu of Arpad, we find the following ritual involving a decapitated lamb.

> This head is not the head of a lamb, it is the head of Mati'ilu,
> it is the head of his sons, his officials, and the people of the land.

---

18. Jer. 37:3–10.

19. Jer. 34:11, 16.

20. Jer. 34:16. The nobles profaned God's name because they broke their covenant to release their slaves which they swore in God's name at God's Temple. This is a clear violation of the third commandment, taking God's name in vain.

21. Jer. 34:17.

22. This is a reference to the Covenant at Sinai.

23. Jer. 34:18.

24. Jer. 34:19–20.

25. See II Kings 25:1–17. The destruction of Jerusalem and the Temple by the Babylonians took place in 587 BCE. Zedekiah, a puppet king who vacillated between loyalty to and rebellion against King Nebuchadnezzar of Babylon, was forced to witness the execution of his sons. Afterwards, his eyes were put out and he was taken into captivity in Babylon along with a remnant of the nobility.

> If Mati'ilu sins against this treaty, so may, just as the head of this spring lamb is torn off, and its knuckle placed in its mouth [...] the head of Mati'ilu be torn off, and his sons [...] be torn off.[26]

Although numerous Assyrian gods, beginning with Ashur, King of Heaven and Earth, are listed as witnesses to this treaty,[27] it is the inherent magical power of the rite, the tearing off of the head of the lamb and the placing of its knuckle in its mouth, that makes the curse effective. Concerning the role of magic in rituals such as this, Yehezkiel Kaufman writes that in ancient Near Eastern pagan cultures "magic may ... appear in a pure form in rites that have no connection with the will of the gods, but are viewed as automatically effective, or even capable of coercing the gods to do the will of the practitioner."[28]

Ultimately, it is important to differentiate the Covenant Between the Pieces ceremonies in Genesis 15 and Jeremiah 34 from their ancient Near Eastern precursors. The most significant difference is that the biblical ceremonies are devoid of magic. In Zedekiah's covenant with the nobility in Jeremiah 34, the halved animals serve as a *symbolic warning* as to how God will punish the nobles should they violate the covenant they are making. In Genesis 15, where God passes between bisected animals, thereby confirming the Covenant of Abraham, any magical elements that may have been associated with this ritual in its original form have been totally suppressed.

B'rit Milah, The Covenant of Circumcision (Genesis 17)

In Genesis 17, it is Abraham's turn to confirm the covenant by means of his own ritual circumcision. In the initial verses of the chapter, God prepares Abraham for an expanded restatement of the covenant and its accompanying covenantal ritual of circumcision with the following charge:

---

26. *ANET*, 532-33. Another example of a sympathetic magical curse occurs in a vassal treaty of the Assyrian monarch Esharhaddon—"If you sin against this treaty ... Just as (these) yearlings and spring lambs, male and female, are cut open and their entrails are rolled around their feet, so may the entrails of your sons and daughters be rolled around your feet." *ANET*, 539.

27. Ibid., 533.

28. Kaufman, *Character of Israelite Religion*, 40.

The Two Covenant Rituals Between God and Abraham

> I am El Shaddai,
> *hithalleich l'phanai vehyei tamim*
> Walk before Me and be whole,
> and I will set *b'riti* My covenant between us
> and multiply you exceedingly. [29]
>
> Gen. 17:1–2

The Rabbis understand *vehyei tamim* "be whole" to refer to a physical wholeness or perfection that results from circumcision, the culminating focus of Genesis 17.[30] It is more likely that God's challenge to "be whole" is a moral exhortation, a restatement of God's initial covenantal charge to Abraham in Genesis 12:2 *vehyei b'rachah* "be a blessing."[31] In Genesis 17:3, Abraham indicates his willingness to accept God's challenge to "walk before Me and be whole" by bowing down in God's presence. God then reiterates the basic terms of the covenant with some important additions including changing the patriarch's name from *Avram* to *Avraham*, which is interpreted to mean *av hamon goyim* "the father of a multitude of nations," an allusion to the promise of countless progeny who in turn will become the founders of new nations. For the first time, God also declares that "kings shall come forth from you," an oracle pointing to the eventual rise of the monarchy in Israel and Judah.[32] This is followed by a restatement of the divine pledge to be God to Abraham and his descendants, and to give them the land as an everlasting possession.[33]

Following this renewal of the terms of the covenant, the Eternal sets forth the stipulations of the ritual of circumcision whereby Abraham can confirm his covenantal partnership with God. God asks Abraham to circumcise all the male members of his household including his slaves, whether

---

29. The translation is mine.
30. Rabbi Judah HaNasi in Mishnah *N'darim* 3:11.
31. The moral, as opposed to the Rabbis' physical dimension of the divine charge to Abraham *vehyei tamim* "be whole" in Gen. 17:1, is strengthened by its allusion to the story of Noah. The reference to Noah's upright character, Gen. 6:9, includes two key words (*tamim* and *hithallech*): "Noah was a righteous man, *tamim* whole (or blameless) in his generation; Noah *hithallech* walked with God." The same two words appear here in God's charge to Abraham in Gen. 17:1—"*Hithalleich* Walk before me and be *tamim* whole."
32. Gen. 17:6.
33. Gen. 17:8.

home-born or purchased. In addition, all of Abraham's descendants are commanded to circumcise their infant sons on the eighth day of life.[34]

Having imparted to Abraham the requirements concerning circumcision, God goes on to inform him that within a year, he and Sarah will have a son who is to be named Isaac.[35] As we observed in chapter 5, once the reluctant Abraham fully grasps that God is determined to make the yet-to-be-born Isaac rather than Ishmael the next covenantal leader, he submits to God's will and demonstrates his full commitment to the covenant by circumcising himself, his thirteen year old son Ishmael, and his entire household.[36] When Isaac is born, Abraham enters him into the covenant on the eighth day as God had commanded.[37]

Circumcision As a Sign of the Covenant

Genesis 17:11 states that circumcision is a "sign of the covenant." When something is a sign, it is a reminder of something else. After the Flood in the days of Noah, the rainbow is designated as the sign of a covenant between God and all flesh, so that when God sees the rainbow, a phenomenon of nature associated with rain storms, God will remember the divine promise to never again let loose a flood of rain that can destroy every living being.[38] H. Eilberg-Schwartz has suggested that the removal of the foreskin from the *male reproductive organ* is a fitting sign for the Covenant of Abraham because it points to the covenantal promise of fertility.[39] Baruch Levine notes that when we look at the metaphorical use of the term *areil* "uncircumcised" in the Tanach as it is applied to the lips of Moses[40] and the ears and hearts of the Israelites,[41] these organs are thought of as being

---

34. Gen. 17:9–14.
35. Gen. 17:19, 21.
36. Gen. 17:23–27.
37. Gen. 21:4.
38. Gen. 9:12–17.
39. Eilberg-Schwartz, *Savage in Judaism*, 146–48.
40. Ex. 6:12, 30.
41. In Jer. 6:10, God says "To whom shall I speak, give warning that they (the Judeans) may hear? Their ears are *areilah* blocked (uncircumcised) and they cannot listen." In Jer. 4:4 God proclaims, "*himmolu* Open (circumcise) your hearts to YHVH, remove *orlot* the thickening (the foreskins) about your hearts . . . "

blocked, thereby impeding faithful speech, hearing, or feeling.[42] Just as the lips, ears, and heart, need to be figuratively "circumcised" so as to restore their proper function, the uncircumcised penis can be seen as in need of uncovering so that it too might better fulfill its basic function of being fruitful. Lawrence Hoffman in *Covenant of Blood* applies the causal connection between circumcision and fruitfulness to biblical horticulture by drawing our attention to Leviticus 19:23–25.[43] There we read "when you enter the land and plant any tree for fruit *va'araltem orlato et piryo* you shall trim its fruit in the manner of a foreskin."[44] For three years, the period in which the fruit tree is being "circumcised," the fruit may not be eaten. In the fourth year, the fruit is to be given as an offering to God, and in the fifth year, the fruit may be consumed by the Israelite farmer. The entire passage concludes with the statement "that its yield to you may be increased: I am YHVH your God."[45] Thus, by observing the religious dictate of pruning the immature fruit as if it were a foreskin for three years and dedicating the fourth year fruit to God, the result will be enduring fruitfulness.[46]

Shaye Cohen posits that the Covenant of Circumcision not only refers to the divine promise of fertility, it also points to the promise of land. Cohen's argument is based on the reasonable assumption that the promise of progeny and the promise of land go hand in hand, for what is the benefit of progeny without a land to inherit? As implicit textual support for his theory, he notes that just prior to entering the promised land, Joshua circumcises the uncircumcised generation of Israelites who had been born in the desert.[47]

---

42. Levine, *JPS Torah, Leviticus*, 131–32.

43. Hoffman, *Covenant of Blood*, 39.

44. I follow Levine's translation of this phrase (Levine, *JPS Leviticus*, 131 note 32).

45. Lev. 19:25.

46. Even though David Bernat acknowledges that "circumcision has fertility connotations in many cultures," and possibly even in ancient Israel, he contends that in all of the P material, including Gen. 17 where we find the commandment concerning circumcision, there are no explicit allusions to sexual imagery or fertility. Bernat argues that this is because the Priestly code seeks to expunge any references to fertility as an intentional reaction to the sexual excesses of Canaanite paganism (Bernat, *Sign of the Covenant, Circumcision in the Priestly Tradition*, 50–52). See addendum 3 for a brief explanation of the Codes—J, E, P and D.

47. S. Cohen, *Why Aren't Jewish Women Circumcised*, 12. See Joshua 5:2–8.

The Significance of the Eighth Day for Circumcision

The seventh day of Creation is the day on which God completes Creation as we read in Genesis 2:2, "On the seventh day God finished the work He had been doing, and He rested on the seventh day from all the work which He had done." Because the work of Creation is concluded on the seventh day, the number seven comes to signify the concept of completion in the Torah. Passover and Sukkot are seven day festivals,[48] priests are ordained in seven days,[49] the altar is consecrated in a seven day ritual[50] and on Yom Kippur, the Holy of Holies is purified by the process of sprinkling sacrificial blood seven times in front of the curtain that protects it.[51] Given the common usage of the number seven to express completion, it follows that when a male child lives for seven days, a complete week, he is thought to have lived a significant unit of time so that on the eighth day,[52] as he commences his second week of life, he can be entered into the covenant by means of *b'rit milah*.

Circumcision Through the Ages Is a Religious as well as an Ethnic Rite

In Jeremiah 9:25, we learn that many of the surrounding nations including the Egyptians, Edomites, Moabites, and Ammonites, practiced circumcision, but Israel seems to be unique in viewing circumcision as having a religious as well as an ethnic significance. Lawrence Hoffman theorizes that circumcision among the early Israelites may have had a variety of cultural and ethnic meanings, but later, under the influence of the post-exilic priestly writers, it took on a religious dimension when it became a sign of the covenant.[53]

---

48. Pesach and Sukkot are designated as seven day festivals in Lev. 23:8 and Lev. 23:34.

49. Ex. 29:35.

50. Ex. 29:37.

51. Lev. 16:14.

52. I have heard from doctors who say that the clotting factor in an infant's blood reaches its normal level by the eighth day.

53. Hoffman, *Covenant of Blood*, 27–38. According to those who adhere to the Documentary Hypothesis, the entire chapter under discussion, Genesis 17, belongs to P, the priestly tradition. Since this material was probably written by priests, whose primary role was to conduct the sacred rituals of the sacrificial cult, it follows that the P author espouses a *ritual* with sacrificial overtones such as circumcision as the essential covenantal act. So

The Two Covenant Rituals Between God and Abraham

In time, circumcision became the primary indication of Jewish identity. Thus, Antiochus Epiphanes, the infamous second-century BCE tyrant associated with Hanukkah, prohibited circumcision among his Jewish subjects in Judea as part of his plan to forcibly assimilate them into Hellenic culture.[54] Three centuries later in the second century CE, the Roman Emperor Hadrian issued another ban on circumcision. It is said that this prohibition was a significant factor leading to the Bar Kochba Rebellion (131 CE). In the Midrash, the Rabbis propose that *b'rit milah* was one of the few pre-Sinai traditions that enabled the Israelite slaves in Egypt to maintain their connection with the God of Abraham, Isaac, and Jacob.[55] In this teaching, the Rabbis may have been addressing their concern about the challenge to circumcision in their Greco-Roman world where some of their Jewish brethren, especially if they wanted to compete in popular athletic competition in the nude, sought to assimilate by undergoing epispasm, a surgical reversal of circumcision.

Circumcision also proved to be a major dividing line between the early Christian Church and Judaism. Influenced by Paul's teachings, Christianity focused on circumcision as a prime example of what Paul thought was the misguided emphasis of Judaism on observance at the expense of belief. He argued that rather than the circumcision of the flesh, God wants the "circumcision of the heart," a metaphor expressing openness to God, an image which is anticipated in Deuteronomy 30:6 and Jeremiah 4:4.[56] The controversy over circumcision epitomized the emerging differences between the two religions, the Christian emphasis on faith versus the Jewish emphasis on observance of the Torah (rites and deeds).

Given the above flash points in Jewish history, it is clear that circumcision was a vital ethnic as well as an important religious element in the life of the Jewish people in the ancient world. This was also true for Jews of the Middle Ages, and as we shall contend in the next chapter, it remains a ritual of primary importance for Jewish continuity today.

---

strong was the priestly investment in circumcision that whoever failed to be circumcised was to be "cut off" from his people since he had broken the covenant (Gen. 17:14).

54. 1 Maccabees. 1:48; 2 Maccabees 6:10.

55. M. Friedmann, ed., *Seder Eliahu Rabba* (Jerusalem: Bamberger and Wahrman, 1960), 123.

56. Although Paul himself was circumcised on the eighth day (Phil. 3:5), he was a proponent of the view that circumcision was not necessary because he saw it as a metaphor referring to the need to open one's heart to faith. In the Christian Bible see Gal. 5:6; 6:15; I Cor. 7:19; Rom 2:29; Col. 2:11.

The Two Covenant Ceremonies Indicate the Unique Nature of the Partnership Between God and Abraham

In this chapter we have discussed the ritual confirmation of the Covenant of Abraham, first by God, in the *B'rit Bein Habittarim* in Genesis 15, and then by Abraham, in the *B'rit Milah* in Genesis 17. The fact that no other covenant in the Tanach features *two ritual confirmations, one by each party*, indicates that even though God initiates the covenant and specifies its terms, God is not just the "One" who must be obeyed, and Abraham is not merely a passive participant. Rather, they are *partners* in a covenantal venture in which each partner has to step forward to ritually confirm the covenant to reassure the other. In this vein, the Covenant Between the Pieces is God's empathetic response to Abraham's outspoken concern about the promise of land. And even though, on two previous occasions God had declared to Abraham that his descendants would inherit the land,[57] the Eternal does not rebuke the patriarch for a lack of faith, but promptly responds to Abraham's challenge by means of the Covenant Between the Pieces ceremony accompanied by the third clear affirmation of the promise of land—"to your offspring I give this land."[58] Two chapters later, Abraham, at the age of ninety-nine, makes a remarkable effort to assure his divine partner that he is totally committed to the covenant by circumcising himself in accord with God's challenging request. As in God's Call to Abraham to leave his father's house, there is no compulsion. Abraham freely chooses to observe the Covenant of Circumcision because he is inspired to continue his covenantal partnership with God which promises to bring the blessings of progeny, land, and meaning, to himself and his descendants.

---

57. Gen. 12:7; 13:17.
58. Gen. 15:18.

CHAPTER 8

Our Son's Inspirational Bris

WHAT MUST ABRAHAM HAVE thought when at the age of ninety-nine God asked him to undergo self-circumcision! The Torah does not tell us, but the difficulty of the task and the pain involved suggest that Abraham's circumcision was a faithful expression of his innermost commitment to God and the covenant. We can also surmise that one year later, at Isaac's *b'rit milah*, upon seeing the fruit of God's covenantal promise before him and recalling his own memorable act of commitment to the covenant, Abraham must have felt overwhelmed with a sense of holiness and joy. I think that Barbara and I experienced similar feelings, when after thirteen years without a child, we entered our new born son into the Covenant of Abraham.

Over the course of my rabbinate, I have attended many *b'rit milah* ceremonies. On most of these occasions, I have had the honor of bestowing a Jewish name upon the infant after the *moheil*, a skilled and licensed traditional officiant, performed the ceremony. The most inspirational *b'rit milah* was our son's. He was born on Friday, November 26, 1976 at 6:07 PM, the day after Thanksgiving. As soon as Barbara and I came down from the high of the birthing experience, we realized that our son was born on a Friday night after sunset; Shabbat had begun. This meant that the eighth day of his life, the day appointed for the circumcision of the male descendants of Abraham,[1] would occur on the following Sabbath. The Covenant of Circumcision is so revered in Jewish tradition that according to *halachah*, a *b'rit milah* may be conducted on the Sabbath, a festival, or even Yom Kippur, when these holy days coincide with the eighth day of an infant's life. If

---

1. "And throughout the generations, every male among you shall be circumcised at the age of eight days" (Gen.17:12).

the child is born via Caesarean, *b'rit milah* is postponed to a regular weekday. If there are health issues such as severe jaundice, *b'rit milah* is delayed until the infant is healthy and performed on a weekday. A *bris*[2] can also be postponed for practical reasons such as the unavailability of a *moheil*,[3] but it should never be conducted prior to the eighth day.

Four decades ago, at the time of our son's birth, there were very few *mohalim* in the Boston area. That situation has been remedied to some extent by two URJ (Union for Reform Judaism) courses, one in 1986 and another in the spring of 2008, to educate and train Jewish physicians to serve the Reform movement and the Boston Jewish community at large as *mohalim* and *mohalot* (female officiants).[4] In the seventies when our son was born, in the absence of a cadre of trained *mohalim/mohalot* in the Reform community, I turned to a very learned scholar, Rabbi Arnold Wieder, an Orthodox rabbi, a beloved teacher at the Hebrew College in Boston, and an experienced *moheil*, with whom I had co-officiated at a number of *b'rit milah* ceremonies. Even though I knew that the ceremony could be postponed if Rabbi Wieder was unable to officiate on Shabbat, I shared with him that Barbara and I wanted to observe our son's *b'rit milah* on the eighth day, because having waited so long for a child, we felt a need to be as faithful as possible to Jewish tradition. He understood and was willing to try to fulfill our request. At that time, we lived in a first floor apartment of a two family house on School St. in Watertown, MA. Rabbi Wieder's home was on Corey Rd. in Brighton, a distance of about four miles which he would have to walk on Shabbat. Early Friday afternoon, I drove to his house. Rabbi Wieder packed up his instruments for the ritual circumcision, and we re-

---

2. The Ashkenazic (German/East European) pronunciation is *b'ris*; the Sephardic (Spanish/Mediterranean) is *b'rit*.

3. Colonial Jews in America observed *b'rit milah* the "Covenant of Circumcision" more than any other ritual except for the rites connected to death. Due to the lack of *mohalim*, the ritual was often not performed on the eighth day, but postponed until a *moheil* was available which sometimes involved a wait of a number of years. See Jonathan Sarna, *American Judaism, A History* (New Haven: Yale, 2004), 25–26, and Jacob R. Marcus, *Early American Jewry: The Jews of New York New England and Canada, 1649–1794* (Philadelphia: Jewish Publication Society, 1951), 1, 79–81.

4. The "Berit Mila Program" came into being through the pioneering efforts of Rabbi Lewis M. Barth, a faculty member at HUC-JIR in Los Angeles, and Drs. David James and Deborah Cohen. The initial offering of the course took place in a number of cities including Los Angeles, New York, Boston, Seattle, Philadelphia, San Francisco and Albuquerque. Dr. James also helped found the Berit Mila Board of Reform Judaism which sponsored the publication of *Berit Mila in the Reform Context* edited by Lewis M. Barth, 1990.

turned to our Watertown apartment where he set out his implements and prepared the room according to his requirements, including turning on all lights that would be needed for the circumcision on the next day.[5] These preparations were done so that Rabbi Wieder could observe the Sabbath prohibitions of not carrying objects outside his home for a great distance and not turning on lights. I then drove him back to his home in Brighton before the setting sun signaled the beginning of Shabbat.

December 4th, Shabbat *Vayeitzey*,[6] was a bright and clear day. The ground was covered with snow and it was very cold, in the single digits. After worship with his congregation and lunch at home, Rabbi Wieder put on his galoshes, heavy gloves, and winter coat, to which he had attached his warmest scarf by means of a safety pin (so as to technically avoid carrying his scarf on the Shabbat) and walked the four miles in the freezing New England cold to our home. He arrived about three in the afternoon.

My father was the *sandek* (the one who has the honor of holding the infant during the *b'rit milah*). I think he turned a few shades whiter than the snow outside as he firmly held his only grandson's legs in position. According to Jewish tradition, it is the father who is responsible for performing the circumcision. I have heard of occasions when once the *moheil* has positioned the protective shield that exposes the foreskin, Jewish fathers have assisted by making the initial cut. I gladly ceded this right to Rabbi Wieder who served as my proxy. After our son was placed on a special tallit-draped chair set aside for Elijah the prophet, whose presence is invoked as the protector of Jewish children as well as the precursor of the Messiah, I remember feeling the embracing warm hands and arms of friends as Rabbi Wieder performed the circumcision. I also distinctly recall feeling an intense presence of the holy. Tears of joy came to my eyes. Every face was beaming for Barbara and me and our newborn son, whom we were entering into the Covenant of Abraham. Even though his *bris* took place on a darkening New

---

5. According to Rabbinic tradition, turning on a light on Shabbat or starting any electrical appliance or device is a violation of the commandment in Exodus 35:3 "You shall kindle no fire throughout your settlements on the Sabbath day."

6. The first significant Hebrew word of each Torah portion provides the name of the portion as well as the name of the Sabbath on which the portion is read. The first such word of the Torah portion for the Sabbath day of our son's *b'rit milah* was *Vayeitzey* which means "And he (Jacob) went forth." The portion includes Gen. 28:10—32:3. It begins with Jacob's departure from Beer-Sheba in flight from his brother Esau's anger. On his first night away from home, Jacob dreams of a staircase (or ladder) with ascending and descending angels.

England winter afternoon, the aura of God's presence and the closeness of loving family and friends made it seem like the brightest of days.

Following the circumcision, we gathered in our living room for the naming and additional words of celebration. We gave our son the Jewish name:

Sh'mu-eil Michah ben Rav Chayyim uBraiyna
Samuel Micah the son of Rabbi Chayyim and Breina

Samuel was the name of Barbara's father, Samuel Shure, who died from a sudden heart attack when she was a senior in high school. He was a man of many talents and experiences. He had attended McGill University, fought in the trenches in World War I, played the violin in the Kansas City Symphony Orchestra, was a great raconteur as well as a skilled business man, and a loving husband and father. Micah, our son's middle name, was in memory of Barbara's grandfather, Morris Shure, who had lived with Barbara and her parents in Cincinnati. Barbara remembers her grandfather as a fount of gentle love and kindness. I regret that I did not have the opportunity to get to know either of them.

After the naming, I read Hannah's prayer from the book of Samuel which she had recited in thanksgiving for her Samuel, who like ours, was a long awaited child.[7] Like the Matriarchs, Hannah struggled with infertility.[8] Every year, along with her husband Elkanah, and her rival wife Peninnah, who mocked her because she was barren, Hannah attended the annual festival sacrifices at the sanctuary in Shiloh where she would ask God to fulfill her request for a child. One time, in the midst of prayer, she made a vow to the Eternal that if God would grant her a son, she would dedicate the child to the Holy One as a lifelong Nazirite so that no razor would touch his head, no wine or strong drink would pass his lips, and he would refrain from contact with a corpse.[9] Because she was moving her lips but her voice could not

---

7. I Samuel 2:1–10. Hannah's prayer is a generic psalm of thanksgiving and praise to God for overseeing many different aspects of life. Only one verse is applicable to Hannah's specific situation—v. 5 "the childless wife has born seven." This psalm makes reference to "His king" (v. 10) which suggests it was written during the period of the Israelite monarchy. Because Samuel's birth took place before the monarchy, it is doubtful that Hannah actually uttered this psalm. A later editor probably inserted it in the text.

8. In chapter 15, I discuss the infertility experienced by Sarah, Rebekah, and Rachel, as well as Leah's period of infertility which took place after the birth of four sons (Gen. 30:9).

9. Numbers 6:1–8.

Our Son's Inspirational Bris

be heard, Eli, the high priest at the Temple in Shiloh, accused her of being intoxicated. When Hannah informed him that her mumblings were words of prayer that came from her intense desire for a child, he promised to pray to God on her behalf. Within a year, a son was born whom she named *Sh'mu-eil*, a name which the biblical text interprets as *mei-YHVH sh'iltiv* "I requested him from YHVH."[10] Even though there is no verification of it in the Tanach, we can assume that Hannah fulfilled her vow to raise Samuel as a Nazirite. After he was weaned, she brought him to Eli to be trained as a priest and said, "*hishaltihu* I lend him to YHVH. For as long as he lives he is *sha-ul* lent to YHVH."[11] According to the book of Samuel, it was then that she offered her famous prayer which I read at our son's *b'rit milah*. The biblical Samuel grew to be the foremost prophet, priest, and Israelite leader of his day (eleventh century BCE).

Our friend Rabbi Larry Kushner was present at the *bris* and with his usual insight, he spoke about Jacob's ladder from the Torah reading of that Shabbat morning. He made the inspirational comment that the presence of children in a family creates holy ladders to God.

After sundown, I drove Rabbi Weider back to his home in Brighton. I remain eternally thankful to him for enabling Barbara and me to fully rejoice in the ritual of entering our son into the Covenant of Abraham on the eighth day of his life.

At a *bris* there is a remembrance of the ancient rite of sacrifice. One Rabbinic tradition says that Abraham's circumcision took place on Yom Kippur at the site where the Temple altar was to stand and that it constituted an atoning sacrifice for Israel.[12] In the Orthodox rabbi's manual, *HaMadrich*, following the circumcision, the *moheil* is instructed to say "Master of the Universe, may it be Your will that this be considered by You—and thus accepted according to Your will—as if I had *sacrificed* him before Your throne of glory."[13] Since the *moheil* stands in place of the father, it is actually

---

10. 1 Samuel 1:20.

11. 1 Sam. 1:27–28 features a leitmotif on the Hebrew root *shin-aleph-lamed* "to ask"—"It was this boy I prayed for, and YHVH granted me *sh'eylati* my request that *sha-alti* I asked of Him. I, in turn, hereby *hishaltihu* lend him to YHVH. For as long as he lives, he is *sha-ul* lent to YHVH."

12. *Pirke de Rabbi Eliezer*, 29. Ginzberg comments that in older sources, Abraham's circumcision is said to take place on the thirteenth or fifteenth of Nisan which corresponds with Pesach (Ginzburg, *Legends of the Jews*, 5: 233, note 126). This imples that Abraham's sacrificial act of circumcision accords with the offering of the Pascal lamb.

13. Hyman E. Goldin, *Hamadrich*, *The Rabbi's Guide* (New York: Hebrew Publishing

the father who symbolically sacrifices his son. As in the case of Abraham and Isaac, the child is not actually sacrificed; he is redeemed by a sacrificial substitute. Isaac was redeemed by the sacrifice of a ram; today, sons are redeemed by the "sacrifice" of circumcision.

The idea of circumcision as a symbolic sacrifice touches on a core concept of the covenant. When we accept the covenant we are declaring that we want to devote our lives to God's hope for a world of goodness and that we, like Abraham, want to be God's instruments by which "all the families of the earth may be blessed." If we are committed to this messianic vision, it follows that we need to dedicate our children to do the same. This is what Abraham did with Isaac on the mountain in the land of Moriah, and this is what Hannah did with Samuel at the Temple in Shiloh. At a *b'rit milah* we follow in their footsteps. In thankfulness to God for a new life, and with the understanding that we are in covenant with God, we dedicate our sons to join us in the hard work of realizing God's will on earth. In some sense we are saying that our sons belong to God. We do the same thing for our daughters at a *bat b'rit* ceremony.[14] The implicit understanding in both ceremonies is that our children are lent to us by God, so that as parents we may prepare them to be God's servants.[15] Thus at a *b'rit milah,* the ancient echoes of God's covenant with Abraham and the act of sacrifice run very deep.

I am aware that in the last forty years or so, some Jewish parents have chosen not to observe *b'rit milah*. My feeling is that the standard arguments against circumcision—the pain, the risk of infection, and the attitude of "leave nature alone" in matters relating to the human body—are not to the point,[16] because they do not address the central issue: circumcision is a

---

Co., 1956), 36.

14. In Reform Judaism it is customary to hold a ceremony for a baby girl known as a *bat brit* "Daughter of the Covenant" (there are a variety of names for the ceremony including *simchat bat, b'rit bat*, etc.) on the Sabbath following her birth, or a subsequent Sabbath. It is most often conducted at home. The ceremony celebrates her entrance into the covenant and her Jewish naming. In traditional Jewish families, on the Sabbath following a daughter's birth, the child's father will celebrate the event with an *aliyah* and special blessing at synagogue.

15. See note 14 in chapter 6, where the concept of our children as being on loan from God is discussed in reference to the biblical interpretation of the name *Sh'mu-eil* "borrowed from God," as well as the story of Beruriah, the wife of Rabbi Meir, who likened her recently deceased sons to precious divine deposits which God had come to reclaim.

16. In regard to the pain associated with infant circumcision, some *mohalim* use a topical anesthetic. Having been present at many *b'rit milah* ceremonies, I can attest that once the procedure has been completed, the crying of the infant subsides rather quickly

basic religious rite in Judaism which brings our sons into the 4,000 year old covenant with the God of Israel. As a Jew, I cannot simply disregard that Abraham, the founder of our faith, confirmed his covenant with God by circumcising himself in his old age, and that he entered his son Isaac into the same covenant by circumcising him on the eighth day of his life.

The historical and ethnic factors in circumcision are also significant. As we observed at the conclusion of the previous chapter, throughout Jewish history, circumcision has been a defining element of Jewish identity and has consequently been a point of attack for tyrants such as Antiochus and Hadrian who sought our assimilation by banning circumcision. I refuse to let those who forcibly sought to assimilate us be victorious.

In the final analysis, I believe that Anita Diamant is right on the mark when she writes, "The significance and ritual power of *b'rit milah* is not the stuff of reason or even of language. *Bris* is a radical act of faith, as well as a tangible, physical, visceral connection to our most ancient past."[17] For Barbara and me, our son's *bris* was indeed an act of faith expressing our thankfulness to God for a child and for the opportunity to enter him into the covenant. It is therefore very difficult for me to hear of Jews who treat *b'rit milah* with disdain or lack any understanding of its religious significance. Even though the *halachah* maintains that a Jew who is not circumcised is still a Jew, I am concerned by the failure of some Jewish parents to observe this ancient ritual which has been central to Jewish existence and religious tradition throughout our history.

Understandably, when there is an interfaith marriage, the situation is more complex. I have spoken to Jewish spouses who are very anxious about the challenge of introducing their gentile husbands/wives and in-laws to a rite which is foreign to their religious and cultural tradition. I sympathize with their concern. Although I attempt beforehand to educate interfaith couples about the importance of *b'rit milah* in the Jewish

---

with the aid of nursing or a little wine on a piece of gauze. Dr. Thomas Goldenberg feels that the restraint that the child experiences by being held still is the most discomforting element and that performing the procedure in a swift manner minimizes an adverse impact on the child. He also maintains that there is evidence that circumcision reduces sexually transmitted diseases such as genital herpes and syphilis, and diseases of the penis such as penile cancer and infant urinary tract infection (Thomas Goldenberg, "Medical Issues and Berit Mila," in Barth, *Berit Milah in the Reform Context*, 192–96, 202). Ample and clear data from recent studies in Africa indicate that circumcision reduces the contraction of AIDS by 60%. See Mark Shoofs, "Challenge for AIDS fighters: Circumcising Africans Safely," *Wall Street Journal*, Sept. 7, 2007, A1.

17. Diamant, *Jewish Baby Book*, 116.

tradition, if they choose a hospital circumcision soon after birth instead of a *b'rit milah* ceremony with family and friends on the eighth day, I reluctantly accede to their request for a separate naming in their home or in the synagogue at a later date.

Some years ago at a fall meeting for new members at my synagogue, I noticed a very pregnant prospective mother. At the conclusion of the meeting, I asked her if she and her husband were planning a *bris* if she gave birth to a boy. She said that she was indeed going to have a son, but they had decided to have the child circumcised in the hospital a day or two after his birth. I then explained to her that a circumcision performed prior to the eighth day is not a *b'rit milah* ceremony and appealed to the precedent which Abraham had set four millennia ago. "But we just moved from Texas, and we have no family or friends here," she lamented. When I offered to provide her with supportive Temple members for the occasion, she consented. She gave birth a few days afterwards, and on the eighth day of her son's life, I arranged for Dr. Richard Fraser, a *moheil* from our congregation trained in the URJ course, to officiate. I also invited about twenty Temple members to attend the ceremony at the synagogue and asked them to provide refreshments to celebrate the occasion. After the ceremony, the parents thanked me saying they found their son's *bris* to be one of the most inspirational Jewish moments in their lives. I would add that the ceremony initiated for them many years of active participation in congregational life. I sense that this couple like many Jewish families today really did not comprehend the religious and historical significance of *b'rit milah* until it was explained to them. More than anything else, *b'rit milah* ceremonies in my rabbinate, and the moving experience of being a father at our son's entrance into the covenant on that wintry Shabbat, reaffirm for me the importance of the continuation of the 4,000 year tradition of *b'rit milah* as vital to the future of Judaism. And at every *b'rit milah* that I attend, I sense that Abraham, who confirmed his covenant with God at the age of ninety-nine, is there as well, empathizing and rejoicing with the new born Jew whose parents are entering him into the Covenant of Abraham.

CHAPTER 9

The Testing of Abraham

The Ten Rabbinic Tests of Abraham

THE STORY OF ABRAHAM'S near sacrifice of Isaac begins with the phrase *v'ha-Elohim nissah et Avraham* "and God tested Abraham."[1] Although this is the only explicit reference to *"testing"* in the Genesis narrative about Abraham, it provides the cornerstone for the Rabbinic motif "The Ten Trials of Abraham."[2] There are a number of versions of the ten trials in the Midrash.[3] One of the most detailed comes from *Pirqey de Rabbi Eliezer*, an eighth century CE midrashic collection. In this list, the first two tests come from the Rabbis' visualization of Abraham's birth and youth.[4] The last

---

1. Gen. 22:1.

2. *Pirqey Avot* 5:1–6 includes the Rabbis' list of seven special groups of *tens*: 1) the ten statements by which God created the world; 2) the ten generations from Adam to Noah as well as the ten generations from Noah to Abraham; 3) the ten tests of Abraham; 4) the ten miracles performed for our ancestors in Egypt; 5) the ten Israelite tests of God in the wilderness; 6) the ten miracles performed in the Temple; 7) and the ten things created on the eve of the first Shabbat at twilight. Prominent examples of the thematic use of the number ten in the Torah are the ten righteous individuals who could have saved Sodom, the ten plagues, the Ten Commandments, and the ten spies who render a negative report about the prospects of invading Canaan.

3. Slightly differing lists of the ten trials of Abraham appear in the following midrashic collections: Jubilees 17:17 and 19:8; *Pirqey De Rabbi Eliezer*, chapters 26–31; *Avot de Rabbi Natan*, chapter 33; Lewis M. Barth, "Lection for the Second Day of Roshanah: A Homily Containing the Legend of the Ten Trials of Abraham," (Hebrew) *Hebrew Union College Annual*, XLVIII (1987) 1–48; and *Midrash on Psalms* 18:25. *Pirqey Avot* 5:3 refers to the ten trials of Abraham without describing them.

4. As we observed at the beginning of chapter 3, in the absence of any information in the Torah about this period of Abraham's life, the Rabbis use their imagination to create stories about his birth and youth, especially in regard to how the young Abraham came

eight tests in *Pirkey de Rabbi Eliezer* arise from the Rabbis' interpretation of specific events in Abraham's life as described in Genesis:

1. **The Threat of Death to the Infant Abraham:** [Before Abraham's birth, King Nimrod reads in the stars that a challenger to his rule and his pagan beliefs is about to be born.] The leaders and magicians seek to kill the infant. [Their plan is to gather all the pregnant women of the kingdom in one place and to have the midwives murder every male child. Abraham's mother flees and gives birth to her son in a cave.] The child remains hidden in the cave for thirteen years.[5]

2. **Imprisonment and Trial by Fire:** After Abraham emerges from the cave, he preaches against idolatry. Nimrod imprisons him for ten years, and at the conclusion of his prison term, Abraham is cast into a fiery furnace from which God saves him.

3. **Leaving His Father's House** (Gen. 12)

4. **Famine in Canaan** (Gen. 12)

5. **Sarah Kidnapped by Pharaoh** (Gen. 12)

6. **The War Against the Kings** (Gen. 14)

7. **The Covenant Between the Pieces** (Gen. 15)[6]

8. **The Covenant of Circumcision** (Gen. 17)

9. **The Banishment of Ishmael** (Gen. 21)

10. **The Binding of Isaac** (Gen. 22)

---

to believe in the one God.

5. Drawing on Ginzberg's composite account of Abraham's birth and early development, I have bracketed the elements of the story that come from midrashic sources that are not present in the text of *Pirqey De Rabbi Eliezer* (Ginzberg, *Legends of The Jews*, 1:186–89). The account of King Nimrod who sets out to kill all male infants with the help of midwives would seem to have been influenced by the biblical story of Pharaoh, who prior to the birth of Moses, seeks help from the midwives in Egypt by ordering them to kill all male Hebrew infants (Ex. 1:15–16). Similarly, in Christian scriptures, King Herod launches a plan to kill the baby Jesus who is seen as a threat to his reign (Matthew 2). For additional midrashic legends about Abraham's birth and youth, see Ginzberg, *Legends of the Jews*, 5:209–10.

6. Ginzberg posits that the Rabbis ascribe a reward to Abraham at the Covenant Between the Pieces because even though he asked for a sign from God as to whether he would inherit the land, *he did not demand a sign* that he would have children because "he trusted in God" (Gen. 15:6) (Ginzberg, *Legends of the Jews*, 1:235).

My List of Abraham's Eight Trials in Genesis

We have seen that the Rabbis propose that Abraham overcomes ten tests. Although I only identify eight such tests, the exact number of tests is immaterial. What is important is that there is a clear motif of testing. After we have explored my list of eight trials, we will attempt to explain why Abraham was continually tested.

The First Test: Leaving His Father's Home (Gen. 12)

Abraham's first test is God's challenge to leave his "father's house" in Haran. Leaving home is not just a physical and emotional uprooting for Abraham, it also calls for a clear and open break with the pagan values and practices of his father Terah, which are alluded to in Joshua 24:2.[7] Evidence for the continued practice of idolatry by Abraham's relatives in Haran can be seen when Laban, Terah's great-grandson,[8] becomes upset about the disappearance of his household gods which his daughter Rachel steals from him when she departs with Jacob on their way to Canaan.[9] Like the Rabbis, we have to infer that sometime before God's Call, Abraham breaks with the paganism of his father and begins to believe in the one God. It is one thing, however, to believe differently from your father in private, and quite another to make that belief public by casting off your father's authority as Abraham did when he left Haran.[10] Breaking away from his "father's house" and the environment of paganism in Haran was the difficult yet necessary step in launching Abraham's new faith.

---

7. "Then Joshua said to all the people, 'Thus said YHVH the God of Israel: in olden times, your forefathers—Terah, the father of Abraham and father of Nahor—lived beyond the Euphrates and worshiped other gods.'"

8. Gen. 24:15 informs us that Rebekah's parents are Bethuel, the son of Nahor (Abraham's brother) and Milcah. Rebekah is therefore Nahor's granddaughter, Abraham's grandniece, and Terah's great-granddaughter. Since Laban is her brother, Laban is Nahor's grandson, Abraham's grandnephew, and Terah's great-grandson.

9. Gen. 31:19, 30–35.

10. While the Rabbis trace Abraham's public rebellion against his father's pagan beliefs to Abraham's childhood in Ur when he smashed the idols in his father's idol shop and went on to preach in public against idolatry, Abraham's departure from Haran is the first *biblical* sign of the patriarch's break with his father.

The Second Test: The Separation of Abraham and Lot (Gen. 13)

After leaving Egypt, Abraham and Lot's herdsmen find that their flocks are too numerous to dwell side by side in the land of Canaan. They quarrel over resources, an argument which sets up a test of familial relations. As the head of the family and bearer of the covenantal promise of the land, we would expect Abraham to decide who should settle where. Abraham, however, gives his nephew Lot the choice of selecting the part of the land that he would prefer. When Lot chooses to go east to the well-watered fertile plain of the Jordan River near Sodom, Abraham agrees to remain in the mountainous western part of Canaan.[11] The effect of this test is to highlight Abraham's generosity.

The Third Test: The War Against the Four Kings (Gen. 14)

In the next trial, in a conflict of five local kings, including the king of Sodom, against an invading alliance of four kings from the east headed by Chedorlaomer of Elam,[12] Abraham's nephew Lot is captured by the invading forces. When Abraham hears of this, he musters a troop of three hundred and eighteen "home born" men and with the help of three allies, Aner, Eshkol, and Mamre, he pursues Chedorlaomer as far as Dan and defeats him. Abraham then rescues Lot and donates a tenth of all the spoils to Melchizedek, the king and priest of Salem. When the king of Sodom, who had previously been defeated by Chedorlaomer and his forces, suggests to Abraham that he plans to take possession of the captives while Abraham should take the rest of the enemies' chattel, Abraham declines to take anything for himself; instead, he requests that his three allies, Aner, Eshkol, and Mamre, should take their share of the remainder of the spoils.[13] By his actions Abraham demonstrates that he is not interested in booty, and even more to the point, he does not want anyone to attribute his wealth to the largesse of the king of the evil city of Sodom.[14] In this military venture, Abraham shows himself to

---

11. Lot's choice of the well-watered rift of the Jordan takes place before God's destruction of Sodom turns the area into a wasteland (Gen. 13:10–12).

12. Since the kingdom of Elam was to the east of Babylon, it is assumed that these kings were an eastern alliance.

13. Gen. 14:24.

14. Gen. 13:13 states "Now the inhabitants of Sodom were very wicked sinners against YHVH." Also, see Gen. 19 where the Sodomites seek to abuse Lot's guests. The town is eventually destroyed by God because there are not ten righteous individuals to be found.

be loyal to his nephew Lot, brave, altruistic, sagacious, a competent leader of troops, unwilling to associate with disreputable individuals, and uninterested in the spoils of war, all fitting attributes for a patriarch who has been challenged "to be a blessing." Although he still owns no land in Canaan, his key role in this conflict establishes him as an important leader and military figure in the area.[15]

The Fourth Test: Circumcision (Gen. 17)

Needless to say, the divine command to confirm the covenant by circumcising himself at the age of ninety-nine, as well as performing the ritual on his thirteen year old son Ishmael and the rest of his household, is a test of major proportions. Abraham, having been convinced of God's intention to bless him and Sarah with a child, performs his self-circumcision without hesitation.

The Fifth Test: Abraham Pleads for the Innocent at Sodom (Gen. 18)

In Genesis 18, confronted by the pervasive evil of Sodom, God recognizes that before taking action, the Eternal has an obligation to consult with Abraham, God's new covenantal partner, since "all the nations of the earth are to bless themselves by him, for I have singled him out, that he may instruct his children and his posterity to keep the way of YHVH by doing what is just and right."[16] Reuven Kimelman of Brandeis proposes that by consulting with Abraham about the fate of Sodom, God is testing the patriarch to determine whether he proves to be a worthy partner by defending the principles of justice and righteousness.[17] Although Abraham uses

---

15. Consistent with Abraham's martial role in the War against the Kings, the Rabbis occasionally refer to Abraham as God's knight or warrior. BT *Sanhedrin* 89b, likens the relationship between God and Abraham to a king who has won many wars with the aid of a great warrior. According to this midrashic perspective, in asking Abraham to sacrifice Isaac, the Eternal turns to Abraham, God's knight, to stand in the breach so that people will not think that all the previous victories on behalf of God were without substance.

16. Gen. 18:18–19.

17. Reuven Kimelman, in a lecture I attended, advanced the idea that Abraham was being tested by God at Sodom and Gomorrah.

deferential language in confronting God,[18] he courageously challenges God to reconsider the consequences of the Eternal's decision—the killing of the innocent along with the guilty in Sodom. As Abraham argues for sparing the city for the sake of fifty, then forty-five, forty, thirty, twenty, and finally ten righteous individuals, it becomes clear to God and to us, that Abraham is a fearless champion of justice.

The Sixth Test: The Banishment of Ishmael (Gen. 21)

Following Isaac's birth, Sarah sees Ishmael *m'tzacheiq*, a word which has been understood in many ways.[19] I believe it refers to Ishmael's "bullying" or "making fun" of Isaac. Regardless of its exact meaning in this setting, it is clear that whatever Sarah sees Ishmael doing, she reacts by demanding that Abraham banish Ishmael and his mother Hagar from their home, so that Ishmael can no longer compete with her son Isaac for family leadership and the inheritance of Abraham's estate.[20] The Torah tells us that "the matter distressed Abraham greatly, because it concerned his son."[21] God is aware of Abraham's anguish about Hagar and Ishmael, for the Eternal says, "Do not be distressed over the boy or your slave,"[22] and tries to put Abraham's concern for his first born to rest by repeating the divine promise that Ishmael will become a great nation.[23] Aware of God's determination to elevate Isaac over Ishmael and reassured by the knowledge that Ishmael will have a significant future, Abraham accepts God's directive to submit to Sarah's demand so that Isaac's place as Abraham's successor

---

18. "I who am but dust and ashes" (Gen. 18:27) is an example of Abraham's deferential language.

19. Gen. 21:9. For some of the various intepretations of *m'tzacheiq*, see my discussion in chapter 15 under the heading "Sarah has Hagar and Ishmael Expelled into the Wilderness."

20. Gen. 21:10.

21. Gen. 21:11.

22. Gen. 21:12.

23. In this passage God tells Abraham to accede to Sarah's demand that Ishmael be removed and says, "as for the son of the slave-woman, I will make a nation of him too, for he is your seed" (Gen. 21:13). Previously, in Gen. 17:20–21 God hearkens to (*sh'maticha*—"I have heard you," an allusion to Ishmael's name) Abraham's plea for Ishmael by blessing Abraham's first born and by promising that Ishmael will be a great nation and the father of twelve chieftains.

in the covenant, as well as his status as the sole beneficiary of Abraham's property,[24] can be secured.

The banishment of Ishmael to the wilderness is a test which challenges Abraham to put aside his feelings as a loving father by endangering the life of his first born son for the sake of God's covenantal plan. No doubt, Abraham is also saddened by the prospect of being separated from Ishmael for an indefinite period of time. The Rabbis sympathize with his anguish by imagining how years later, Abraham makes surreptitious visits into the desert to visit his banished son.[25] Abraham's expulsion of Ishmael foreshadows what is to come in regard to his near sacrifice of Isaac his second son.

The Seventh Test: The *Aqeidat Yitzchaq*—the Binding of Isaac (Gen. 22)

Abraham's most famous trial, God's command to offer Isaac as a burnt offering on one of the mountains God will show him, is, as we have observed above, the only trial that is specifically designated as a test—*v'ha-Elohim nissah et Avraham* "and God tested Abraham."[26] If we read the *Aqeidah* out of context as an isolated event in Abraham's life (as we do at every Rosh Hashanah in synagogue), we can easily fail to grasp the momentum in the narrative that conveys the idea that by the time of the *Aqeidah*, Abraham's doubts about God's covenantal promises have been vanquished. (We highlighted this dynamic in chapter 5 "Abraham's Suspenseful Journey from Doubt to Faith.") Thus, when Abraham hears the divine command to sacrifice Isaac, he is ready to serve as God's knight of faith. Abraham's silence in

---

24. Gen. 21:12. See 147 for my discussion of how Abraham's banishment of Ishmael may be an act of disinheritance. When Abraham dies, he wills all he owns to Isaac. During his lifetime, Abraham gives gifts to "the sons of his concubines," a phrase which presumably includes Ishmael as well as the six sons that Abraham had with his wife Keturah (Gen. 25:5–6).

25. On Abraham's first visit, Ishmael is absent, and Abraham does not reveal his identity to Ishmael's wife who fails to be hospitable to him. Instead of introducing himself, he leaves a message with Ishmael's wife that Ishmael should replace his tent peg. Ishmael understands that his father has left him a message to divorce this wife and get another. On Abraham's second visit, Ishmael is once again away from home. Ishmael's new wife, however, is very gracious and hospitable, so that Abraham leaves a message that Ishmael has found a very good tent peg that should not be discarded. The Midrash also imagines that eventually Ishmael takes his family and comes to live with Abraham in the land of the Philistines for an extended period. See Ginzberg, *Legends of the Jews*, 1:266–69.

26. Gen. 22:1.

the face of God's unfathomable command speaks of his belief that the God who miraculously fulfilled the divine promise of progeny with the birth of Isaac, will somehow, despite this test which threatens Isaac's life, actualize the divine pronouncement that Isaac will be the one to carry on the covenant after Abraham.[27]

I cannot imagine that Abraham makes the fateful trek with Isaac without trepidations. Isaac is the one, however, who gives voice to the mounting tension when he asks his father, "Here are the firestone and the wood; but where is the sheep for the burnt offering?"[28] Abraham's response "God will see to the sheep for His burnt offering, my son,"[29] is not offered as a deceptive sop to calm Isaac's anxiety; it is a profession of Abraham's faith which he makes in the throes of his anguish that somehow God will fulfill the divine promise in regard to Isaac's future.

When they arrive at the appointed place, and Abraham binds Isaac upon the altar and goes to the extent of picking up the knife to slay his son, God calls off the sacrifice and openly declares "now I know you fear God since you have not withheld your son, your only one, from Me."[30] With this conclusive declaration, God's testing of Abraham comes to an end. After Abraham passes this final test of tests, God reaffirms the covenantal promises of progeny and land to Abraham and his descendants and asserts an unshakable trust in Abraham that "all the nations of the earth shall bless themselves by your descendants, because you have obeyed my command."[31] Now that God is wholly convinced that Abraham is a God-fearing and trustworthy covenantal partner, the suspense in regard to Abraham's suitability as God's partner in the covenant has been resolved.

The Eighth Test: The Purchase of the Cave of Machpelah (Gen. 23)

Although God's testing of Abraham concludes with the *Aqeidah*, I believe there is one more test which arises from a human source—the purchase of the Cave of Machpelah as a burial ground for Sarah.[32] When Sarah,

27. Gen. 17:21.
28. Gen. 22:7.
29. Gen. 22:8.
30. Gen. 22:12.
31. Gen. 22:18.
32. The Book of Jubilees (2nd Century BCE) lists Abraham's purchase of the Cave of

The Testing of Abraham

Abraham's beloved wife dies, at the age of 127, Abraham needs to secure a burial plot for her. At this point, Abraham owns no land in Canaan. He is, as the Torah reminds us, a *geir v'toshav* "a resident alien."[33] Abraham's attempt to purchase a burial site for Sarah is a test of his skill and self-confidence at negotiations with his Canaanite neighbors. The polite and studied verbal exchange between Abraham and the local gentry, and later between Abraham and Ephron the Hittite, the owner of the specific property which Abraham seeks to purchase, is very precise and formulaic. Everything must be done according to the proper protocol, since this purchase of the first "Jewish" real estate in Canaan must be legal to ensure the acquisition in perpetuity.[34] One false word or mistake, and the negotiation might fail. In the end, Abraham is successful and "the field, its cave, and all the trees in the field within its boundaries, passed to Abraham by purchase, in the sight of the Hittites and all the town leaders."[35]

The *Aqeidah* marks the climax of the *five divine tests* I have identified—leaving his father's house, the commandment to circumcise himself and his household, the dialogue with God at Sodom, the banishment of Ishmael, and the binding of Isaac. In my list of eight tests, *three are human tests*. The first two human tests are the contest over resources between Abraham and Lot's shepherds and the War against the Kings. The third human test is Abraham's attempt to purchase the Cave of Machpelah, where we see that the patriarch has attained the respect of his Canaanite neighbors who say to him *n'si Elohim atah b'tocheynu* "you are a mighty prince among us."[36] With the acquisition of the cave and its surrounding property, Abraham passes this trial and obtains the first tangible down payment on the divine promise of land.

Machpelah as the tenth trial (Jubilees 19:3–9). There, it is viewed as a test of self-control because Abraham negotiates the purchase without revealing to the town council of Hittites that God has already promised him and his descendants the land of Canaan. I too see this event as a trial, but for different reasons as stated above.

33. Gen. 23:4.

34. See Sarna's thorough discussion of all the aspects of this important negotiation in Sarna, *JPS Genesis*, 156–57.

35. Gen. 23:17–18. The translation is mine.

36. Gen. 23:6. See chapter 3, note 43 for an explanation of *n'si Elohim* as "a mighty prince."

The Significance of the Tests of Abraham

Why, from the moment Abraham leaves Haran for Canaan to the time of the *Aqeidah*, is Abraham tested? In regard to the divine tests, the explicit reason is that God wants to determine whether Abraham *y'rei Elohim* "fears God" (is thoroughly devoted to God) so that he qualifies as the Eternal's covenant partner. And so, following Abraham's passage of the final divine test of the *Aqeidah*, God states, "Now I know *ki y'rei Elohim atah* that you fear God."[37] A second reason for testing Abraham is that by successfully overcoming his trials, both divine and human, the first patriarch demonstrates to his Canaanite neighbors that he possesses the attributes of righteousness, courage, integrity, generosity, leadership, diplomacy, sagacity, compassion, and of course, faith in God. Abraham's trials then, not only prove Abraham's loyalty to God from the divine perspective, they are also for the benefit of his neighbors and future generations of non-Jews, who will look to Abraham as a moral exemplar, and as a result come to Abraham's belief in the one God. The Rabbis in *Avot de Rabbi Natan A* expound upon the patriarch's messianic role when they say that Abraham's love of the Eternal, as demonstrated by his faith in overcoming his ten trials, "is to be made known" to the nations of the earth who will say "More than all of us, more than everyone, is Abraham worthy of getting his reward [in heaven]."[38] Lewis Barth, Professor of Midrash at HUC-JIR in Los Angeles, draws the implicit teaching from this passage, that the result of the peoples of the world learning about Abraham's ten acts of faith is that they will convert to the patriarch's belief in the one God.[39] A similar Rabbinic teaching on Abraham's missionary role is a word play on "and God *nissah*

---

37. Gen. 22:12.

38. *Avot de Rabbi Natan A*, ch. 33.

39. Lewis Barth, "Introduction to the Ten Trials of Abraham" 16 (unpublished) and in personal conversations with Rabbi Barth. The Rabbis' understanding of Abraham and Sarah as being involved in converting pagans to the belief in the one God is based on the Rabbinic interpretation of the phrase in Gen. 12:5 that on his journey to Canaan, Abraham took with him "the souls *asu* they had made in Haran," that is, the individuals whom Abraham and Sarah had converted to monotheism (*Genesis Rabbah* 39:14). I doubt that this is the *p'shat* "the plain meaning" of this phrase in the Tanach, since conversion to Judaism did not really come into being until the Rabbis. I understand "the souls that they had made in Haran" to refer to the servants or household attendants they (Abraham and Sarah) had acquired in Haran.

tested Abraham" from the *Aqeidah*, where the Rabbis propose that Abraham is God's *neis* "banner or ensign" to the nations, a model for non-Jews to follow.[40]

We, Abraham's descendants who have inherited the covenant that God initiated with the first patriarch, may not be asked to banish our children to the wilderness, or sacrifice them on a mountain top, but surely we understand that a life worth living is a life that is tested. When we remember that Abraham, despite his initial doubts and impatience, passed the many divine and human trials that he encountered, we can draw inspiration for our own trials in our effort to carry out the the objective of the Covenant of Abraham, the messianic quest for universal peace and justice.

---

40. *Genesis Rabbah* 55:6.

CHAPTER 10

The Test of Leaving My Father's House

ABRAHAM'S LIFE WAS FULL of tests; the more he was tested, the more he grew as a mature man of faith. He passed most of his tests with flying colors, so much so, that we view him as an exemplary leader, the founder of our people and our faith. Although the *Aqeidah* may have been Abraham's most famous test, I believe that his most significant trial was the first one, the challenge of *lech l'cha* "Go forth . . . from your father's house." Leaving his father's house meant making a break with Terah's parental authority, religious views, and practices. It also involved abandoning all those material, communal, and emotional supports that we associate with "home." In retrospect, we see that Abraham's positive response to God's startling challenge to leave his home in Haran was well worth it, for if Abraham had never summoned up the courage to break away from his father's house, there would be no Jewish people, no Judaism.

Leaving home is a major American theme. We live in a culture in which maturity is often attained only after leaving our parents' home, usually at the cost of a few broken idols. If we fail this test, our lives may be seen by ourselves and others as unfulfilled. In my teens, I had numerous experiences of leaving home in the physical sense—eight years of overnight camp in Maine, the Quaker work camp trip to England in the summer of my junior year of high school, and then four years of college in Boston followed by five years of rabbinic preparation in Cincinnati and a year of study in Israel. During the decade of my higher education, even though I often made brief trips home, I became accustomed to being away from

The Test of Leaving My Father's House

"my father's house." In my final year of rabbinical school, my mother subtly brought up the idea that I should consider a pulpit in the Philadelphia area. My rabbi, David Wice, suggested that I should think about serving as his assistant at Rodeph Shalom, but I decided not to. I instinctively felt that if my parents were nearby, I would not feel free to develop into the kind of rabbi I wanted to become.

Looking back, I think that the fear that I held of being a rabbi in the same community in which my parents lived was an indication that I had not totally left "my father's house," a term which I see as a metaphor for the powerful parental influence of my father and mother. My parents were rather formidable individuals. They were both accomplished lawyers. My mother had been a valued member of a prestigious law firm in Newark, New Jersey. My father headed up his own law firm in Philadelphia known as Zoob and Matz. He was primarily an estate lawyer but practiced general law as well. He was very respected by his legal peers. He was also an excellent pianist and musician. In 1919, as a freshman at the University of Pennsylvania he wrote the music for the football fight song "Fight On Pennsylvania," which is still played after every Penn touchdown. This made him somewhat of a celebrity in Philadelphia. While at Penn, he also composed much of the music and provided piano accompaniment for the Mask and Wig, a drama club at Penn that produced original all male musicals. He accomplished this without actually belonging to the Mask and Wig, which in the 1920s did not have any Jewish members.

My father cut a rather dashing figure. Although he was only five foot seven, he held himself very erect. He had a broad bushy mustache, something which I may have adopted in his honor (My mustache is on the neat and trim side rather than bushy). In winter, he wore a black derby to work; in the summer, he often sported a straw boater. He smoked a long-stemmed curved pipe; I came to love the sweet smell of his tobacco smoke. In his office and in public, he was at times ebullient and charming and at other times serious and dignified. At home, these two sides of his personality were turned down a notch. Because of the stern component of his persona, he did not need to exercise much discipline on his two sons; we were instinctively disinclined to engage in bad behavior. Underneath his serious demeanor, however, he was very kindhearted. He hugged his sons frequently, engaged in lighthearted tusseling, and rarely scolded or reprimanded us.

My father and mother were not only proven professionals, they were also very cultured and well read. They were voracious readers of novels, history, biography, and classic literature. My father subscribed to *Scientific American* magazine, an indication of the breadth of his intellectual interests. My parents attended the Philadelphia Orchestra often, especially taking in the Friday afternoon concerts in their later years. They loved theater and were knowledgeable about fashion, gourmet food, and wine. My mother was a remarkable cook. My father in addition to playing classical and popular music on the piano was also a knowledgeable and skilled gardener. He grew his own seedling flats for the beautiful flowers that adorned the flower beds in our back yard. Above all, their marriage of over fifty years was a loving and good one, with clearly demarcated roles—my mother ran the house and our social life, while my father was in charge of financial planning and house maintenance. In sum, professionally and personally, they cast a large shadow for their two sons. Measuring up to the public and domestic images of my parents, as well as their implicit high expectations for their children, was not easy.

Although my mother often told me that I had brought them a great deal of gratification as parents, my father rarely mentioned his pride in any particular accomplishment that I had achieved in the classroom or on the athletic field. Looking back, I think my father thought of himself as an exceptional person. He therefore took for granted that his sons would also be exceptional. I yearned to know that he really thought of me as a competent, caring son, and human being. I sensed that he did, but I don't recall his saying so. As a result, I always felt a slight cloud of doubt about his appreciation of me and my talents.

Although I was usually able to anticipate their preferences, my parents were very considerate about giving me space to make my own decisions. When I was a teen, my mother once suggested that I might make a good lawyer, the chosen profession of both my parents, but she did not push it. At college, I was on a pre-med course with the vague intention of becoming a psychiatrist. I think my sudden decision after my junior year to become a rabbi both surprised and pleased my parents. Although they were certainly educated Americans, neither of my parents was an educated Jew. From their reading they knew some basics of Jewish history, but they were not at home in the Bible or any of the great texts of our tradition. In fact, as children, neither of them had been taught how to read Hebrew, and as adults they made no effort to learn. (In their day not many synagogues were offering classes for adults to learn how to read Hebrew, a situation which fortunately has been remedied today.) Thus, by the time I finished my first year at rabbinic school, I had easily surpassed their Jewish knowledge and skills. I was careful never to embarrass them by pointing out their educational deficiencies in Judaism, but it was secretly satisfying to know that my parents looked to me for guidance in all things Jewish. Quite a role reversal!

By choosing the rabbinate, I may have thought that the test of leaving my parents' home was over, but as time passed, I discovered that was not the case. As mentioned previously, after my first three years as an assistant rabbi in Worcester, I found that I missed the joys of study. I was so involved with adult education, the youth group, the religious school, and other responsibilities of the active rabbinate that I had little or no time for Jewish learning. And so I applied to and was accepted at graduate school for a degree in Bible at Brandeis. In addition to the attraction of learning, another voice nudged me towards the pursuit of a doctorate. My father knew that I enjoyed academics. I think he himself regretted that he had not become a college professor. From time to time, he openly fantasized about teaching. I think he would have made an excellent college or law school teacher, for even though he was a bit verbose, he could break down a complicated problem and present it in a very clear and understandable manner. And so, part of my reason for continuing my education was his suggestion that I might look into a doctorate in Jewish studies with the goal of college teaching. My mother was also an ardent admirer of anyone with a PhD from a first rate university, so I certainly stood to gain some points with her. Thus, at the age of thirty, when I embarked on a course of graduate studies at Brandeis, I saw my academic venture as providing my parents with another reason to be proud of me.

Ultimately, I think that my decision to go on to graduate work was prompted by a confluence of my interests and my insecurities. Part of me decided to do it because I love the study of anything Jewish. Another part of me was somewhat fearful of going out on my own in the rabbinate. In addition, deep down, as mentioned above, there was also a desire to fulfill the expectations of my father, as well as those of Dr. Jacob Marcus, one of my revered teachers at Hebrew Union College, known as the "Dean" of American Jewish historians, who had encouraged me to pursue a doctorate after ordination.

The first years of combining graduate study at Brandeis and a part-time rabbinate in Westwood, MA were very fulfilling. I enjoyed the learning as well as my first solo pulpit experience. Like many graduate students, however, after completing my course work, I got stuck on my thesis. My thesis advisor had proposed that I write about divine anger in the Bible. The suggested approach was to do a thorough word study of each anger word in the Tanach to determine how it is used in reference to God's wrath. I knew that Dr. Nelson Glueck, the President of the Hebrew Union College, who had ordained me, had written a very successful and famous doctoral thesis on the meaning of the word *chesed* in the Bible. His major contribution in this study was to determine that *chesed* in reference to the relationship between God and the Israelites refers to "covenantal loyalty."[1] I thought that I could do something similar, but after a preliminary exploration of the many words and expressions for God's anger in the Bible *za-am, za-ap, chemah, charon aph, ka-as, evrah, rogez,* and *qetzeph,* I found no significant patterns or concepts that were worthy of a thesis. I did not, however, have the self-confidence to inform my advisor that this was the case. Instead, month after month, year after year, I kept writing chapters on each anger word, hoping that some important ideas would emerge, but they never came. In retrospect, I feel that my advisor was at fault for not helping me confront the fact that I really did not have a viable thesis topic. As this process dragged on, I naturally began to re-examine my decision about pursuing a doctorate. While I love learning, I realized I did not have a passion for the kind of detailed scholarship that was required to become a biblical scholar. In the meantime, as my congregation grew in size, my congregational duties became more demanding, and I became more accomplished as a pulpit rabbi. The choice should have been obvious. Quit academics and devote myself to serving my congregation and the Boston Jewish community. For a long time, however, I could not do it. I did not want to be judged a quitter, and I thought I would be disappointing my parents. Barbara was very supportive as I underwent periods of intense work on my thesis followed by long stretches of time when I barely looked at it. I knew I had her love and support, regardless of what I decided. Not once did she say, "What's with your thesis?"

It took me a decade after I had started my graduate work to finally throw in the towel. I should have done it much earlier, but I could not muster up the courage to leave "my father's house." Once I did, at the age of forty, I knew I was on the right path to becoming the adult that I wanted to be. Having made the decision to cut my losses, I felt truly liberated. I had

---

1. Dr. Glueck's thesis was translated from German into English by Alfred Gottschalk—Nelson Glueck, *Hesed in the Bible*, (Cincinnati: Hebrew Union College Press, 1967).

The Test of Leaving My Father's House

finally come to understand that while my parents were free to make suggestions about the course of my life, ultimately as an adult, I had to make my own decisions on the basis of what I believed was the best direction for me and not whether my father or mother would approve or be pleased. Not surprisingly, it turned out that my parents really didn't care that I had not obtained my doctorate. They just wanted me to be happy with my life choices. The necessity of pleasing them by getting a doctorate and going on to teach at a college or university was mainly a construct of my own mind. Despite my initial disappointment at not achieving my goal, I have come to realize that I learned a lot about the Tanach in my graduate studies and for that I am grateful. I could not have attempted this book without the knowledge that I gained in my studies at Brandeis. Once liberated, I also discovered that I enjoyed participating in the Jewish community at large. In addition to my contribution as the Founding Chair of the Rashi School, I served on the founding boards of Gann Academy, the pluralistic Jewish high school in the Boston area, and Mayyim Hayyim, the Living Waters Community Mikveh located in Newton. I also served a two year term as the President of the Massachusetts Board of Rabbis. My major regret is that it took me so long to get out from under the shadow of what I thought were my parents' expectations so that I could emerge into the light of what I now know to be my true calling, the congregational rabbinate and community leadership.

Even though Abraham was seventy-five years old when he left his father's house, *only a little less than half his life had passed*, for he lived to the age of 175. If I live, God willing, to a ripe old age, I will have left my father's house by jettisoning my doctoral studies and focusing my energies on the rabbinate about the same stage of life that the first patriarch broke away from his father Terah to set out on his life's mission. I take some comfort in that realization.

CHAPTER 11

Isaac Puts Down Roots in the Land of Canaan

Abraham's Merit Provides the Dynamic for God's Covenant with Isaac

Before Isaac's birth, God informs Abraham that Isaac will succeed him as the second patriarch:

> But My covenant I will maintain with Isaac,
> whom Sarah shall bear to you at this season next year.
>
> Genesis 17:21

The Torah, however, does not mention the covenant again in connection with Isaac until after his marriage to Rebekah and the birth of their twin sons, Jacob and Esau. At that time, there is a famine in the land of Canaan, and before Isaac has a chance to flee to Egypt as his father did, God challenges him to enter into the covenant:

> *Do not go down to Egypt;*
> *stay in the land which I point out to you;*
> Reside in this land, and I will be with you and bless you;
> I will give all these lands to you and your offspring,
> fulfilling the oath that I swore to your father Abraham.
> I will make your descendants as numerous as the stars of heaven,
> and give to your descendants all these lands,
> so that all the nations of the earth shall bless themselves by your offspring—

Isaac Puts Down Roots in the Land of Canaan

Inasmuch as Abraham obeyed Me and followed My mandate:
My commandments, My laws, and My teachings.

Genesis 26:2–5

As was the case with Abraham, there is no reference to the word *b'rit* when God invites Isaac into the covenant by promising progeny and land and by setting forth the vision of a day when all the peoples of the earth will be blessed by Isaac's seed. God also tells Isaac that if he stays in the land and does not go down to Egypt, he and his descendants will enjoy the covenantal blessings of progeny and land "inasmuch as Abraham obeyed Me and followed My mandate: My commandments, My laws, and My teachings."[1] Abraham's merit, then, provides the primary dynamic for the establishment of the covenantal relationship between God and Isaac.

Abraham Establishes the Foundation for Isaac's Claim to the Land

With the charge "Stay in the land!" God's call to Isaac to take up the challenge of covenantal leadership focuses on the task of maintaining and strengthening a physical presence in the land of Canaan. In order to fully understand this challenge, we need to explore in greater detail how Abraham's act of staking claim to the land prepared the way for Isaac.

God makes the initial promise of the land to Abraham when the patriarch takes his first steps in the land at Shechem, "I will give this land to your offspring."[2] It is ironic that immediately after Abraham receives the promise of the land, famine forces him to abandon it for Egypt. Upon his return from Egypt, Abraham graciously invites Lot, his nephew, to choose where he would like to settle. Lot decides to claim the land to the east, in the vicinity of Sodom, which at that time is described as "well-watered" like "the garden of YHVH, like the land of Egypt."[3] Abraham is left to settle in the west, the hill country of the land of Canaan. At first glance, Abraham's territory seems less desireable, but Speiser notes that there is a "gentle irony" in that with

---

1. Gen. 26:5. The reference to Abraham keeping God's commandments, laws, and teachings, seems premature as these terms are more appropriate for the Covenant at Sinai. The Rabbis use this verse to suggest that Abraham was already observing the laws given at Sinai. See BT *Yoma* 28b.
2. Gen. 12:7.
3. Gen. 13:10.

God's destruction of Sodom and Gomorrah, Lot's lush garden-like valley in the Jordan rift will be turned into a wasteland, while Abraham's rugged hill country is destined to become the land of milk and honey.[4]

After Lot departs for Sodom, Abraham stands at a site between Bethel and Ai where he had previously built an altar, while God directs him to visually survey the land in all four directions. What he sees constitutes his inheritance and that of his offspring.

> Look around from where you are,
> to the north and the south,
> to the east and the west,
> for all the land that you see,
> I am giving to you and your descendants forever.[5]
>
> Genesis 13:14

God goes on to instruct Abraham to confirm his visual claim by traversing the land.

> Get up and walk about the land,
> its length and its breadth,
> for it is to you that I am giving it.[6]
>
> Genesis 13:17

Sarna comments that throughout the ancient world, walking around a plot of land was a symbolic act of acquisition; the Rabbis call this *chazaqah*.[7] Similarly, Abraham's sojourning in a multitude of Canaanite sites,[8] his building of altars at some of these locations,[9] his struggle to secure the use

---

4. Speiser, *Genesis*, 98.
5. Translation by Chaim Stern, (Plaut and Stein, *Torah*, 94).
6. Ibid., 94.
7. Sarna, *JPS Genesis*, 100. In BT *Baba Batra* 100a, Rabbi Eliezer understands Abraham's traversing the land in Gen. 13 as an act of acquisition.
8. Abraham is found at the following sites in Canaan: Shechem—Gen. 12:6; between Ai and Bethel—Gen. 12:8; Negev—Gen. 13:1; Hebron—Gen. 13:18; Dan—Gen. 14:14; Valley of Shaveh in the vicinity of Salem (Jerusalem)—Gen. 14:17–18; between Kadesh and Shur in the Negev, in the territory of Gerar—Gen. 20:1; Beer-sheba—Gen. 21:33; the land of Moriah—Gen. 22:2. The deeds of Abraham at some of these sites (Shechem, Bethel, Hebron, and Jerusalem) foreshadow significant events at the same sites in the history of the kingdoms of Israel and Judah.
9. Abraham builds sacrificial altars at Shechem (Gen. 12:7), between Ai and Bethel (Gen. 12:8), and at Hebron (Gen. 13:17).

Isaac Puts Down Roots in the Land of Canaan

of a well that he had excavated in the territory of King Abimelech,[10] and his purchase of a family burial site in Hebron,[11] are all actions that help establish his claim to the land that God had promised him and his descendants.

Isaac's Obedience to God's Charge "Stay in the Land" Helps Sustain Abraham's Claim to Canaan

Unlike his father, Isaac is not called on to be God's ensign or knight. Instead, Isaac's specific covenantal challenge, which he receives in the midst of famine, is "Do not go down to Egypt. Stay in the the land that I point out to you. Reside in this land and I will be with you and bless you."[12] God's insistent call for Isaac to stay in the land may reflect the Eternal's concern that if Isaac goes down to live by the banks of the Nile, he might be tempted to stay there. Isaac's commitment to remain in Canaan is needed to maintain and strengthen the covenantal claim to the land that Abraham initiated. Sarna points out that God's call to Isaac to stay in Canaan is not as simple a task as it appears, since the challenge for a "pastoralist" to remain in a land that is periodically subject to famine involves risking the loss of livestock and starvation.[13]

Isaac Follows in Abraham's Footsteps but Breaks New Ground as the Only Patriarch to Farm the Land

There is a midrashic maxim that states *"whatever happened to Abraham, also happened to his children."*[14] "His children" in this midrashic context does not refer to Abraham's actual children, Ishmael, Isaac, and the six sons whom he fathered with Keturah,[15] but rather Abraham's descendants,

---

10. Gen. 21:22–30.
11. Gen. 23.
12. Gen. 26:2.
13. Sarna, *JPS Genesis*, 183.

14. *Tanchuma, Lech L'cha*, 9:60, in reference to Abraham, says *kol she-eira lo eira l'vanav* "all that happened to him happened to his children." *Genesis Rabbah* 40:6 has the same concept with slightly different vocabulary—*kol mah shekkatuv b'Avraham katuv b'vanayv* "Whatever is written [in the Torah] about Abraham, is written about his children."

15. After Sarah dies, Abraham marries Keturah with whom he has six sons: Zimran, Jokshan, Medan, Midian, Ishbak, and Shuah (Gen. 25:2).

the *b'nai Yisrael* "the children of Israel." Thus, according to the Midrash, as Abraham was chosen from his family, his descendents were chosen among the seventy nations; as Abraham was brought out from Haran to Canaan, his children were brought out of Egypt to Canaan; as God promised to bless Abraham, the Eternal promised to bless his seed, etc.[16] There is ample reason, however, to apply this Rabbinic adage to Isaac, for Isaac reenacts many of his father's experiences. Thus, Isaac and Rebekah participate in a wife-sister incident with King Abimelech of Gerar,[17] similar to the one Abraham and Sarah had experienced with the same king.[18] Later, Isaac, like his father, becomes involved in a controversy over water with the envious herdsmen of Gerar, who block up the wells that Abraham had excavated. Isaac digs his father's wells anew, but his quarrels with the shepherds continue until he excavates a well that he names *R'chovot* "ample space," and they finally leave him in peace.[19] From there, Isaac goes up to Beer-sheba, a site where his father also resided,[20] and God blesses him "for the sake of My servant Abraham."[21]

While Isaac is in Beer-sheba, he reenacts another important event in his father's life. King Abimelech, Ahuzzath, his councilor, and Phicol, chief of his troops, come to visit Isaac. The patriarch is surprised to see them because they and their subjects have been hostile to him by contesting access to the wells in Gerar that Isaac had excavated. When he asks them the reason for their visit, they respond that they have seen how God has blessed him, and they are now ready to offer him a peace treaty.[22] And so, just as Abraham secured a *b'rit* "a treaty" with Abimelech in Beer-sheba which resolved a dispute over water,[23] now Isaac does the same thing, in the same place.[24]

Since so many of Isaac's experiences echo those of his father, and because the Torah affirms that God's covenant with Isaac was initiated as a result of Abraham's merit, we feel compelled to ask, "Does Isaac make any

16. See the references in *Tanchuma* and *Genesis Rabbah* cited in note 14 above.
17. Gen. 26:6–11.
18. Gen. 20.
19. Gen. 26:17–23.
20. Gen. 22:19.
21. Gen. 26:24.
22. Gen. 26:26–31.
23. Gen. 21:22–34.
24. Gen. 26:31.

unique contributions to the continuity of the Covenant of Abraham?" A partial response to this question is to point out that Isaac does something that neither Abraham nor Jacob does. With God's help, he becomes a successful farmer; his harvest in relation to the unit of seed planted is one hundred to one.[25] Isaac's bountiful agricultural venture expresses the idea that he does not just conserve the covenantal claim to the land, he strengthens it by putting down living roots in the promised land.

Despite a Tendency Towards Passivity, Isaac Becomes a Resilient Patriarch

Many have characterized Isaac in a disparaging way as the "passive patriarch." I have to admit that there are a number of valid reasons for this epithet. As a boy he is bullied by his older brother Ishmael so that Sarah has to step in to protect him by having the aggressive Ishmael banished to the desert. Perhaps the most frequently cited example of Isaac's passivity is the *Aqeidah,* when Isaac offers no physical or verbal resistance to being bound upon the altar. Also, Isaac, unlike his sons Jacob and Esau, makes no effort to select his own wife; Abraham has to take the initiative by sending his servant to obtain a wife for Isaac among Abraham's relatives in Haran. On that occasion, Abraham admonishes the servant not to consent to a marriage arrangement in which Isaac leaves Canaan to live with his wife's family in Haran.[26] Abraham may be fearfull that should this happen, his compliant son might remain in Haran, with the result that the patriarchal claim to the land of Canaan could be jeopardized. Fortunately, this never comes to pass, because Rebekah, agrees to return with Abraham's servant to live with Isaac in Canaan.

When Rebekah arrives in Canaan, we read, "Isaac then brought her into the tent of his mother Sarah, and he took Rebekah as his wife. Isaac loved her and thus found comfort after his mother's death."[27] Apparently, Isaac is unable to bring closure to his mourning for his mother on his own. It is only when the love he holds for his mother is replaced by his love for Rebekah that he finds solace. Later, Rebekah deftly deceives the nearly blind Isaac by orchestrating Jacob's theft of the blessing of the first born.

---

25. Gen. 26:12. Sarna offers this view of a seed to harvest ratio of "a hundred fold" according to the understanding of the medieval commentator, Rashbam, Rabbi Samuel ben Meir (Northern France, c. 1080–1174), a grandson of Rashi (Sarna, *JPS Genesis,* 185).

26. Gen. 24:6.

27. Gen. 24:67.

And when Rebekah learns that the aggrieved Esau intends to kill Jacob after Isaac dies, fearful of revisiting her initial deception, Rebekah conceals from Isaac her knowledge about Esau's plans for revenge and persuades her husband to send Jacob away with the rationale that Jacob should not marry an objectionable local Hittite woman as Esau has done. Taken in by her argument, Isaac blesses Jacob and sends him off to Haran to marry one of Rebekah's nieces.[28]

Although these incidents provide a picture of an individual whose life is primarily shaped by others, if we take Isaac's entire life into account, I do not believe that he merits the label the "passive patriarch" with its negative connotations. Isaac is to be especially admired for the way he affirms life after the *Aqeidah*. The Torah suggests that following that harrowing experience, while Abraham and his servants return to Beer-sheba, Isaac goes off alone into the Negev.[29] I suspect that he seeks solitude in order to recover from the trauma of the *Aqeidah*. Isaac's subsequent actions attest to his attainment of a resolute state of mind: he marries the wife that Abraham obtains for him, raises a family, actively strives to follow God's covenantal charge to "stay in the land," becomes a successful farmer, repeatedly excavates new sources of water (even more than Abraham),[30] becomes a recognized local leader,[31] concludes a peace treaty with Abimelech, and in his parting blessing to Jacob seeks to transmit covenantal leadership to his son.[32] That he meets these challenges following the *Aqeidah* is a tribute to his faith, maturity, and resiliency.

---

28. Gen. 27:41—28:5.

29. On two occasions during the *Aqeidah* the text says *vayyeilchu sh'neyhem yachdav* "and the two of them walked off together" (Gen. 22:6, 8). This clearly refers to Abraham and Isaac. After the sacrifice of the ram, we find almost the exact same phrase but with a significant difference—"Abraham returned to his servants and *vayyeilchu yachdav* they went on together to Beersheba" (Gen. 22:19). In this verse, the word *sh'neyhem* "the two of them" is absent, meaning that this time, Abraham returns to Beer-sheva with his servants but not with Isaac. The next time we read of Isaac, we learn that he has been dwelling, presumably by himself, in the "vicinity of Beer-lahai-roi" (Gen. 24:62).

30. In Gen. 26:18 we read that Isaac digs anew all the wells that Abraham had excavated that had been stopped up by Abimelech's servants. Isaac goes on to excavate three more wells in Gerar—Esek, Sitnah and Rehoboth (Gen. 26:20–22), and a well in Beer-sheba which he names *Shivah* "oath," because of the covenant he made with Abimelelch in that place (Gen. 26:33).

31. I infer Isaac's enhanced status as a local leader from the fact that Abimelech and his officers change course and come to Isaac for a peace treaty because they have become aware of how God has blessed him in wealth and power.

32. Gen. 28:3–4.

Isaac Puts Down Roots in the Land of Canaan

As Abraham overcame his doubts about God's covenantal promises so that he achieved success as the first patriarch, so too Isaac rises above his tendency toward passivity as well as his ordeal at Moriah, to make a significant contribution to the covenant. While we tend to overlook Isaac in comparison to Abraham and Jacob, his pioneering father and his God-wrestling son, we should remember that Isaac is the only patriarch who farms the land, and despite famine and conflict with his neighbors, he is the only patriarch who never abandons the land of Canaan.[33] Not every son of a pioneering father can or needs to be an innovator. Those like Isaac who conserve and enhance the achievements and ideals of a larger than life father are to be valued in their own right. Above all, we should acknowlege that by means of his steadfast commitment to maintain the covenantal claim to the land of Canaan, Isaac provides what is needed in his generation.

---

33. Abraham's brief stay in Egypt is recounted in Gen. 12:10–20; Jacob spends twenty years in Haran and later has a seventeen year stay in Egypt which ends with his death (Gen. 47:8).

CHAPTER 12

How I Came to Love Israel and Its People

LIKE HIS FATHER, ISAAC's career as a patriarch in the land of Canaan begins with a famine. Abraham's response to famine was to flee to Egypt. Before Isaac can do the same, God stops him—"Do not go down to Egypt; continue to dwell in the land that I tell you of, soujourn in this land, and I will be with you and give you blessing—for to you and to your seed I give all these lands . . ."[1] From that moment on, the meaning of Isaac's life and his connection to the land are inextricably bound together as he seeks to gain a foothold in Canaan by struggling to find water, to farm, and to try to live in peace with his contentious neighbors. And when the time comes for Isaac to transfer covenantal leadership to his son Jacob, Isaac's fervent attachment to the land is foremost in his mind—May God "grant the *blessing of Abraham* to you and your offspring; that *you may possess the land* where you are sojourning, which God gave to Abraham."[2] And so from the very beginning of Isaac's commitment to the covenant until the end of his life, strengthening his father's claim to the land of Canaan was central to his role as a patriarch.

I had a very different experience in regard to my beliefs and feelings about the land of Israel. My love of Zion took a long time to develop. It did not really mature until I was in my late twenties. I trace the first stirrings of my consciousness about *M'dinat Yisra-eil* (the State of Israel) to a single

---

1. Gen. 26:2-3. Translation by Fox, *Five Books*, 117.
2. Gen. 28:4. Note that the text equates *"the blessing of Abraham"* with the possession of the land.

How I Came to Love Israel and Its People

day—May 15, 1948. It was *Shabbat K'doshim*, the day on which David Alpers, the middle son of Ben and Lillian Alpers, our family's best friends, celebrated his *bar mitzvah* at the famous Mikveh Israel Synagogue in Philadelphia, a Sephardic congregation whose founding dates back to colonial days. After the singing of *Ein Keiloheinu* at the conclusion of the service, small blue and white flags with the Star of David appeared out of nowhere, and everyone stood up and waved them over their heads. The women and girls who were in the balcony, as well as the men and boys downstairs, began to sing and dance. I was eight years old at the time. I wasn't quite sure what was happening until my parents told me that the congregants of Mikveh Israel were celebrating the birth of the one-day-old State of Israel. I can still feel the surprise and thrill of that spontaneous celebration.

My maternal grandmother, Helen Lowenstein, provided the most consistent connection to Israel during my childhood. She was an enthusiastic Zionist who was known at times to carry a blue and white Jewish National Fund *pushke* (*tz'dakah* or charity box) so that she could be ready when an opportunity arose to collect funds for her beloved Israel. She lived in Newark, New Jersey, and when she came to stay with us in Philadelphia or on the Jersey shore in the summer, she often shared with me some remembrances of her trips to Israel.

In their characteristically quiet way, my parents were also supporters of Israel. My father was an active member of the Philadelphia chapter of the American Friends of Hebrew University in Jerusalem. He persuaded one of his wealthy non-Jewish clients, Mr. Graham French, a lawyer from the French family of the Philadelphia pharmaceutical firm Smith, Kline and French, to donate money for a new building at Hebrew University.[3] My parents went to Jerusalem with Mr. French for the dedication. My dad was a very modest person and didn't make a big to-do about it, but I was very proud of him.

In the spring of 1949 we joined Congregation Rodeph Shalom, two years after Rabbi Louis Wolsey retired following a twenty-two year tenure. Rabbi Wolsey was one of the leaders of the American Council for Judaism, an anti-Zionist organization that espoused the idea that supporting a Jewish nation in the land of Israel was contrary to the mission of the Jewish people to be an *or lagoyim* "a light to the nations."[4] According to

---

3. My recollection is that it was a building for the study of agriculture.

4. The popular phrase *or lagoyim* "a light to the nations" is a corruption of *livrit am l'or goyim* "a covenanted people, a light of nations" (Is. 42:6).

the Council, a *Jewish nation* would inevitably become enmeshed in the political and military evils that befall all nation states, a situation which would divert us from our covenantal mission. While there is some truth in what the Council foresaw, I believe that the major unspoken reason that the members of the ACJ were opposed to the establishment of the State of Israel was their fear of being accused of dual loyalty—as American Jews they did not want to be seen as placing their allegiance to Israel on a par with or even above their loyalty to the United States. They were afraid that the Christian community might think of them as un-American. Today, it is clear that one can be loyal to one's country and at the same time an advocate for Israel. Living in democratic America and being supportive of a different national entity does not necessarily mean that one must choose one at the expense of the other. When Rabbi Wolsey's successor, Rabbi David Wice, a committed Zionist, arrived at Rodeph Shalom in 1948, the year that Israel declared its independence, he immediately introduced the Israeli flag on the pulpit alongside the American flag. I imagine that some of Wolsey's followers in the congregation must have been in shock, but in that same year, the fledging State of Israel successfully defended itself from its attackers and in doing so won the admiration of American Jewry. I later learned that in retirement, Rabbi Wolsey recanted his anti-Zionist position. I did not know him, but I respect him for publicly disavowing a position that he had advocated throughout his career. Not many rabbis have the courage to openly acknowledge that they made a major ideological mistake.

When I went off to Hebrew Union College–Jewish Institute of Religion in Cincinnati in the fall of 1961 to begin my rabbinical studies, I was not a Zionist. I believed in the need for a Jewish homeland for oppressed Jews from other parts of the world, but that was the extent of my thinking on Israel. The summer after my first year at rabbinical school, I took advantage of a postponed college graduation gift from my parents to travel in Europe. While on a mini-cruise through the Greek islands, I made friends with several English girls. They were not Jewish, but upon learning that I was a rabbinical student, they wondered why I had not taken this opportunity to go to Israel since it was so close. I was taken aback by their question. It had never occurred to me to visit Israel on this trip, but their question pushed me to ask myself, "Why was Israel a lower priority on my trip than Greece, Italy, France or England?"

By the time Barbara and I were married during my third year at HUC-JIR, my interest in Israel had grown considerably. At that time, the College did not have the Year in Israel program for all first year rabbinical and cantorial students as it does now, but a number of students took an extra year for study in Israel. I decided to do the same. I wanted to improve my conversational Hebrew, but more importantly, I hoped to explore in greater depth my relationship to the land and its people. The College had recently opened a beautiful new campus in Jerusalem. Many members of the HUC-JIR faculty in Cincinnati had a history of being opposed or indifferent to Zionism. By contrast, Dr. Nelson Glueck, the President of the College, was a staunch supporter of Israel. He was also a famous archaeologist, who was well known and admired by many Israelis for his archaeological surveys of the Negev and his work on the Nabateans.[5] The new campus in Jerusalem with its archaeological school came into existence primarily because of his efforts and fame. The archaeological rationale for the Jerusalem School was useful in allaying the fears of the Orthodox in Israel, who could not have been pleased that a Reform institution had gained a toehold on prime Jerusalem real estate just down the street from the King David Hotel.

Everyone remembers their first day in Israel. Barbara and I certainly do. On a blazing hot July day in 1964, we climbed into a crowded *sheyrut* at Ben Gurion Airport, twelve miles south of Tel Aviv, to begin our first *aliyah* (ascent) to Jerusalem. A *sheyrut* is a communal taxi. It takes as many passengers as it can handle at one time and drops them off at different places along the way. Our *sheyrut* driver introduced us to the dangers of driving in Israel. The road from Tel Aviv to Jerusalem in those days was only two lanes. This made no difference to our driver. Regardless of whether we were on a curve or going up a hill, he was determined to pass the cars in front of him. Time and again he swung his fully loaded, groaning *sheyrut* across the dividing line, only to have to whip back in line just barely avoiding a head on collision. I thought that Barbara's finger nails would be permanently imbedded in my leg. By the time we reached Jerusalem, we were the last passengers in the *sheyrut*, and we had no idea where we were going to stay. Our driver sensed our anxiety and delivered us into the capable hands of the manager of the small aging Hotel Moriah near Montefiore's windmill in Yemin Mosheh.[6] I don't remember the manager's name, but he mercifully

---

5. Dr. Glueck conducted important archaeological surveys in the Negev which helped determine the chronology and pattern of ancient settlement in the area. He also made significant contributions to Nabatean archaeology. The Nabateans, c. 400 BCE–100 CE, were an Arab people who established a trading and agricultural community in what is today, southern Jordan. Their capital was Petra.

6. The Hotel Moriah has since been rebuilt as a large modern hotel in the same area.

took us under his wing until we found an apartment on Rechov Usishkin in the lovely section of Jerusalem known as Rechavia and began our exciting year of study in Israel.

During that year, Barbara and I enrolled in ulpan (classes for conversational Hebrew in which Hebrew is taught by total immersion in the language) and studied archaeology at HUC-JIR in Jerusalem, where I also took Talmud with John Tepfer and Bible with Matt Tsevat. At Hebrew University, Nehama Leibowitz, a truly gifted teacher, opened the world of medieval commentators to me. I also studied conversational Hebrew with a private tutor. Oh how I enjoyed the study of Torah in Jerusalem that year! Barbara and I also strengthened our friendship with another young pre-rabbinic couple who were spending the year in Israel, Donald and Greta Lee Splansky. We had met them the previous summer when we served on the staff at the UAHC Olin Sang Ruby Institute at Oconomowoc, Wisconsin. Don and Greta Lee and Barbara and I were married one week apart in December, 1963, and have remained close friends for over fifty years.[7] Don, who was a student at the New York campus of HUC-JIR, and I, participated in a thought provoking discussion group with Chanan Brichto, who was heading up the Jerusalem branch of HUC-JIR that year. From Rabbi Brichto, I learned concepts about God and insights into the Bible that have remained a source of faith and inspiration to me throughout my rabbinate. I feel fortunate to have had him as a teacher and friend.

In addition, we learned about the archaeology and topography of Israel by traveling throughout the land with Dr. James Ross of Drew University, the director of the College's archeological program that year. Under Dr. Ross's supervision, Barbara and I spent a week as volunteers at Tel Gezer, an important archaeological site between Tel Aviv and Jerusalem that had been fortified by King Solomon.[8] We also took many *tiyyulim* (hikes) with our HUC-JIR friends and left our footprints near the source of the Jordan river in the Galilee, on the shores of the Red Sea at Eilat, and at the summit of Masada. As the Patriarchs must have experienced awe and wonder at the great variety of landscapes in the promised land, I too was struck by its many beautiful features—the golden glow of the sun on the Judean mountains, the lush greenery of the Galilee dotted with red and purple anemonies in springtime, and the stark beauty of the starlit night sky in the Negev.

---

7. Rabbi Splansky is the Rabbi Emeritus of Temple Beth Am in Framingham, MA.
8. 1 Kings 9:15.

How I Came to Love Israel and Its People

I especially remember a day of touring with Dr. Glueck at Tel Dan near the northern border of Israel. He casually walked through the ruins as if he were in his own backyard. Suddenly, I spotted a round edge of black stone sticking up from the ground. I bent down to pick it up, but it was lodged in the earth. I cleared the soil around it with my fingers and gently pulled out a semicircular black stone object with a smooth depression in the center. It fit into the hollow of my hand. There were incised decorative lines encircling the smooth central depression. It was clearly half of a broken artifact, but what was it? I showed it to Dr. Glueck who matter of factly said, "Oh, that's an Iron Age cosmetic palette." Suddenly, I visualized an Israelite noble woman three thousand years ago dipping her fingers into this cosmetic palette to darken her beautiful eyes or rouge her lovely cheeks. It was a little thing, but it made a momentary personal connection for me with an ancestor from another age.

Shabbat in Jerusalem was unlike any other Barbara and I had experienced. On Friday afternoons, as traffic and business in the Holy City gradually slowed down, I was always delighted by the ringing of a bell on a little red truck which made the rounds of our Rechavia neighborhood to signal the coming of the Sabbath. Only in Jerusalem! On Friday nights we would invite guests to our apartment or go to the apartments of other HUC-JIR couples for Shabbat dinner. Sometimes I would attend *Kabbalat Shabbat* (the service to welcome the Sabbath) at a local *shtiebel* (a small room or apartment which serves as a house of prayer) where in traditional fashion only the men attended while their wives prepared the Sabbath meal at home. On Shabbat morning, Barbara and I worshipped at the lovely chapel at HUC-JIR. It was a joy to walk to synagogue down the middle of the streets of Jerusalem without worrying about traffic. We loved the flute enhanced Sabbath music and would often spend Shabbat afternoon with friends from the College or with Israelis who attended services there. On Shabbat as well as other times, the favorite activity of Israelis is to invite guests to one's home or to unexpectedly drop in on friends and family. No one seems to mind. How wonderful it is that the traditional Jewish value of ha<u>ch</u>nasat or<u>ch</u>im "hospitality" flourishes in *Eretz Yisra-eil*.

I particularly remember one Shabbat when we attended services at a fledgling Israeli Reform congregation in a suburb of Tel Aviv. Rabbi Tovia Ben-Chorin, a sabra[9] whom I knew from his HUC-JIR student days in

---

9. A *sabra* is the word used to describe a native born Israeli. Like the fruit of a *sabra* cactus, Israelis are thought to be tough and prickly on the outside but tender on

Cincinnati, was the rabbi. After services, he arranged for us to have lunch at the home of an Israeli family from his congregation. We had a wonderful meal and very much enjoyed getting to know our hosts. Suddenly, the discussion, which I had joined in my halting conversational Hebrew, became serious. What would Barbara and I do if war broke out in Israel? Would we stay to help, or would we return home to America? I promptly answered that we would return to the States. Our hosts were surprised by my answer and politely challenged my position. How could we abandon our Israeli brothers and sisters in their hour of need? While I stuck to my position, the discussion rattled me. What did I believe was my responsibility to Israel and its people? Was I, like many American Jews, just a check book Zionist? From that moment, I knew I had more work to do on my relationship with the people and the State of Israel.

I was ordained at HUC-JIR in 1967, and even though I was profoundly affected by my year of study in Israel, I was not a committed Zionist. In my first pulpit as an assistant rabbi to Rabbi Joseph Klein at Temple Emanuel of Worcester, I was strongly influenced by his deep-seated love for the land and the people of Israel. Rabbi Klein, having grown up as the son of a traditional cantor in a Zionist home in Cleveland, was an ardent supporter of Zion. On the High Holydays, he always dedicated a major sermon to Israel. During my three years at Temple Emanuel, under his influence and the strong support of the congregants of Temple Emanuel for Israel, a positive connection to the land and its people became an integral part of my Jewish identity. And so, two decades after that memorable Bar Mitzvah at Mikveh Israel in Philadelphia in May of 1948, I finally became a fullfledged Zionist. Since then, whenever I recall the discomforting discussion that took place in the home of our Israeli hosts in Tel Aviv, I believe I would answer their question differently—if Israel was attacked while I was there, I hope I would have the courage to remain in the land as a volunteer to aid my Israeli brothers and sisters in their time of need.

While I am a lover of Zion, I do not believe that God specifically dedicated the land of Israel to the Jewish people. Rather, I hold that God's revelation to our ancestors, and for that matter to all humanity, is comprised of universal ideals such as the oneness of God and humanity, the sacredness of life, and the paramount importance of ethical living. I am aware, however, that for the last four millennia, the Jewish people have lived with the conviction that God promised the land of Israel to the Patriarchs and

---

the inside.

to us, their descendants. When that long standing belief is coupled with the reality that Judaism was born in the land of Israel, that there was a Jewish kingdom or Jewish political entity in the land for a thousand years, that during the two thousand year Diaspora, Jews, though often small in number, continued to live in the land, and that Jews in every corner of the earth have continued to recite daily prayers which look forward to a return to the land, it is clear that the Jewish people has a strong and enduring claim to the land of Israel as a homeland.

After I became the rabbi of Temple Beth David in Westwood, I led a number of congregational trips to Israel. Following every trip, Barbara and I would briefly fantasize about the possibility of making *aliyah*, but our fantasy never materialized into action. The primary reason for not settling in Israel was my awareness that I was not equipped educationally, culturally, or temperamentally, to be a Reform rabbi in Israel, where I would have to cope with the challenge of the Orthodox monopoly in all areas of Jewish religious life.[10] Currently, a new cadre of native Israeli Reform rabbis are being ordained at HUC-JIR in Jerusalem; they are far better suited than I to enlist in this important struggle. I am hopeful they will help usher in a bright future for Reform Judaism in Israel where an option to Orthodoxy is sorely needed. Here in the States, I have tried to support Israel by diligently educating the children and adults in my congregation about Israel, by leading congregational trips to Israel, by helping to establish ways to fund trips to Israel for our youth and by encouraging my congregants to make financial contributions to Israel.

Looking back to Isaac's relationship to the land, I see him as the first "Zionist" because his primary covenantal challenge was to stay in the promised land and to strengthen the covenantal claim to the land. In the face of famine, Isaac, at God's urging, remained in Canaan and resisted the temptation to flee to the lush banks of the Nile. Although I have chosen not to put down roots in the promised land, I admire and applaud all those, like

---

10. Because of the numerous political parties in Israel and the parliamentary system of government inherited from the British, the dominant political party usually needs the support of the Orthodox representatives in the Israeli Parliament to maintain a working majority. In return for the votes of the Orthodox parties on political issues, the majority governing party surrenders to the Orthodox Rabbinate control of all religious affairs. In this way the Orthodox, who comprise 15–20% of the population of Israel, have a disproportionate voice on issues such as government support for synagogues and schools; policies affecting conversion, marriage, divorce; and guidelines for determining Jewish identity.

Isaac, who have made that heroic choice. To live in Israel at the crossroads of history is to live courageously.

As Isaac, like his father Abraham, was expected to be a blessing,[11] I believe we need to call on the current leaders of the State of Israel to adhere to the high standards of Jewish morality. There are those who contend that this is not necessary. "Why," they ask, "can't Israel act like all the other nation states? Why does it have to be better?" I believe that any organization or community that defines itself as "Jewish," as is the case with the State of Israel, takes upon itself the covenantal responsibility of accepting God's challenge to Abraham to pursue "righteousness and justice." Israel has often tried to live up to its covenantal heritage by sharing technology and Israeli know-how with developing countries in the third world and by humanitarian efforts within its borders and abroad. Indeed, as I write these words, I am aware that just this week, young Israelis traveled to the Greek island of Lesbos to take in Arab boat refugees from the civil war in Syria and to provide them with medical care and general assistance. I am extremely proud of this kind of deed of loving-kindness that has become the hallmark of Israel's relationship with people in crisis throughout the world. But at the same time, when Israel strays from the high standards of ethical behavior enjoined in the covenant, I cannot refrain from calling on its leaders and its citizens to rise to its historic covenantal calling.

If Isaac were alive today, I think his approach to the Palestinian question would be the same as his approach to Abimelech and his contentious herdsman—he would carry a sword in one hand and a hoe in the other. The sword would signify Isaac's determination to defend himself and his people from suicide bombers, missiles, and any armed threat; the hoe would represent his deep-seated desire to develop the land for the benefit of Israelis and Palestinians alike. Perhaps, such a combination of restrained strength and a genuine proactive spirit of cooperation might bring a much needed peace to the land. *Lu Yehi,* "Would that it may be!"[12]

---

11. Isaac exemplified moral excellence when he used restraint rather than a rush to bloodshed in his controversy with Abimelech and his herdsmen (Gen. 26:12–30).

12. During the Yom Kippur War of 1973, Naomi Shemer composed and recorded a song that gave voice to the sentiments of the people of Israel. The key phrase in the song is *lu yehi* "May it be," a plea for peace in the midst of conflict.

CHAPTER 13

Jacob Stays the Course

The Motif of the Younger Superseding the Elder

IN THE TANACH THE first born son is entitled to the largest share of his father's estate as well as family leadership.[1] It is therefore surprising that in Genesis the younger sibling consistently supersedes the first born: God favors Abel over Cain, Isaac precedes Ishmael, Jacob overtakes Esau, Rachel is preferred over Leah,[2] Perez pushes past Zerah, Joseph gains ascendancy over first born Reuben and his nine other elder brothers, and Ephraim displaces Manasseh.[3] This consistent reversal of the preferential status of the first born in Genesis reflects the idea that patriarchal leadership is not determined by custom but by God's purposeful agenda. A significant aspect of that agenda is that the Eternal favors leadership skills and an appropriate

---

1. Deut. 21:17 states that the first born son inherits a double portion of his father's estate. This means that the father's estate is divided into portions according to the number of sons plus one. The first born gets a double portion; the other sons receive a single portion. In Num. 8:16–18, we learn that the first born in a family was the religious leader prior to the divine assignment of religious leadership to the tribe of Levy.

2. Rachel's ascendancy over Leah, her elder sister, stems from the fact that she is Jacob's beloved. There are several verses which suggest her primacy—when the sisters are about to depart from their father Laban's house, Rachel's name is mentioned before Leah's (Gen. 31:3, 14), and when the people at the gate invoke a blessing over Boaz and Ruth, Rachel's name precedes that of Leah, "May YHVH make the woman who is coming into your house, like Rachel and Leah, both of whom built up the House of Israel" (Ruth 4:11). This is probably the source of the customary blessing over a daughter in which Rachel precedes Leah—"May God make you like Sarah, Rebekah, Rachel and Leah..."

3. Two other significant biblical examples of younger siblings who surpass their elder brothers are Moses and David.

temperament over the order of birth. Thus, the prudent Isaac is preferred over the aggressive, war-like Ishmael.[4] And in the third generation, our focus in this chapter, Jacob's shrewd intellect and perseverance are seen by God as a better fit for patriarchal leadership than the shortsighted impulsiveness of Esau, the first born twin.

God's Oracle to Rebekah: The Elder Shall Serve the Younger

The story of Jacob and Esau is the quintessential biblical example of sibling rivalry. The twins' struggle commences before birth as they wrestle within the womb of their mother Rebekah who implores God to tell her the reason for her intense pain. God responds "two nations" are in your womb; they will separate, and "the elder shall serve the younger."[5] The two nations are: Israel who descends from Jacob, and Edom whose origin goes back to Esau.[6]

God's oracle to Rebekah begins to be actualized when the famished Esau returns from the hunt and sells the right of his first born inheritance to his wily brother Jacob for a bowl of lentil soup.[7] The second assault on Esau's first born status is managed by Rebekah, who, with the aid of goat skins, disguises Jacob as Esau, enabling Jacob to purloin the blessing of the first born from Isaac, his aging, nearly blind father.

> May God give you of the dew of heaven and the fat of the earth,
> Abundance of new grain and wine,
> Let peoples serve you,
> nations bow down to you;
> *Be master over your brothers,*
> *And let your mother's sons bow down to you.*[8]

---

4. In Gen. 16:12 an angelic oracle foretells that Ishmael will be "a wild ass of a man; his hand against everyone, and everyone's hand against him."

5. Gen. 25:23.

6. In Gen. 36:9 Esau is called *Avi Edom* "the father of the Edomites." The identification of Esau with Edom is also alluded to at Esau's birth. The territory of Edom, which is situated across the southern part of the Jordan rift, has a reddish appearance due to the color of the soil. Appropriately enough, when Esau is born, he emerges from the womb *admoni* "red," a word play on *Edom* (Gen. 25:25).

7. Gen. 25:27–34.

8. One wonders why "brothers" and "sons" are in the plural since Jacob has but one brother. It may be that the parallel words "peoples" and "nations" in the preceding phrase attracts the plural usage, or perhaps the verse looks to the future when the Edomites,

> Cursed be they who curse you
> Blessed they who bless you.
>
> Genesis 27:28-29

A question arises in regard to Isaac's blessing as to when Jacob will be a "master" over Esau so that Esau "bows down" to him? As the story of the twins unfolds, the opposite seems to be true, for when Jacob returns to Canaan after a twenty year hiatus, he bows down to Esau seven times![9] I believe that Jacob's mastery over Esau does not refer to the struggle between the twins during their lifetimes, but rather to the days of David's conquest of Edom when the Edomites, the descendants of Esau, become subservient to the Israelites, the descendants of Jacob.[10]

Isaac's Parting Blessing of Jacob Invokes God's Covenant with Abraham

When Rebekah learns that Esau is nursing his anger in the wake of Jacob's theft of his blessing, and that once Isaac dies, Esau intends to kill Jacob,[11] she persuades Isaac to send Jacob to Haran to find a wife among the daughters of her brother Laban with the pretext that Jacob should not repeat the objectionable choice that Esau has made in marrying two Hittite women.[12] Before Jacob leaves, Isaac seeks to prepare his younger son for covenantal leadership with a parting benediction.

> May El Shaddai bless you,
> make you fertile and numerous,
> so that you become a community of peoples.
> May He grant you the blessing of Abraham,
> to you and your offspring;

Esau's descendants, are recognized as Jacob's "brothers" as well as his "mother's sons."

9. Gen. 33:3.
10. II Samuel 8:13–14.
11. Gen. 27:41–45.
12. Gen. 27:46. In the very next verse, Isaac instructs Jacob not to take a wife "from among the *Canaanite* women" (Gen. 28:1). There is no contradiction here for Canaanite is a generic term for all the different ethnic groups in the land including the Hittites. The Hittite Empire ruled the area of Anatolia, present day Turkey and northern Syria, from about 1600 to 1200 BCE, a period roughly parallel to patriarchal times. It is therefore not surprising to read of Hittites living in Canaan at this time, such as Ephron the Hittite, from whom Abraham buys the cave and surrounding field of Machpelah (Gen. 23:7–18).

> that you may possess the land where you are sojourning,
> which God gave to Abraham.
>
> Genesis 28:3-4

Now that Isaac is fully reconciled to the idea that his younger son will carry on the Covenant of Abraham, unlike Isaac's initial blessing of the disguised Jacob, Isaac's parting benediction explicitly connects Jacob to Abraham's covenantal legacy of numerous progeny and the inheritance of the land.[13]

In a Dream About a Stairway, God Invites Jacob to Join the Covenant

In flight from his brother's anger, Jacob sets out for Haran. As the sun begins to set, Jacob halts his journey, takes a stone from the place, and puts it under his head as he lays down to sleep. He then has a dream of a stairway (or ladder) with ascending and descending angels whose "top touches the sky."[14] In the dream, God appears to Jacob for the first time and invites him to enlist in the Covenant of Abraham.

> And YHVH was standing beside him and He said,
> "I am YHVH, the God of *your father Abraham*
> and the God of Isaac: the ground on which you are lying
> I will give to you and to your offspring.
> Your descendants shall be as the dust of the earth;
> you shall spread out to the west and to the east,
> to the north and the south.
> All the families of the earth shall bless themselves
> by you and your descendants.
> Remember, I am with you: I will protect you
> wherever you go and will bring you back to this land.
> I will not leave you until I have done what I have promised you.
>
> Genesis 28:13-15

---

13. Isaac's initial blessing of Jacob (disguised as Esau) speaks in general terms of God's blessings of plenty and family leadership (Gen. 27:28–29). There are no references to Abraham or to the divine promises of progeny and land that comprise the essential components of the Covenant of Abraham.

14. Gen. 28:12. Jacob's *sullam* "stairway" suggests the image of a *ziggurat* such as the great cultic tower of Babylon. The text states in regard to Jacob's stairway *v'rosho maggi-ah hashamaiymah* "its top was touching the sky." This is reminiscent of the phrase describing the Tower of Babel *v'rosho vashamaiyim* "its top in the sky" (Gen. 11:4).

How is it that in the blessing above, God asserts that Abraham rather than Isaac is Jacob's father? From the perspective of the covenant, *Abraham is Jacob's father*, since God's pact with Jacob, as was the case with Isaac, derives from the Eternal's foundational covenant with Abraham. And despite the absence of the word *b'rit* "covenant" or any synonyn, it is evident that here in Genesis 28, God seeks to establish the Covenant of Abraham with Jacob, since God's offer includes the same divine promises of progeny and land, as well as the vision of universal blessing to "all the families of the earth" that God had declared in covenantal invitations to Abraham and Isaac.

Jacob Is Filled with Awe but Responds with a Conditional Vow

In the immediate aftermath of his dream and God's covenantal promises, Jacob awakens and is filled with awe:

> Jacob awoke from his sleep and said,
> "Surely YHVH is present in this place, and I did not know it!"
> Shaken, he said, "How awe-inspiring is this place!
> This is none other than the abode of God,
> And this is the gateway to heaven."
>
> Genesis 28:16-17

Jacob then takes the stone that he had placed under his head, sets it upright as a pillar, and anoints the top with oil. The consecrated pillar serves as a witness to Jacob's response which he offers in the form of a *conditional* vow.[15]

> If God remains with me,
> if He protects me on this journey that I am making
> and gives me bread to eat and clothing to wear,
> and if I return safe to my father's house—
> YHVH shall be my God.
> And this stone, which I have set up as a pillar,
> shall be *beit Elohim* God's abode;
> And of all that You give me,
> I will always set aside a tithe for You.
>
> Gen. 28:20-22

---

15. Gen. 28:22; 31:13. The function of the pillar is akin to the mound of stones that will later serve as a testament to the peace treaty between Jacob and his father-in-law Laban (Gen. 31:48–54).

We have seen that in the course of Jacob's dream oracle of a stairway, God concludes with a promise to protect Jacob while he is away from Canaan—"I will protect you, wherever you go and bring you back to this land. I will not leave you until I have done what I have promised you."[16] It is therefore puzzling that when Jacob awakes from his dream, he responds with three conditions that need to be met before he can make a total commitment to the covenant: God has to protect him on his journey to Haran, provide him with bread to eat and clothing to wear, and safeguard his return to his father's house. Why doesn't Jacob trust God's initial promise of support and protection? I think the answer lies in Jacob's youth, his precarious circumstances, as well as his cautious personality.[17] Away from home, totally alone, headed for an indeterminate stay with an uncle he has never seen, and hearing God's voice for the very first time, Jacob is understandably apprehensive about his immediate future. Despite God's assurance, Jacob wants to make doubly sure of God's support and protection before consenting to a lifelong covenantal commitment. And so, at this initial stage in Jacob's relationship with God, God's word alone will not do; only Jacob's experience of God's support and protection will suffice; hence, Jacob's *conditional* acceptance of the covenant.

After Twenty Years In Haran, Jacob is Reminded by God that the Time has Come to Return to Canaan

Jacob labors fourteen years for Laban in Paddan-aram as a bride price for Rachel and Leah, and an additional six years as the steward of Laban's flocks, a total of twenty years in all. Despite Laban's attempts to cheat Jacob of his fair wages, God blesses Jacob so that he becomes wealthy like his father and grandfather before him.[18] Now that God has satisfied the major conditions of material support and protection that Jacob had sought in his provisional

---

16. Gen. 28:15.

17. In Gen. 27:11–13, Jacob's cautious personality is revealed when he expresses to his mother Rebekah his concern about the possibility of his father reaching out to touch him and discovering that he is the smooth-skinned Jacob rather than the hairy Esau. If that should happen, Jacob fears that his father Isaac will consider him a trickster and curse him rather than bless him. Jacob agrees to participate in the deception when his mother says that if Isaac discovers his identity, she will take his father's curse upon herself.

18. "So the man (Jacob) grew exceedingly prosperous, and came to own large flocks, maidservants and menservants, camels and asses" (Gen. 30:43).

vow, all that remains is for God to watch over Jacob on his return home. And so God reminds Jacob that the time has come for him to return to the land of Canaan in order to fulfill the vow he made twenty years before to serve as God's covenantal partner.[19]

Wrestling at the Jabbok

When Jacob finally decides to leave Haran, he has a great deal of trouble disengaging from his devious father-in-law, Laban, but eventually, he heads home with a large entourage including his wives, children, servants, and flocks. As he nears Canaan, his thoughts naturally turn to Esau, the brother whose anger he had fled twenty years before. In fearful deference to Esau, Jacob sends messengers to Seir[20] (Esau's home territory) announcing that he is on his way back to Canaan. His apprehension about seeing his brother is heightened when the messengers return to inform him that Esau is coming to meet him with four hundred men![21] Jacob's response is to divide his household into two camps, thinking that if Esau encounters one camp and attacks it, the other may escape.[22] He then prays to God, "Save me, I pray, from my brother's hand, from Esau's hand! I am afraid of him, lest he advance on me and strike me down, mothers and children alike."[23] Jacob implores God not to allow this to happen by reminding God of the divine promise to make his offspring "like the sands of the sea."[24] In addition, Jacob, seeks to win Esau's favor by sending forth several droves of flocks as gifts for his brother.[25] Michael Fishbane of the University of Chicago sees these gifts as an atonement offering by which Jacob seeks foregiveness from Esau. And so, Jacob says to Esau, "*qach birchati*" a phrase which Fishbane understands as a double entendre—"Take my gift" or "Take my blessing."[26] The blessing Jacob is returning to Esau is the first born's blessing of additional material wealth that Jacob bought by guile from his famished brother

19. Gen. 31:3, 13.
20. Seir is located across the Jordan rift, east of the Negev wilderness. It is destined to become the territory of the nation of Edom.
21. Gen. 32:7.
22. Gen. 32:8–9.
23. Gen. 32:12.
24. Gen. 32:13.
25. Gen. 32:14–22.
26. Fishbane, *Text and Texture*, 52.

for a bowl of lentil soup. The second blessing, the blessing by which Isaac conferred familial and covenantal leadership on Jacob,[27] is a blessing that Jacob cannot return.

That night, after transporting his family and his possessions across the Jabbok River[28] into Canaan, Jacob crosses back over the river and lies down alone, just outside the boundary of the promised land. There he wrestles with "a man" until dawn.[29] It is commonly understood that the mythic background of this story is the folk belief in a river demon whose harsh embrace is embodied by the strong current.[30] As to the contextual identity of Jacob's adversary, it may be a psychic manifestation of Esau. On the eve of his reunion with Esau after twenty years, Jacob is understandably obsessed with anxious concerns about the brother whom he had wronged.[31] Richard E. Friedman of the University of Georgia writes that Jacob initially thinks he is wrestling with a man, but in the course of the struggle, he comes to realize it is an angel, an "hypostatization" (a physical manifestation) of God.[32] The angel wrenches Jacob's hip dislocating it, but the injured Jacob refuses to release his divine opponent until the angel gives him a blessing. The blessing comes in the form of a change of name from *Ya-aqov* to *Yisra-eil*—"*ki sarita*[33] for you have contended with beings divine (the angel/God) and human (Esau and Laban) and have prevailed."[34] Jacob's new name suggests that this is a juncture of positive growth and transformation, an evolution from *Ya-aqov* "the supplanter"

---

27. Gen. 27:29 and Gen. 28:3–4.

28. Note the use of consonance—the repetition of the consonant *qof* in the name of the river *Yabboq* (Gen. 32:23) and in the word for wrestling *vayei-aveiq* two verses later (Gen. 32:25).

29. Gen. 32:25.

30. Sarna, *JPS Genesis*, 403.

31. A midrash proposes that the mysterious being is Esau's patron angel who makes one final effort at the border of the promised land to prevent Jacob from claiming Canaan as his inheritance (*Genesis Rabbah*, 77:3).

32. Friedman points out the similarity of Jacob's angel to the three visitors to Abraham's tent who come to tell him of the birth of Isaac. At first, the Torah refers to these visitors as *anashim* "men" (Gen. 18:2, 16, 22); later, two of the visitors are described as *hammalachim* "angels" (Gen. 19:1). Similarly, Jacob's adversary in Gen. 32:25 is an *ish* "a man," but in Hosea 12:5, Jacob's adversary is understood to be an angel, "He strove with *malach* an angel and prevailed" (Friedman, *Hidden Face of God*, 9–13) and (Friedman, *Commentary on the Torah*, 63).

33. *Sarita*, "you contended," is a word play on the name *Yisra-eil*.

34. Gen. 32:29.

(Esau's negative interpretation of Jacob's name following Jacob's theft of Esau's blessing)[35] to the heroic *Yisra-eil*, "one who contends with God."

After God Changes Jacob's Name, Does Jacob Change?

In regard to Abraham's change of name from *Avram* to *Avraham* in Genesis 17:5, we noted that the name Abraham displaces the name Abram in the succeeding narrative. At the same time, we proposed that the change of name indicates an internal change in the first patriarch from one who retains doubts about God's promises to a steadfast believer in the word of the Eternal.[36] The change of Jacob's name in Genesis 32 reveals a different pattern. Despite the divine pronouncement "No longer shall you be called Jacob, but Israel,"[37] Jacob's new name *Yisra-eil* does not replace *Ya-aqov*; both names continue to occur in the Jacob narrative in Genesis, so that instead of Israel being a substitute for Jacob, it becomes an alternate name. A particularly clear example of the interchangeable usage of the two names occurs in the divine call to Jacob before his departure for Egypt, "God called to Israel in a night vision, 'Jacob! Jacob!'"[38]

It is still important to ask, however, does the climactic contest at the river, as well as the acquisition of the name *Yisra-eil*, signal a change in Jacob's character? My response is yes, but not completely. After the Jabbok, some of Jacob's deeds reveal a continuation of the crafty, cautious behavior of his youth, but at the same time, on a number of occasions, Jacob acts in a courageous, visionary way. Let us examine the blameworthy as well as the praiseworthy events of Jacob's life after his wrestling with the angel so that we may make an appropriate assessment of his covenantal contribution.

---

35. When Esau learns that Jacob has stolen the blessing of the first born through deception, he cries out in Isaac's presence, "Was he then named *Ya-aqov* Jacob *vayyaqveini* that he might supplant me these two times?" (Gen. 27:36). The two times are Esau's loss of his birthright in exchange for lentil soup and the theft of the blessing of the first born.

36. See chapter 5, "Abraham's Journey from Doubt to Faith."

37. Gen. 32:29.

38. Gen. 46:2. The synonymous use of the names Jacob and Israel can also be observed in poetic passages in other books of the Tanach where they appear in parallel. In such passages the name Jacob (referring to the people) most often precedes Israel, as in Balaam's famous saying in Numbers 24:5, "How lovely are your tents O Jacob, your dwelling places O Israel." Jer. 46:27 is an example from the Prophets, "But you, have no fear, My servant Jacob, be not dismayed, O Israel."

The Tense Reunion of Jacob and Esau

To his credit, on the morning after he acquires the name Israel, Jacob no longer hides behind propitiatory gifts as he did on the previous day. Now, he assumes a position at the head of his household, as he sets forth to meet Esau and his four hundred retainers.[39] Although still fearful of Esau, as can be seen from his seven bows as he limps ever closer, he prepares to meet his brother face to face.[40] Esau, the spontaneous, more emotional brother is clearly moved by the sight of his younger twin. Benno Jacob suggests that it is Jacob's injury, his clear vulnerability, that disarms any resentment that Esau may have harbored.[41] He runs to greet Jacob, embraces him, and kisses him. They both break into tears.[42]

But immediately following the dramatic reunion, Jacob's capacity for deception resurfaces. Esau, hoping to initiate a stronger bond of brotherhood, offers to escort Jacob and his entire entourage to Esau's home in Seir. Jacob declines his brother's offer saying that he must go at his own pace because of the frailty of his children and the nursing flocks, but he promises to come to "my lord" later.[43] Esau then proposes to have some of his attendants escort Jacob to Seir, but Jacob again demurs, "Oh no, my lord is too kind to me."[44] So Esau leaves for home with the expectation that Jacob will arrive at Seir in the not too distant future. Jacob, however, knowing that his covenantal destiny is in Canaan not in Seir, and wishing to disengage himself from his brother, whom he still does not completely trust, bypasses Seir and continues his journey to the promised land[45] thereby deceiving Esau once again.

Later, when their father Isaac dies, the brothers reunite to bury him,[46] but there is no other mention of their being together in the period immediately before or after Isaac's death. It therefore appears that Jacob never makes an earnest attempt to fully repair his relationship with Esau.

---

39. Gen. 33:1–3.
40. Gen. 33:3.
41. B. Jacob, *Genesis*, 226.
42. Gen. 33:4.
43. Gen. 33:12–16.
44. Gen. 33:15.
45. Gen. 33:17.
46. Gen. 35:29. Long separated sibling rivals Isaac and Ishmael also come together to bury their father (Gen. 25:9).

Jacob Fails to Respond to the Rape of Dinah and the Massacre Committed by Simeon and Levi

Soon after separating from Esau, Jacob is involved in a series of related events that suggest cowardice. Dinah, Jacob's only daughter is raped by a young man by the name of Shechem, the son of Hamor, from whose clan Jacob had just purchased a field.[47] Despite the disgrace[48] and the realization that Dinah may not be marriageable because she has lost her virginity, the ever-cautious Jacob maintains an embarrassing silence while waiting for his sons to return from tending the flocks. When they learn what has happened to their sister, the enraged brothers hurry home, but before they can formulate a plan of action, Hamor and his son Shechem come to Jacob to propose a unification of their two peoples, beginning with the marriage of Dinah and Schechem. Jacob's sons agree to the marriage and the merging of the two familial groups, provided Hamor and his followers undergo circumcision so that they can truly become *am echad* "one people" with Jacob's household.[49] Hamor and Shechem consent to these terms, but as they and all their warriors are lying about in their painful recovery, two of Jacob's sons, Simeon and Levi, slaughter all the males, including Hamor and Shechem, while the other brothers plunder the town. Following this shameful act, Jacob addresses Simeon and Levi as follows:

> You have brought trouble on me,
> making me odious among the inhabitants of the land,
> the Canaanites and Perizzites;
> my men are few in number,
> so that if they unite against me and attack me,
> I and my house will be destroyed.
>
> Genesis 34:30

Much to our surprise and dismay, Jacob makes no comment about the deception and mass murder that Simeon and Levi have perpetrated; he only

---

47. Gen. 33:18–20. As Abraham's purchase of the cave of Machpelah and its environs near Hebron (Gen. 23) helps establish a claim to territory in the future Kingdom of Judah in the south, perhaps Jacob's purchase of the field near Shechem is the first down payment on the territory of the Kingdom of Israel in the north.

48. Tikva Frymer-Kensky asserts that Dinah's loss of her virginity brings shame to Jacob and his sons because it implies they have not protected her (Frymer-Kensky, *Reading the Women of the Bible*, 188–90).

49. Gen. 34:22.

seems concerned with his own reputation and the danger of retaliation from the inhabitants of the land. His comments are more like those of a craven tribal chieftain interested in damage control than a self-assured patriarch whose children have committed a moral atrocity. Many years later, on his deathbed in Egypt, Jacob castigates Simeon and Levi for their "cruel anger" and "wrath" in regard to this incident,[50] but it is too little, too late.

Jacob Dedicates a New Altar at Bethel while God Reissues the Covenantal Offer

Although Jacob's lack of response to the rape of his daughter and the subsequent massacre committed by his sons might qualify as the moral low point of his life, it is immediately followed by a praiseworthy action. God calls on Jacob to "go up promptly to Bethel and remain there; and build an altar there to the God who appeared to you when you were fleeing from your brother Esau."[51] Jacob responds, since God "answered me when I was in distress and has been with me wherever I have gone,"[52] he will fulfill the conditional vow he made two decades before, by building a new altar to God at that site. In preparation for this sacred act, Jacob directs his household to purify themselves by donning new clothes[53] and by getting rid of their idolatrous objects,[54] which he buries under a tree near Shechem.[55] When he reaches Bethel, Jacob constructs an altar as God had commanded and renames the sacred site *Eil Beit-eil*, "El (the God) of Bethel."[56]

God now confirms Jacob's change of name to Israel and issues a second covenantal offer:

50. Gen. 49:5–7.
51. Gen. 35:1.
52. Gen. 35:3.
53. Gen. 35:2. Because they are about to enter a sacred place to participate in the holy act of building an altar, there is a need for purification. This is similar to Sinai when the Israelites are commanded by God to stay pure and wash their clothes in preparation for the revelation (Ex. 19:10–14).
54. Perhaps the objects which Jacob buries include the idols Rachel stole from her father as well as those of his other wives and servants who left Laban's household with Jacob.
55. Gen. 35:4–7. Jacob's route of Shechem to Bethel may be an intentional repetition of the route of Abraham's first journey in the land in Gen.12.
56. Gen. 35:7 He had named it *Beit Elohim* "the House of God" following his dream of a stairway (Gen. 28:19).

> "You whose name is Jacob,
> You shall be called Jacob no more,
> But Israel is your name."
> Thus He named him Israel.
> And God said to him,
> "I am El Shaddai,
> Be fertile and increase;
> A nation, yea an assembly of nations,
> Shall descend from you.
> Kings shall issue from your loins,
> The land that I assigned to Abraham and Isaac,
> I assign to you;
> And to your offspring to come
> Will I assign the land."
>
> Genesis 35:10–12

The promises of progeny and land which appear in God's initial covenantal invitation to Jacob (Gen. 28) and in the covenants with Abraham and Isaac are repeated in this second divine offering of a covenant to Jacob. There is also a significant parallel to God's covenant with Jacob's grandfather; as God informed Abraham, "kings shall come forth from you,"[57] Jacob is also told that *m'lachim* "kings" will proceed from his loins, a reference to the future kingdom of Israel.

Jacob's Unconditional Positive Response to God's Second Covenantal Offer

Jacob's response to God's second offering at Bethel to become God's partner in the Covenant of Abraham is strikingly different from his former reply. At that earlier time, the young, awestruck, insecure Jacob, could only bring himself to make a provisional pledge—if God protects and cares for me and brings me home safely, YHVH will be my God. Two decades later, Jacob responds without hesitation or reservations of any kind by erecting a second pillar at Bethel, no doubt next to the stone "pillow" or marker he had consecrated on the night of his stairway dream. He anoints this pillar with oil as he had done with the first,[58] but he then does something different—he pours a *nesech* "a libation" (a wine offering) upon the pillar which imparts

---

57. Gen. 17:6.
58. Gen. 35:14.

a priestly element to the rite of consecration.[59] In this way, Jacob makes a faithful, unconditional commitment to the covenant, something he was not prepared to do as a young man in flight from Esau's anger. Any doubt that God and Jacob have concluded a covenant is erased by the reference in Leviticus 26:42 to *b'riti Ya-aqov* "My (God's) covenant with Jacob."

Why Jacob Receives the Name Israel for a Second Time

Since Jacob's name is changed to Israel at the wrestling match at the Jabbok (Gen. 32), why does God repeat the change of name here at Bethel (Gen. 35)? Speiser explains the repetition by asserting that the two passages stem from different documentary sources—he assigns the first change of name story to the J code and the second to the P code.[60] Even if this is correct, I believe that the Narrator had a specific lesson in mind when he included both name-changing stories in the final text. Sarna suggests that the second reference is needed because when Jacob wrested the name Israel from his angelic opponent, he was on the banks of the Jabbok *outside* the border of Canaan; now that he has entered the promised land, the name Israel requires confirmation on the soil that is to become the nation of Israel.[61] Robert Alter, Professor of Hebrew and Comparative Literature at the University of California, understands the repetition of Jacob's acquisition of the name Israel as an example of a biblical editor making use of differing accounts of an event to convey a more complex perspective.[62] Alter suggests that the

---

59. Gen. 35:14. The word *nesech* "drink offering" or "libation" occurs only here in Genesis. It's normative context is material related to priestly matters such as in Lev. 23:37 and Num. 4:7.

60. Speiser, *Genesis*, 255, 271. See addendum 3 for a brief explanation of the codes or documents J, E, P, and D, and the Documentary Hypothesis.

61. Sarna, *JPS Genesis*, 241–42. This perspective is supported by the wording of God's covenantal offer in Gen. 35:11 which features a particular nationalistic component—"a nation, yea, an assembly of nations shall descend from you. Kings shall issue from your loins."

62. Alter proposes that biblical authors intentionally include differing versions of an event to express a more complex perspective on biblical characters and events. He compares this kind of narrative to a film montage, a splicing together of contrasting images of the same subject which results in a more nuanced vision (140), or the technique of a post-Cubist painting which might provide "a profile and a frontal perspective of the same face" on a single canvass (146). As an example in biblical narrative, he cites the variant stories of how David comes to Saul's attention. In I Sam. 16, Saul hears from one of his attendants about David's skill as a musician. When Saul is visited by an evil spirit, David

name change on the banks of the Jabbok in Genesis 32 is folkloristic and mysterious; it serves as an allusion to Jacob's past struggles with humans and God. Similar to Sarna, Alter posits that the change of Jacob's name at Bethel in Genesis 35 points to Jacob's glorious *national* future when his descendants will have established the kingdom of Israel.[63]

Jacob's Covenantal Charges: Be A Blessing, Be Fruitful, and Stay the Course

In God's initial covenantal offer to Jacob in Genesis 28 he is told "all the families of the earth shall bless themselves by your descendants."[64] From this, we can infer that Jacob, like his grandfather Abraham and his father Isaac, is being challenged to "be a blessing," a moral exemplar for others. In this sphere of behavior, Jacob lags behind his father and grandfather. At heart, Jacob is a pragmatist, not a moralist. Turning to God's second offer of a covenant at Bethel, in words reminiscent of God's instructions to the first man and woman at Creation,[65] Jacob is told *p'reih ur'veih* "be fruitful and multiply."[66] At the time of this divine exhortation, Jacob already has eleven sons and a daughter.[67] It is therefore apparent that this divine charge, "Be fruitful," is addressed primarily to Jacob's descendants, the "House of Jacob." Although there is no other specific task that God assigns to Jacob

---

is brought to court to soothe Saul with his music. In the second account, in I Sam. 17, David the shepherd lad, brings provisions from his home to his three older brothers, who are preparing for battle against the Philistines. When the Philistine hero Goliath challenges the Israelites to a contest of single combat, David steps forward and persuades Saul to let him represent Israel. After David kills Goliath with his slingshot, Saul asks Abner, his commander, about David's parentage and is told that he is the son of Jesse. If Saul had already summoned David to court to soothe him with his music, why does Saul need to ask Abner about David's origins? Despite this apparent contradiction, Alter contends that both variants are needed because they project two significant aspects of David's character—his musical talent in I Sam. 16 and his courage and combat skills in I Sam. 17 (Alter, *The Art of Biblical Narrative*, chapter 7 "Composite Artistry," 131–154). While we, being heirs of the Greek tradition of logic and consistency, may have trouble with differing accounts, apparently, our biblical ancestors did not.

63. Alter, *Genesis*, 197.
64. Gen. 28:14.
65. Gen. 1:28.
66. Gen. 35:11.
67. We learn of the birth of the twelfth son, Benjamin, later in the same chapter, Gen. 35:16–20.

in the two covenantal invitations at Bethel, I believe that Jacob's primary challenge can be understood from the larger context of his life. Throughout all his difficulties, God is asking Jacob *to stay the course*, to hold fast to the covenantal vision of a great nation in its own land, dedicated to the ideal of serving as a blessing to "all the families of the earth."[68] His life's task of *staying the course* is symbolized by Jacob's heroic perseverance during his night-long wrestling match with his divine opponent at the Jabbok.

Despite His Many Trials, Jacob Holds Fast to the Covenant

In addition to the rape of Dinah and the perfidy of Simeon and Levi, Jacob endures a number of other familial trials in the land of Canaan: the death of his beloved wife Rachel in childbirth;[69] the sordid affair of his son Reuben with Bilhah, Jacob's concubine;[70] and the disappearance and presumed death of his favorite son Joseph.[71] Such setbacks might have sidelined a less dedicated leader, yet Jacob stays the course.

The self-sacrificing dimension of Jacob's personality is especially evident when, in the midst of a devasting famine, he is confronted with the difficult decision of whether to allow Benjamin, his remaining favorite son,[72] to accompany his older brothers to buy grain in Egypt, something Jacob did not do on their first expedition to Egypt out of fear that something might happen to Benjamin. As the famine becomes more severe, Benjamin's brothers are forced to make a second trip to Egypt to purchase grain from the imperious Egyptian vizier (Joseph) who had warned them not to return without their youngest brother. This time, Jacob consents to let Benjamin go and prays that God may incline the Egyptian to be merciful to his sons. In the same breath, he stoically accepts the possibility of losing Benjamin

---

68. Gen. 28:14.

69. Gen. 35:16–20.

70. In Gen. 35:22. Jacob learns that Reuben has slept with Bilhah, but we do not hear any reproof until Jacob's deathbed blessing when he castigates Reuben for "mounting your father's bed" (Gen. 49:4). To sleep with your father's concubine is a clear challenge to parental authority.

71. Gen. 37.

72. We learn of Benjamin's favored position from Judah's words to the Egyptian official (Joseph), "We told my lord, 'We have an old father, and there is a child of his old age, the youngest; his [full] brother (Joseph) is dead, so that he alone is left of his mother, *and his father dotes on him*'" (Gen. 44:20).

as he has lost Joseph—"If I am to be bereaved, I shall be bereaved."[73] Here we see Jacob as a loving father, besieged by an excruciating dilemma. Reluctantly, he decides to do what must be done for the welfare of his entire family, even if it means risking the loss of a favorite son a second time.

After his sons return with the surprising news that Joseph is alive and well in Egypt, Jacob's commitment to the covenant is tested by Joseph's invitation to his father to come live with him in Egypt. Jacob is concerned about abandoning Canaan, presumably because there will be no covenantal claimant remaining in the promised land.[74] God seeks to dispel Jacob's anxiety—"Fear not to go down to Egypt, for I will make you there into a great nation. I Myself will go down with you to Egypt, and I Myself will also bring you back." With God's covenantal promises vouchsafed, Jacob departs for Egypt to be reunited with Joseph.

In Egypt, Jacob Seems Discouraged but Eventually Recommits to the Covenant

Soon after his arrival in Egypt, Joseph introduces his father to Pharaoh. The king asks the patriarch a very straightforward question "How many are the years of your life?" Jacob responds with more information than Pharaoh requested: "The span of the years of my lifetime has been 130; *m'at v'ra-im* few and miserable have been the days of my life. They have not attained the years of my fathers when they were alive."[75] From Jacob's comment to Pharaoh concerning the brevity of his life when compared with his father and grandfather (Abraham died at the age of 175, Isaac at 180), it would appear that at the age of 130, Jacob senses that his death is imminent and laments that he will not live as long as his father and grandfather.[76] Despite Jacob's premonition, he lives for another seventeen years in the land of Egypt until his death at the age of 147. Interestingly, the Torah says that

---

73. Gen. 43:14.

74. We encountered this problem in chapter 11 in regard to Abraham and God's concern about Isaac's potential abandonment of the land.

75. Gen. 47:9. This is Chaim Stern's translation. He understands *ra-im* as "miserable" (Plaut and Stein, *Torah*, 294). NJPS has "hard."

76. It is disappointing to observe that Jacob puts greater stock in longevity than the quality of life. Perhaps this can be attributed to the biblical idea that living an especially long life is a clear sign of God's blessing.

when Abraham and Isaac die, they expire at *b'seivah tovah* a "ripe old age,"[77] a term which expresses a sense of completion and fulfillment, but this phrase is not present when Jacob's death is recorded.[78] Given its absence and Jacob's depressing comments to Pharaoh, Jacob appears to be the only patriarch who looks back on his life with a sense of disappointment and bitterness. It would seem that *at this particular moment in his life*, even though all his sons and their families, having survived the famine in Canaan, are safely reunited with him in Egypt, the pain that he has endured during his many ordeals, especially the death of Rachel in childbirth,[79] outweighs a sense of thanksgiving at having survived the threat of starvation along with his entire family. In addition, although God has assured him concerning a return to the promised land, Jacob does not see any sign that it will happen in his lifetime.

Despite his discouraging assessment of his life, at some point during his seventeen years in Egypt, Jacob reengages in his life's mission. Thus, near death, Jacob summons Joseph and makes him swear that when he dies, Joseph will take his remains and bury them in the burial place of his ancestors—the Cave of Machpelah in Hebron.[80] Jacob extracts this promise in the hope that his interment in Canaan will serve as a vivid reminder to his family that their ultimate covenantal destination is to the north in the land of Canaan. Shortly thereafter, Jacob adopts Joseph's sons, Ephraim and Manasseh as his own, and blesses them with words that speak of a future of many descendants[81] and the honor of having their names used when the people of Israel invoke God's blessings—"By you shall Israel invoke blessings saying: God make you like Ephraim and Manasseh."[82] Jacob goes on to assure Joseph that "God will be with you and bring you back to the land of your fathers."[83] Jacob then calls all of his sons together and blesses them with a visionary benediction about the glorious future,[84] when the twelve

---

77. Gen. 25:8; 35:29.

78. Gen. 47:28; 49:28–33.

79. Upon his deathbed in Egypt, Jacob recalls the enduring sadness he has felt from the death of Rachel (Gen. 48:7).

80. Gen. 47:28–31.

81. Gen. 48:16.

82. Gen. 48:20. The custom of blessings one's sons by Ephraim and Manasseh exists to this day.

83. Gen. 48:21.

84. Jacob's blessing of his sons in Genesis 49 invokes a "glorious future" for all except Reuben, Simeon and Levi, who have caused him trouble.

tribes, destined to descend from each son, will dwell in the promised land.[85] Just as he would not relinquish his hold on his opponent at the Jabbok until he obtained a blessing, Jacob, in the last days of his life in a foreign land, holds fast to the covenantal vision of his offspring prospering in the land God assigned to him, his father, and his grandfather.

Looking back over the story of Jacob, we can see that he had a tumultuous life, full of disappointments and moral shortcomings as well as accomplishments and victories. My assessment of Jacob is that he was successful in his patriarchal role, because by staying the course, he, like his father Isaac, did what was necessary in his generation to sustain the covenant. I am therefore inclined to affirm that the steadfast, visionary component of his character ultimately eclipses the cautious, calculating dimension. From this perspective, by the end of his life, Jacob has become Israel.

---

85. Gen. 49.

CHAPTER 14

Wrestling with My Brother and Depression

JACOB'S WRESTLING AT THE Jabbok serves as a metaphor for his life. Whether it is with Esau, Laban, God, or the many challenges that he confronts, Jacob continues to wrestle. The image of Jacob as a wrestler resonates with me in regard to two distinct struggles in my own life—wrestling with my brother and wrestling with depression.

Wrestling with My Brother

My brother Mike was born on September 2, 1935, while I was born one week short of his fourth birthday on August 24, 1939. (I like to remind him that for one week in the year, we are only three years apart.) One of my most enduring childhood memories is wrestling with my brother. We often wrestled in our bedroom in Trenton, but our most memorable tussles took place in our two tone blue Hudson on eight hour car rides from Trenton, NJ to Gloucester, MA to visit our Uncle Mel and Aunt Evelyn. I would usually initiate the action with a sharp poke to Mike's ribs, and then, locked together like a pretzel, we would roll around the back seat of the car (there were no seat belts in those days) until Mike, who has always been stronger than I, would twist my arm or neck, and I would start to cry. Our parents were rather tolerant of these brotherly battles, but my crying usually prompted an exasperated shout from our mother, "Cut it out!" A truce might last for a half hour or so until I would begin the contest anew with a sly glance and an "accidental" kick to Mike's shins.

WRESTLING WITH MY BROTHER AND DEPRESSION

In recalling these brotherly bouts, I cannot help but be reminded of the wrestling between Esau and Jacob that began in Rebekah's womb. Were the twins at play or were they trying to do away with each other? And on the fateful night at the Jabbok, the river of "wrestling," after twenty years of separation, Jacob was surely tormented by dire thoughts as to what would happen in his reunion with the brother whom he had wronged. And so the wrestling with the man/angel that night may have seemed to Jacob like a life or death contest with Esau. On the following day, when the brothers come together, Esau sees Jacob limping and bowing towards him. Overcome with brotherly affection, he runs to greet him, "embraces him, falls on his neck, and kisses him."[1] In the Torah scroll there are six dots over the word *vayyishaqeihu* "and he kissed him," one for each Hebrew letter in the word, a sign that there is something very unusual going on. According to Rabbi Jannai, the dots indicate that the kiss of Esau, from the Hebrew root *nun-shin-qof*, has overtones of an angry "bite" from an almost identical root *nun-shin-kaph*.[2] Rabbi Jannai is suggesting that Esau was simultaneously expressing his love for and his anger with Jacob. This speaks to what I felt as Mike and I were locked in combat for hours in the back seat of our parents' car—playful affection commingled with competitive anger.

Mike was a very bright child, but he was handicapped by dyslexia, which in the forties and fifties when he was growing up, was just beginning to be diagnosed. Because of his dyslexia, he wasn't really reading in grammar school; he survived by memorizing much of what he heard. It wasn't until Mike reached adolescence that our parents discovered that he was dyslexic. Add that to his being the first born who was trying to live up to the high expectations of very accomplished parents, one can understand why as a teenager, Mike sometimes reacted to the pressures he was experiencing by not applying himself in school. Our parents made the mistake of expressing their anxiety about his situation in my presence without telling me what it was all about. They assured me that they had faith that Mike would eventually succeed in school, but they did not really try to explain what was going on. As a result, I began to feel unwarranted resentment towards my brother. "How," I thought to myself, "could he intentionally hurt our parents? Hadn't they given him plenty of love and support! How could he do this to them!" In response to my anger with my brother, I adopted a rather simplistic Jacob and Esau perspective, similar to the stereotyping

---

1. Gen. 33:4.
2. *Genesis Rabbah* 78:9.

of the twins by the Rabbis.[3] I would be Jacob, the "good son," by bringing worry-free pleasure to our parents to compensate for the anxiety that Mike, the "bad son," the Esau of our family, had wrought. And so as a teenager, this is how I perceived things, even though underneath my resentment, I still loved and admired my brother. Eventually, our parents had the wisdom to send Mike to a private boarding school, the Solebury School in New Hope, PA, where with small classes and no one to look over his shoulder, he thrived as a student, athlete, and leader.

Early in my rabbinic career, I attended a study session led by Rabbi Norman Cohen, a professor of Midrash at HUC-JIR in New York. I learned from him that in the Tanach a number of the warring siblings in Genesis such as Isaac and Ishmael, Jacob and Esau, and Rachel and Leah find a measure of reconciliation.[4] My study of these sibling struggles helped me realize that the relationships between children in a family are often quite complex, and that there can be competition, anger, love, and envy all mixed together. In addition, in therapy, I discovered a lot about my own limitations, and as a consequence, I began to identify with the problems and pressures Mike had experienced in his youth. I also came to realize that our parents had done a very poor job of helping me appreciate what my brother was undergoing. Having attained a more mature level of insight about our family dynamics, I discarded my simplistic way of thinking about my brother and began to reach out to connect with him in a more empathetic way. I now know him as a devoted husband to his wife Rose, who to our sorrow died of ovarian cancer in May of 2002, a great father to his daughters Jessica and Rachel, and a fantastic grandfather to his four grandchildren Gwen, Evelyn, Theo and Nathaniel. I admire him for having overcome his learning disability to earn a BA from Trinity College in Hartford and a law degree from Harvard Law School, and I have tremendous respect for him for having become a successful leading executive for many years as Vice President of Elderhostel (now known as Road Scholar), an organization with headquarters in Boston that sponsors educational programs for seniors throughout the

---

3. The Rabbis view Jacob and Esau as personifications of Israel and Rome. Thus, for the Rabbis, Jacob/Israel is almost always good, while Esau/Rome is the idol worshiper, innately evil. See the Introduction, ii, note 1, for midrashic examples of rabbinic stereotyping of Esau and Jacob.

4. Isaac and Ishmael come together to bury Abraham in the Cave of Machpelah (Gen. 25:9). Jacob and Esau unite to bury their father, Isaac (Gen. 35:29). Rachel and Leah work together to help Jacob separate from Laban after twenty years of service. (Gen. 31:14–16).

world.[5] He has also held important volunteer positions such as Chair of the Allocation Committee of the Boston United Way. Ultimately, I discovered that I like and love him as a brother, and I know that he feels the same about me. I now understand our childhood wrestling as an initial stage in our development as brothers who sought in competition with each other to establish our places in our family and in the world. We have emerged from those sibling struggles secure in our professional and familial identities, and I take pride in the fact that we have created a much better brotherly bond than Jacob and Esau ever did.

Wrestling with Seasonal Depression

In the previous chapter, I commented on the incident after Jacob arrives in Egypt, when Joseph presents his father to Pharaoh who asks the patriarch, "How many are the years of your life?" After informing Pharaoh that he is 130, Jacob goes on to tell Pharaoh that those years have been *m'at v'ra-im* "few and miserable" and that he feels he has not approached the longevity of his father and grandfather.[6] My sense is that Jacob's dour assessment of his life and premature focus on his death are signs of depression. Surely, a mentally healthy Jacob would have tried to make a better first impression on the King of Egypt. No doubt, his many losses, particularly the death of his beloved Rachel in childbirth, contribute to his sad assessment of his life. Another important reason for his depression may be that he and his entire family are in Egypt with no immediate prospects of a return to the promised land. Certainly Jacob was excited by the opportunity to see Joseph alive and well,[7] but at the same time, he was very reluctant to leave Canaan knowing that he would be creating a situation in which not a single member of his family of seventy dwelt in the land. God's convincing pledge of an eventual return to Canaan gave Jacob the incentive to depart,[8] but the dispiriting effect of his major relocation, is evident in his depressing comment to Pharaoh. By the end of his life, however, Jacob's mental attitude has dramatically improved. Apparently, Jacob wrestled with his sadness,

---

5. Elderhostel began in 1975. My brother joined the organization a few years after it began and has been involved in every major initiative including the first international programs.
6. Gen. 47:9.
7. Gen. 45:28.
8. Gen. 46:3.

and came to the conclusion that it was futile to obsess about the situation. And so, in his waning years Jacob returns to his original covenantal objective by setting out to instill in his twelve sons a desire to return to the land promised to him, his father, and grandfather.

Like Jacob, I wrestled with depression. For about two decades, from my early forties to the age of sixty-two, I suffered from seasonal depression for four to five months every year. Starting in March and extending into June and sometimes even July, I became seriously depressed. I was not ill enough to require hospitalization, but every day was a brutal test of my endurance.

The beginning of my depressive periods often coincided with the festival of Purim. I am aware that some people experience depression on the anniversary of a traumatic event or the recurrence of a specific holiday. Some Christians, for example, get depressed at Christmas time, because they feel they can never attain the inflated expectations of joy that are associated with the Christmas season. Perhaps, this is similar to what happened to me at Purim, a holiday whose motto is *mishenichnas Adar, marbeh b'simchah*, "when Adar (the month in which Purim is celebrated) arrives, joy begins to flourish." When I was a pulpit rabbi, I used to spend days trying to come up with a unique costume for Purim. I also put in a lot of time thinking up jokes, games, and silly *shticks*. I became known in our congregation for my original costumes and creative Purim programs, but looking back, I think the intense pressure to be "funny" may have had the opposite effect of triggering depression. For me, "when Adar arrived," sadness began to flourish. Other factors that might have contributed to the onset of my annual spring depression are allergies (I suffer from hay-fever in the spring and fall) or a sense of disappointment that by springtime, I had not been able to accomplish the high goals that I had set for myself in the previous fall at the Jewish New Year.

Everyone experiences sad moments or days, but clinical depression, feelings of extreme sadness which last for an extended number of days, weeks, months, or even years, is said to affect fifteen million Americans, about 6.7 per cent of the population.[9] Researchers do not thoroughly understand the causes of depression nor do they agree on how to treat it. Each individual has a unique genetic, physical, mental, familial, and cultural

---

9. This statistic comes from a 2014 fact sheet of the Anxiety and Depression Association of America.

profile, so that every person who experiences depression needs to be treated according to his/her specific situation.

The name that is applied to seasonal depression is ironically enough SAD, an acronym for Seasonal Affective Disorder. My psychiatrist told me that my experience of seasonal depression was somewhat unusual. Most individuals who suffer from SAD become depressed as winter approaches. Their depression usually begins to abate in spring when there is more sunlight and the days begin to lengthen. Sunlight is thought to help our bodies suppress the production of melatonin, a hormone which affects our biological clock. Darkness causes the opposite, an increase in melatonin. Researchers theorize that when there is a surplus of melatonin, it can disrupt our sleep patterns as well as our mood, and lead to depression. This problem is sometimes treated by sitting for half an hour each day in front of a "light box" which emits radiation similar to the sun's thereby reducing the body's output of melatonin. Although I would sometimes experience the onset of depression as early as February and even tried light box therapy, it eventually became clear to me that I was not suffering from winter seasonal depression, because most years I really did not begin to feel sick until the spring.

What was my depression like? Most days, I felt extremely tired, and when nighttime came, I could hardly wait to go to bed. Unfortunately, I usually awoke at four or five in the morning and could not fall asleep again. Mornings were the worst time; I felt full of anxiety and worry and dreaded getting out of bed. During the day, I had trouble making decisions. Every little challenge or problem seemed overwhelming. I had no appetite so that I would lose around ten pounds every spring. My eyes felt heavy and sad. Every activity required a tremendous amount of effort. I often felt that I was walking through ankle deep mud. I also felt very bad about myself. When I began to engage in a specific task such as leading a service or teaching a class, my mood usually lifted, but that didn't last long. By sheer willpower I was able to mask my depression so that my congregants were not aware of it. I tried to combat it by physical exercise such as swimming laps, hoping that sensations of well-being induced by the famous but elusive endorphins would kick in, but that never happened. In thinking back on it, I don't know why I chose swimming. Although I enjoy playing in ocean surf, I never liked swimming laps in a pool. I should have tried some physical activity that I enjoy such as hiking, basketball, or racquetball, but for some reason, I didn't think of it; I suspect my depression affected my judgment. Thank

A Lifetime of Genesis

God, I was never suicidal. Barbara, who understandably dreaded my annual bouts of depression, would help me get through those tough times with sympathetic listening and encouragement.

For many years, I sought psychiatric counseling to find some relief, but I was very reluctant to take medication. I tried some natural products that are said to help with depression such as St. John's Wort and Sam-E, but they had no effect. I think my resistance to taking chemical antidepressants stemmed from my associating it with drug addiction.[10] I also thought that if I could just get to the psychological roots of my depression by talk therapy, I would find out what was bothering me and be cured. But year after year my depression was waiting for me.

Finally, under the expert care of Dr. Elizabeth Childs, a Boston psychiatrist who is very knowledgeable about psychopharmacology, I decided to try some medication. At first she prescribed several of the newer antidepressants—Prozac, Wellbutrin, Effexor, and Zoloft—but they did not help. They also brought some unwelcome side effects. Our Temple used to sponsor a Mitzvah Day when congregants were given the opportunity to select a social action project among a variety of volunteer activities. One year, I decided to join a group that was scheduled to visit Waltham Fields Community Farm which grows vegetables to be distributed to the poor in the Boston area. When we arrived at the farm, we set out to do some weeding in long rows of carrots. I chose gardening because I usually love being outdoors, but this day the side effects from my medication began to give me a rough time. As I bent over the rows of tiny green carrot tops, I experienced extreme light-headedness. I had to blink my eyes and shake my head so as not to lose consciousness. I tried to tough it out, but after an hour of weeding, my dizziness increased. I finally sat down in the shade, dragged myself to my car, and returned home, disappointed in myself because I had abandoned the group and did not have the staying power to finish the job.

At that point, I was very discouraged. I was convinced that there was no relief for my depression and that I would just have to suffer my springtime curse every year for the rest of my life. Finally, Dr. Childs suggested a first generation antidepressant.[11] She urged me to be patient and said, "I know you are discouraged because the other medications that you tried did

---

10. Currently, there is an "opioid crisis" in Massachusetts and elsewhere due in part to the overprescription of painkillers, antidepressants, and other drugs.

11. Psychiatrists today tend to prescribe second generation, newer antidepressants, such as Prozac, Zoloft, etc., because they have fewer side effects.

not work, but you should know it often takes four or five trial medications before one finds something that helps." She then prescribed Nortriptyline. The first few days that I took it, I knew we had hit on something. The cloud began to lift, and in a short time I felt much better. I was cautiously optimistic. That was in the spring of 2002. I continued to take the medication throughout the year without any serious side effects, and when I survived Purim, 2003, without the onset of depression, I was elated. Then, for a day or two I thought I might be slipping back as some of my classic symptoms of heavy eyes and feelings of sadness surfaced, but when Dr. Childs increased my dosage, my mood picked up, so that I survived the spring of 2003 without a serious bout of depression. For the most part, I have spent the past fourteen years with depression-free springs.

A valuable lesson that I learned from my experience with depression is that treating mental illness is a very complex process. While the trial and error method of discovering the right medication was crucial, counseling with my psychiatrist, frequent exercise, prayer in the midst of the congregation as well as private prayer, listening to healing music (my favorites are light jazz and classical music), attempting to eat well balanced meals with smaller portions, and trying to get about eight hours of sleep at night, have all helped in my struggle with depression. It also doesn't hurt that for the past decade I have been retired from the pulpit so that my stress level has been considerably reduced. Nevertheless, like an alcoholic, I do not for one minute feel that I can ever ignore my proclivity toward depression. I know this is true because from time to time I have experienced the return of depressive symptoms. When that occurs, Dr. Childs adjusts my medication until I regain my equilibrium. It is clear that if I stop taking my medication and do not attend to my mental and physical health, my depressive periods would probably return. I feel especially blessed, however, to live at a time when the understanding of mental illness and the methods of treatment are known to the extent that I can be helped. I am also aware of how fortunate I am, because I know that there are some who suffer from depression who get little or no relief by taking medication.

Because of my struggle with depression, I have come to understand that mental illness is something that cannot be overcome by willpower. Some years ago during the NFL football playoffs, an all-star lineman for the Oakland Raiders did not show up for a crucial playoff game. His teammates and many in the press excoriated him for failing the team at the most important time. Eventually, it came out that he was suffering from mental illness and that he had experienced some problems with his medication. But even when that came to light, he was castigated as being a wimp and a laggard. If he had suffered a broken leg in practice, no one would have said anything, but how could a rugged football player be felled by something going on in his head! If his teammates and some of the sports writers who were so hard on him knew more about how debilitating mental illness can be and how difficult it is to treat, I don't think they would have been so critical. I would also point out that in the military there is a tremendously high rate of suicide of individuals suffering from depression.[12] The armed forces are sometimes home to a culture which, like professional sports, tends to label mental illness as character weakness. This fits in with the larger American culture that looks favorably upon the athlete or soldier who overcomes all obstacles on his or her own. Conversely, the individual who needs counseling or medication to cope with life is sometimes thought of as a mental weakling. It is evident, then, that there is still a lot of work that needs to be done to make mental illness better understood and more accepted in twenty-first-century America.

A basic truth about mental illness or illness of any kind is that those who are stricken need the help of others. There is a beautiful story in our tradition that speaks to this point. Rabbi Yochanan once became ill and his friend Rabbi Chanina went to visit him. Rabbi Chanina asked, him "Are your sufferings welcome to you?" Rabbi Yochanan answered, "Neither they nor their reward." (The Rabbis taught that sometimes we are rewarded by God for enduring our afflictions.)[13] Then Rabbi Chanina said, "Give me your hand." Rabbi Yochanan reached out his hand, Rabbi Chanina raised him up, and Rabbi Yochanan felt better. While the raising up of Rabbi Yochanan by Rabbi Chanina can be seen as a kind of miracle, it also suggests that the human touch accompanied by heartfelt concern can be theraputic. The Talmud then asks why Rabbi Yochanan could not raise himself up? The answer the Talmud provides is "the prisoner cannot free himself from jail,"[14] that is, the person who is ill is unable to cure him/herself; he/she needs help from others. While the mentally ill person has to be willing to wrestle with

---

12. For a contemporary discussion about the increasing number of suicides in the military see Yochi Dreazen, *The Invisible Front: Love and Loss in an Era of Endless War* (New York: Crown Publishers, 2014).

13. The Rabbis call such afflictions *yissurin shel ahavah* "afflictions of [God's] love." It is not a belief which appeals to me.

14. BT *B'rachot 5b*.

his/her illness, professional help from a psychiatrist or psychologist as well as the support of friends and family are vital for improved mental health.

Seemingly insignificant acts of human kindness for the mentally ill can be extremely important. Many years ago, I went to visit a congregant at a local mental hospital. I spent about half an hour with her. I talked to her about her family, about the temple, and about the events of the day. Throughout the entire visit, she did not say one word. She maintained a blank expression and looked down at the ground; our eyes never met. Months later, after she had been released from the hospital, I ran into her. She looked much better. She gave me a hug and said, "Thanks so much for visiting me in the hospital. I really appreciated it." I was stunned. I did not think that she had been aware of my presence. The lesson that I learned is to try to interact with individuals suffering from mental illness as one would with any sick invidividual. Even though they may not be able to respond at the time of a visit, you never know what they are able to comprehend or what they are thinking or feeling. Just your presence can be comforting. Indeed, when I was at my lowest, a loving word from Barbara meant an awful lot to me even though I had difficulty responding to it.

I shared my struggle with depression with my congregation in a Yom Kippur sermon. I did so because I wanted to provide some comfort and understanding to those members of the congregation who suffered from mental illness. I also wanted to acknowledge how difficult is for their families. I received more positive response from that sermon than from any other sermon in my thirty-six years at Temple Beth David. I concluded my sermon with the following prayer, which I adapted from the Reconstructionist Sabbath Prayer Book.[15]

> *Mi Shebeirach Avoteinu V'imoteinu*
>
> May the God Who blessed our Fathers and Mothers, grant healing to all those members of our congregation and members of our own families living near or far from us who struggle with mental illness. May God give them courage, patience, and hope.
>
> May God so endow their healing physicians and therapists with insight and skill that they may be helpful in the restoration of their health.

---

15. *Sabbath Prayer Book*, The Jewish Reconstructionist Foundation, Inc., New York, 1965, 491.

May God bring strength and forbearance to the members of their families who seek to provide comfort and compassion to their loved ones.

May God remove their anger and wipe away their feelings of guilt and sadness.

May God bless them with life and with love so that they may enjoy health and vigor of body and mind.

May God bind up the wounds of those who are mentally ill so that they may embrace life once again and come to thank God for the renewal of body and the renewal of spirit.

And let us say. Amen.

CHAPTER 15

The Matriarchs and the Covenant

The Motif of Matriarchal Infertility

IN ANCIENT ISRAEL, a male heir was considered essential for the preservation of the ancestral holding and for family continuity. It is therefore not unexpected that the hopes, plans, and actions of the four Matriarchs are for the most part centered on their quest to continue the covenantal line by bearing sons. Three of the four Matriarchs, Sarah, Rebekah, and Rachel, have great difficulty conceiving, and the fourth, Leah, after bearing four sons to Jacob, also experiences a period of infertility.[1] The ongoing matriarchal struggles with infertility give rise to familial frustration, jealousy, and strife, which leads us to ask "Why does infertility occur with each matriarch?"

The Tanach assumes that God determines whether a woman conceives or not. Thus, Sarah complains to Abraham "YHVH has kept me from giving birth."[2] Leah has the opposite experience, for when God sees that Leah is second in Jacob's affections, God "opens her womb" so that she gives birth to Reuben.[3] The Tanach does not mention God's involvement every time a woman becomes pregnant, as for example, in the case of Yocheved, the mother of Moses—"A certain man of the house of Levi went and married

---

1. Gen. 30:9.
2. Gen. 16:2.
3. Gen. 29:31–32.

a Levite woman. The woman conceived and bore a son."[4] When God is mentioned in connection with a specific conception, it usually means that the Tanach has something to teach us. Thus, *God's involvement in the initial pregnancy of each matriarch* as well as many of the subsequent matriarchal conceptions call for an explanation.[5] I would suggest that the reason behind the continuing recurrence of matriarchal infertility followed by God's decisions to enable the Matriarchs to conceive at a certain times is that the Narrator wants us to understand that the course of the covenant is shaped by God's will, not happenstance.

Let us examine each matriarch's effort to bear sons, to influence the course of covenantal succession, and to support their covenanted husbands.

Sarah Seeks a Son By Means of a Surrogate

A fourteenth-century BCE Akkadian text from Nuzi (an ancient Hurrian site 150 miles north of present day Bagdad) tells of a married woman acquiring a second wife for her husband for the purpose of adopting the son of that union as her own child.[6] Sarah uses this stratagem when she offers her Egyptian handmaiden, Hagar, to Abraham as a secondary wife.[7] Although Hagar conceives, the Torah says nothing about God "opening her womb," "taking notice of her" or responding to the prayer of her patriarchal

---

4. Exodus 2:1–2a.

5. *With God's help*, Sarah conceives and gives birth to Isaac (Gen. 21:1–2), Rebekah becomes pregnant and gives birth to Esau and Jacob (Gen. 25:21), Leah conceives and gives birth to Reuben (Gen. 29:31–2), and Rachel becomes pregnant and gives birth to Joseph (Gen. 30:22–3). God's "opening" of Leah's womb in Gen. 29:31 not only accounts for the conception of Reuben, it may also extend to her next three sons, Simeon (Gen. 29:33), Levi (Gen. 29:34) and Judah (Gen. 29:35). God is not said to be involved in the conception of the four sons of the concubines Bilhah and Zilpah, but Rachel interprets the name Dan, Bilhah's first son, to mean "God has vindicated me" (Gen. 30:6), suggesting divine intervention. Leah, after a period of infertility, is "heard" by God who assists in the conception of her fifth son Issachar (Gen. 30:17–18) and perhaps by extension her sixth son Zebulun and her daughter Dinah. Although the Torah does not credit God with opening Rachel's womb for the conception of Benjamin, her second son, Rachel's prayerful interpretation of the name of her first son Joseph, "May God add another son for me" (Gen. 30:24), suggests that Rachel is hopeful of divine help in the conception of a second.

6. *ANET*, 220.

7. Gen. 16:3 indicates that Sarah gives Hagar to Abraham after she and Abraham had been in the land ten years, a decade after God's initial promise of progeny. The couple's period of infertility at this point in the story is actually longer than a decade, because Sarah and Abraham were childless when they left Ur (Gen. 11:31).

husband, as it does when each of the four Matriarchs becomes pregnant for the first time.[8] This distinction suggests that God does not intend to have Hagar's child participate in the covenant. During Hagar's pregnancy the Torah tells us that "her mistress (Sarah) was lowered in her esteem."[9] Sarah becomes so incensed by Hagar's haughty attitude that she mistreats Hagar who flees into the wilderness. Eventually, God, through the agency of an angel, persuades Hagar, with promises of a son and countless progeny,[10] to return to her mistress despite the clear expectation of more abuse.

Apparently, Hagar's arrogance causes Sarah to change her mind about adopting Hagar's child, for once Ishmael is born, she does not say or do anything to make him her son. Later, after the birth of Isaac, Sarah denies any relationship to Ishmael when she speaks of him as "the son of that slave."[11] This differs markedly from Rachel and Leah, both of whom adopt the sons of their handmaidens Bilhah and Zilpah.[12]

God Tells Abraham About the Change of his Wife's Name from Sarai to Sarah and that Sarah will Give Birth to a Son

Near the beginning of Genesis 17, God changes the patriarch's name from *Avram* to *Avraham*, a name which features the addition of the letter *hey*. Since the letter *hey* occurs twice in God's name—*Yod-Hey-Vav-Hey*—the addition of the *hey* in the patriarch's new name may be a sign of divine blessing.[13] At the same time, the covenantal blessings of progeny and land are repeated along with the divine announcement that nations and kings

---

8. "YHVH *paqad* took note of Sarah as He had promised, and YHVH did for Sarah as He had spoken. Sarah conceived and bore a son to Abraham . . ." (Gen. 21:1); "Isaac pleaded with YHVH on behalf of his wife, because she was barren; and YHVH responded to his plea, and his wife Rebekah conceived" (Gen. 25:21); "YHVH saw that Leah was not preferred *vayephtach et rachmah* and opened her womb; but Rachel was barren. Leah conceived and bore a son" (Gen. 29:31–2a); "Now God *vayyizkor* remembered Rachel; God heeded her and opened her womb. She conceived and bore a son (Joseph)" (Gen. 30:22–3a).

9. Gen. 16:4.

10. Gen. 16:9–11.

11. Gen. 21:10.

12. Gen. 30:3–8 records Rachel's adoption of Dan and Naphtali, the sons of Bilhah. Gen. 30:9–13 recounts Leah's adoption of Gad and Asher, the sons of Zilpah.

13. David Stein holds that the additional *hey* in the names Abraham and Sarah represents the "Divine Presence" (Plaut and Stein, *Torah*, 101).

will spring from the patriarch. Later, in the same chapter, God *informs Abraham* that his wife's name will be changed from *Sarai* to *Sarah*, a change of name which also features the additon of the letter *hey*. This is the sole biblical example of God changing the name of a woman. The Eternal promises that Sarah will give birth to a son and that she too will be a progenitor of kings and nations.

> As for your wife *Sarai*, you shall not call her name *Sarai*
> for *Sarah*/Princess is her name!
> I will bless her, indeed I will give you a son from her.
> I will bless her so that she becomes nations,
> kings of peoples shall come from her![14]
>
> Genesis 17:15-16

In light of the striking similarities between the divine promises to Abraham and Sarah in Genesis 17, we need to ask whether God is initiating a covenant with Sarah comparable to the covenant the Eternal has made with Abraham.

Does God Enter Into A Covenant with Sarah?

There are two factors that convince me that God does not make a covenant with Sarah in Genesis 17. The first is that every time God enters into a covenant in Genesis with a patriarch, the Eternal speaks directly to the covenantal partner be it Abraham, Isaac, or Jacob. By contrast, when God speaks about Sarah's name change and the promise that a son, nations, and kings will descend from her, the Eternal reveals this information to Abraham but not to Sarah. Secondly, when God adds a *hey* to Abraham's name, the Eternal says, "I will maintain My covenant between Me and you, and your offspring to come."[15] But when God adds a *hey* to Sarah's name, there is no mention of a covenant.

Isaiah 51:2 also supports the view that a divine covenant with Sarah is not part of biblical tradition.

> Look back to Abraham your father,
> and to Sarah who brought you forth.
> For he was only one when I called him,

14. The translation is from Fox, *Five Books*, 73.

15. The addition of the *hey* to Abraham's name is in Gen. 17:5. Two verses later in Gen. 17:7, we read this reference to the covenant between God and Abraham.

but I blessed him and made him many.

Isaiah 51:2

Since the first couplet mentions the joint parentage of the Hebrews by Abraham and Sarah, it is reasonable to expect that the second couplet of the verse should also refer to their mutual role in the covenantal history of Israel, but only Abraham is called and blessed by God, while Sarah is not mentioned at all! It is apparent, then, that even from the perspective of later biblical tradition, God does not establish a covenant with Sarah.

Miraculously, Sarah Conceives and Gives Birth to Isaac

In Genesis 18, we read that standing at the entrance of the family tent, the ninety year old post-menopausal Sarah,[16] is startled to overhear in her husband's conversation with three visitors that she will have a son. Laughing inwardly, she mutters "Now that I am withered, am I to have enjoyment, with my husband so old?"[17] Sarah's laughter and remark, expressing surprise and disbelief, reveal that Abraham had not told her about God's announcement to him that she would have a son.[18] (Perhaps, Abraham withheld the information because of his ambivalence about Ishmael's displacement by Sarah's yet-to-be-born son.) God, in the person of one of the three angelic visitors then says to Abraham "Why did Sarah laugh saying 'Shall I in truth bear a child, old as I am? Is anything beyond YHVH?'"[19] And so within a year, at the time appointed by God, Sarah gives birth to *Yitzchaq*.[20] In her joy at attaining motherhood she exclaims "God has brought me *tz'choq* laughter; everyone who hears *yitzchaq li* will laughingly rejoice with me."[21]

---

16. Gen. 18:11 states that "Sarah had stopped having the periods of women."

17. Gen. 18:12.

18. Gen. 17:16, 19.

19. God reports to Abraham that Sarah said, "Shall I in truth bear a child, old as I am?" (Gen. 18:13). This differs from what she actually said, "Now that I am withered, am I to have enjoyment, with my husband so old?" (Gen. 18:12). A midrash suggests that in speaking with Abraham, God alters Sarah's remark in order to preserve *shalom bayit* "peace in the house" by not informing Abraham that his wife had implied that he was too old for sexual activity (*Genesis Rabbah* 48:18).

20. Gen. 21:1–3.

21. Gen. 21:6. Note the motivic use of the name *Yitzchaq*. The translation is mine.

Sarah Has Hagar and Ishmael Expelled Into the Wilderness; Ishmael is Disinherited

The half-brothers Isaac and Ishmael,[22] grow up in the same household, but one day, Sarah observes Ishmael *m'tzacheiq*.[23] Suddenly, Sarah says to Abraham: "Cast out that slave-woman and her son, for the son of that slave shall not share in the inheritance of my son Isaac."[24] What is Ishmael doing that attracts such a drastic reaction in Sarah? Alter makes the creative suggestion that *m'tzacheiq* means that Ishmael is "Isaac-ing-it," acting like he is to be the next patriarch.[25] I think *m'tzacheiq* indicates that Ishmael is engaged in some sort of dangerous bullying of his younger brother, making fun of him. In the Midrash, the Rabbis give credence to this idea when they propose that Ishmael is using Isaac as target practice with his bow and arrow![26] When Sarah observes Ishmael's aggressive treatment of Isaac,[27] it dawns on her that with Ishmael on the scene, Isaac may suffer physical harm, or he may not be able to mature sufficiently in order to assume his role as the next patriarch. And so she demands that Abraham expel Ishmael.

Sarah's explicit rationale for Abraham's banishment of Ishmael is that "the son of that slave shall not inherit with my son, Isaac."[28] God has told Abraham that Isaac will be the covenantal leader in the next generation, but this does not necessarily ensure that Isaac will *inherit* the major portion of Abraham's property, which by custom belongs to Ishmael, the first

---

22. Ishmael's relative age seems to vary in the Genesis narrative. Gen. 16:16 says that Abraham was eighty-six years old when Ishmael was born. He is one hundred at Isaac's birth (Gen. 21:5). Accordingly, Ishmael is fourteen at Isaac's birth and probably a young man when Sarah seeks to banish him from their home in order to separate him from Isaac. This seems to be at variance with the narrative in Gen. 21:15, where we read that when Hagar and Ishmael run out of water in the wilderness, Hagar places her son under a bush so that she does not have to witness his death, a depiction which suggests that he is not a teen but a young child at the time of his banishment.

23. Gen. 21:9.

24. Gen. 21:10.

25. Alter, *Genesis*, 98.

26. *Genesis Rabbah* 53:11.

27. In chapter 13, note 4, we called attention to the divine oracle to the pregnant Hagar after her flight into the desert, where we encounter a prophecy concerning Ishmael's aggressive nature when an angel tells her that her yet-to-be-born son "shall be a wild ass of a man; His hand against everyone and everyone's hand against him" (Gen. 16:12).

28. Gen. 21:10.

born.[29] Sarah's objective in having Abraham disinherit Ishmael is to have all of Abraham's wealth pass on to Isaac, providing him with the necessary resources to become, like his father, a respected leader in the land. Despite the patriarch's concern for Ishmael, God tells him to accede to Sarah's demand.[30] The question arises as to whether the expulsion of Ishmael constitutes an act of disinheritance. There is a precedent in the Laws of Lipit-Ishtar (nineteenth-century BCE Babylonian Law Code) that states when a slave and her son are given their freedom, they forfeit their inheritance.[31] Years later, near the end of Abraham's life, we encounter a confirmation of Ishmael's disinheritance when the Torah says that Abraham "willed all that he owned to Isaac," and that during his lifetime, he gave gifts to the "sons of his concubines."[32] The sons of his concubines are Ishmael, the son of Hagar,[33] and the six sons of Keturah,[34] whom Abraham married after Sarah's death. Just as Abraham sent Ishmael away from Isaac, he sends the six sons of Keturah eastward "away from Isaac."[35] Both measures are designed to protect Isaac's inheritance and hegemony as the second patriarch.

Sarah's Role in the Covenant

Even though God does not make a covenant with Sarah, we should not underestimate Sarah's role as Abraham's helpmate in sustaining the covenant. When God suddenly calls Abraham to leave his home in Haran, Sarah accompanies her husband on his covenantal mission to Canaan, and after their flight from famine to Egypt, at great risk to herself, she protects him in the courts of Pharaoh and Abimelech when she agrees to pretend she is

---

29. We see the same distinction between the property rights of the first born and the first born's prerogative of family leadership in the story of Jacob and Esau. Esau sells his birthright, his inheritance of the first born, presumably a double portion as described in Dt. 21:17, for a bowl of lentil soup (Gen. 25:29–34); he loses family leadership when Isaac gives the disguised Jacob the blessing of the first born (Gen. 27:18–29).

30. Gen. 21:11.

31. In the laws of Lipit-Ishtar the father may grant freedom to a slave woman and the children she bore him, in which case they forfeit their share of the paternal estate (*ANET*, 160).

32. Genesis 25:5–6.

33. There is no record of a gift from Abraham to Ishmael in the text. Perhaps Abraham gifted Ishmael when he sent him into the wilderness with his mother.

34. Gen. 25:2.

35. Gen. 25:6.

Abraham's sister. Finally, Sarah helps secure Isaac's position as the second patriarch by having Ishmael sent into the wilderness. Ishmael survives to become the father of twelve tribes.[36] His banishment at Sarah's insistence seems cruel. From the perspective of God's covenantal plan, however, it is a necessary cruelty.

Rebekah and the Twins

In Genesis 25 we learn that Rebekah and Isaac have been childless for twenty years. Finally, Isaac prays to God "on behalf of his wife."[37] The Eternal responds to Isaac's plea so that Rebekah conceives. During her pregnancy, she is in such great discomfort that she goes "to inquire of YHVH:"[38]

> And YHVH answered her,
> Two nations are in your womb,
> Two separate peoples shall issue from your body;
> One people shall be mightier than the other,
> And the older shall serve the younger.
>
> Gen. 25:23

From this oracle, Rebekah, the only matriarch who receives a divine message of more than a few words, learns that she will give birth to twins who are destined to give rise to two nations (Edom and Israel), and that the elder will be subservient to his younger brother.

Rebekah's Role in the Covenant

Having heard God's oracle concerning Jacob's supplanting of Esau, why does Rebekah not leave the fulfillment of the oracle up to God? My understanding is that even though Rebekah has been granted foreknowledge of God's covenantal plan for Jacob, she believes that her active participation is essential to its fulfillment. While we might fault Rebekah for favoring one

---

36. Gen. 25:13–15. See chapter 5 note 30 for a listing of the twelve tribes of Ishmael.
37. Gen. 25:21.
38. Gen. 25:22. The text states that Rebekah *vatteile__ch*_ "went" to inquire of YHVH. Where did she go? Some suggest she went to a seer, but the text does not mention such a person. Perhaps, she went to a sacred tree or site which was known as a place where a divine oracle might be received.

of her sons over the other,[39] and for seeking to manipulate her husband by means of deception, Rebekah, like Sarah, sees herself as engaged in the vital task of furthering God's covenantal design.

Rebekah, as was the case with Sarah, is more than just a mother actively promoting her favorite son as the next patriarch; she is also a fitting marriage partner for her patriarchal husband, Isaac. When Rebekah arrives from Haran to become Isaac's wife, the Torah informs us that Isaac "found comfort after his mother's death."[40] Without Rebekah's love and support, Isaac may not find the strength to overcome his grief from the loss of his mother.

Leah and Rachel Compete to Become the Mother of Jacob's Children

The institution of polygamy, which was common in the ancient Near East, had the obvious advantage of increasing the potential for male heirs. The marriage of Jacob to four wives—two primary wives, Leah and Rachel, and two concubines (secondary wives), Zilpah and Bilhah—illustrates how polygamy can aid in the challenge of producing sons. Leah and Rachel, unlike their matriarchal predecessors, Sarah and Rebekah, receive no direct or indirect divine message providing them with prescience about their offspring. Once married to Jacob, they become enmeshed in an intense competition to have sons.[41] Because Leah is not favored by Jacob, God has compassion on her so that she is the first to bear children.[42] Leah gives birth to Jacob's first four sons—Reuben, Simeon, Levi and Judah—heightening Rachel's frustration to an almost unbearable level so that she turns to her husband and cries out, "Give me children, or I shall die!"[43] Jacob's brusque response, "Can I take the place of God who has denied you fruit of the womb?"[44] seems in-

---

39. Although Rebekah favors Jacob, she still loves Esau. We see this when at the conclusion of her words to Jacob urging him to flee from Esau's anger, she says "Let me not lose you both in one day!" (Gen. 27:45). Her cry reflects her fear that should Esau kill Jacob, the custom of blood vengeance might bring about the death of Esau whom she also loves.

40. Gen. 24:67.

41. Norman Cohen writes at length about the competition between Rachel and Leah (Cohen, *Self, Struggle & Change*, chapter 5, 125–148).

42. Gen. 29:31–32.

43. Gen. 30:1.

44. Gen. 30:2.

sensitive in the extreme. As Sarah had tried to do with Hagar, Rachel resorts to providing a surrogate, giving Jacob her handmaiden Bilhah as a secondary wife. Rachel adopts the fruits of that union, Dan and Naphtali, as her own.[45] Leah also experiences a period of infertility so that she too decides to use the convention of concubinage by giving her handmaiden Zilpah to Jacob as a secondary wife. Zilpah gives birth to two more sons, Gad and Asher, both of whom are adopted by Leah.[46]

The rivalry between the sisters takes a new turn when Rachel makes a proposal to her sister. As the favored wife who decides who will have access to Jacob's bed, Rachel offers Leah a night with Jacob in exchange for mandrakes (a plant thought to have aphrodisiac as well as fertility powers) which Leah's son Reuben has found in the field.[47] Following this incident, Leah has three more children with Jacob—two sons, Issachar and Zebulun, and Jacob's only daughter, Dinah.[48] Then, at long last, God "remembers" Rachel so that she gives birth to Joseph.[49] Later when the family returns to Canaan, Rachel dies in childbirth with Jacob's twelfth and final son Benjamin.[50]

Rachel and Leah's competition to bear sons in order to win favor from their husband and to attain self-fulfillment goes hand in hand with God's intent to have the covenant carried on by the twelve tribes of Israel. Among the twelve sons of Jacob, six are by Leah (Reuben, Simeon, Levi, Judah, Issachar, and Zebulun), two by her handmaiden Zilpah (Gad and Asher), two by Rachel's handmaiden Bilhah (Dan and Naphtali), and two by Rachel (Joseph and Benjamin). Each son, except for Joseph,[51] becomes the epony-

---

45. Gen. 30:3-8.

46. Gen. 30:9-13.

47. See Gen. 30:14-16 for the account about Rachel, Leah, and the mandrakes. Sarna details the aphrodisiac powers of mandrakes, a flowering regional plant with large forked roots that can have a humanoid appearance. He also points out the homophonic and thematic connection between mandrakes and love in Song of Songs 7:13-14, "There I will give *dodai* my love to you, *hadduda-im* the mandrakes yield their fragrance . . . *dodi* my beloved" (Sarna, *JPS Genesis*, 209). Alter notes the tradition that mandrakes were also thought to promote fertility, which is surely the primary reason why the barren Rachel wants them (Alter, *Genesis*, 160).

48. Gen. 30:17-21.

49. Gen. 30:22-4.

50. Gen. 35:16-20.

51. Although Genesis 49 and Deuteronomy 33 lists Joseph as one of the twelve tribes, there is no actual tribe of Joseph. In most lists of the twelve tribes such as Numbers 1:5-15, the tribes of Ephraim and Manasseh take the place of their father Joseph. Levi is

mous ancestor (the name of the tribe derives from the name of the son) of one of the twelve tribes of Israel, the next link in the covenant.

While Leah and Rachel do not mention the covenant, we can infer that they know of the covenantal traditions of Abraham and Isaac, and that they are aware of the significance of the covenant for Jacob and for themselves and their sons. After twenty years of serving Laban, Jacob gathers Rachel and Leah together to tell them of their father Laban's machinations concerning his wages. He also tells them about his recent dream in which God reminded him about the pillar he had set up at Bethel as testimony to his vow to serve God and return to Canaan.[52] If Leah and Rachel did not know about the covenant, Jacob's review of his oath surely helps them understand the significance of their husband's covenantal relationship with God. The sisters respond that all the wealth (the flocks) that God has taken away from Laban and given to Jacob is rightfully their property since their father squandered *kaspeinu* "our [bridal] money."[53] They are now prepared to depart from their father's house with their husband and their rightful bridal property in order to join in God's covenantal mission for their husband.[54] Their final encouraging words to Jacob are "Do just as God has told you!"[55] Jacob, no doubt, appreciates Rachel and Leah's support for him over their father Laban, as well as their readiness to follow him to Canaan.

Jacob's Relationship with Rachel

Jacob's relationship with Rachel is intense. From the very first moment that Jacob sees Rachel at the well, he is lovestruck. Jacob is so energized that he shows off his prowess by rolling away the stone from the mouth of the

---

deleted from these lists because as the priestly tribe, Levi has no landed inheritance in Canaan. Although there may have been more than twelve tribes in the period prior to the monarchy, the final number of the tribes of Israel according to the Tanach is twelve. The number twelve is particularly useful since it allows each tribe to have a turn at providing offerings at the Temple in a year of twelve months.

52. Gen. 31:4–13.
53. Gen. 31:15. Bridal money is my understanding of *kaspeinu*, literally, "our money."
54. Gen. 31:14–16. Sarna suggests that the money or inheritance they are claiming is the bride price which Jacob paid to Laban by means of his fourteen years of labor. The monetary equivalent of his labor was to be settled on each bride. Thus, Rachel and Leah are accusing "their father either of the improvident disposition of this money or of outright larceny" (Sarna, *JPS Genesis*, 215).
55. Gen. 31:16.

well, a task usually performed by several men. He then waters all of Laban's flocks that Rachel has brought to the well, and without identifying himself, kisses her, and breaks into tears.[56] Twenty years later, when Jacob is finally ready to depart from Haran, Rachel's support at the expense of her father is manifest by her theft and concealment of Laban's household gods.[57] Her motivation for this theft is not clear. Perhaps, she believes that these small idols (they had to be small enough to fit under Rachel's camel saddle where she hid them)[58] have the power to ward off evil. Speiser, on the basis of documents from Nuzi, suggests that possession of the family gods could signify legal title to an estate which may explain why Laban is so anxious to find them.[59] Rachel is the mother of Jacob's last two sons, Joseph and Benjamin, who become his favorites because they are the sons of his old age (his final two sons) as well as the sons of his favorite wife.[60] Many years later upon his deathbed in Egypt, Jacob recalls the sadness that he has carried with him since the day when his beloved Rachel died in childbirth with Benjamin. In memory of her, he adopts Ephraim and Manasseh, Joseph's sons, and his and Rachel's grandsons, as his own sons.[61]

In the generation after Jacob, familial leadership passes to Rachel's son, Joseph. Unlike Sarah and Rebekah, there is no particular course of action that Rachel takes to help elevate her son to the head of the family. The fact that she is Jacob's beloved certainly contributes to Jacob's preferential treatment of Joseph as a youth in Canaan. After father and son are reunited in Egypt, Jacob's selection of Joseph to carry forward the leadership of the covenantal mission of a return to Canaan[62] is influenced not only by Jo-

---

56. Gen. 29:10–11.

57. Gen. 31:19. See Sarna, *JPS Genesis*, 216, for a detailed discussion about Laban's "household gods."

58. When Laban conducts a search for the idols, Rachel tells her father that she cannot dismount her camel because she is having her period (Gen. 31:34–35).

59. Speiser, *Genesis*, 249–251.

60. Gen. 37:3 states that "Israel loved Joseph best of all his sons, for he was the child of his old age; and he made him an ornamented tunic." Jacob's favoritism in regard to Benjamin is made evident by his keeping Benjamin at home when his older brothers go down to Egypt for the first time to purchase grain and by Judah's recollection of his father's words that his beloved Rachel had two sons, one of whom (Joseph) has been torn by a beast. If Jacob should lose Benjamin as well, it would kill him, because "his own life (Jacob's life) is bound up with his" (Gen. 44:27–31).

61. Gen. 48:5–7.

62. We know of Jacob's selection of Joseph as the family leader because he has a separate dialogue with Joseph before he speaks to all his sons at his deathbed to tell them

seph's position of power in the Egyptian court, but also by the fact that Joseph is the son of his beloved Rachel.

Jacob's Relationship with Leah

It is difficult to assess the relationship between Jacob and Leah. Genesis 29:17 states "Leah's eyes were *rakkot*; Rachel was shapely and beautiful." The word *rakkot* is often translated as "weak"[63] and understood as a defective physical trait of Leah, who suffers in comparison to Rachel's overall beauty described in the second part of the verse. Fox points out, however, that the verse can be read as an example of synonymous parallelism. If Rachel is described as "shapely and beautiful," *rakkot* may be a reference to Leah's most positive feature. In that case, it might mean that her eyes are "delicate" or "tender" in the sense of sympathetic.[64]

We know that Jacob is smitten by Rachel's beauty the first time he meets her at the well, and that he contracts with Laban, her father, to marry Rachel in exchange for seven years of his labor. When the seven years are up, in the dark of night, Laban places Leah in Jacob's tent instead of Rachel, so that the elder sister becomes Jacob's first wife.[65] Jacob, who deceived his father Isaac when he stole the blessing of the first born, now complains to Laban about being the victim of deception. Although it is difficult to believe that Jacob was totally unaware that it was Leah rather than Rachel who had come to him in the night, it is nevertheless possible. Having waited seven years for this night, he may have been blinded by passion so that Jacob was unable to distinguish between the sisters. It is also important to point out that even though Jacob has to make a commitment to work for Laban for another seven years to acquire Rachel, Laban allows him to have his younger daughter *within one week*![66] My sense is that despite his

---

of their future. Also in the blessing of his sons, Jacob refers to Joseph as *n'zir echayv* "the elect of his brothers," (Gen. 49:26) namely, their leader.

63. NJPS. The understanding that Leah's eyes are weak may be related to a possible derivation of the name Leah from the root *lamed-aleph-hey* meaning to be "weak" or "tired."

64. Fox, *Five Books of Moses*, 137.

65. Gen. 29:23.

66. Following Jacob's complaint, Laban says to him "It is not our practice in our place to marry off the younger before the older. Wait until the bridal week of this one is over, and we will give you that one too, provided you serve me another seven years." (Gen. 29:26–7).

protestation, the wily Jacob is rather pleased that he has acquired two wives in the span of seven days.

Genesis 29:31 tells us that because Leah is s'nu-ah, God opens her womb first. S'nu-ah can be understood as "unloved" or even "hated," but Sarna notes that in this context the term does not denote hatred, but rather the wife who is less preferred.[67] In the previous verse, the Torah tells us that "Jacob loved Rachel more than he loved Leah,"[68] which means that he loved Leah, just not as much as Rachel. It is, nevertheless, clear that Leah's secondary position in Jacob's affections troubles her. We know this because of her interpretation of the names which she gives to her first three children. The name of Leah's first born is R'uvein which she interprets as "YHVH has seen my affliction."[69] Leah adds a second interpretation of the name R'uvein which is even more replete with pathos, "Now my husband ye'e-havani will love me."[70] Leah names her second son Shimon from the root shin-mem-ayin "to hear" because "YHVH shama heard that I was not preferred."[71] To her third son she gives the name Leivi in the hope that "my husband yillaveh will become attached to me."[72] By the time Leah's fourth son is born, she seems to have found some resolution of her sense of disappointment, for she names this child Y'hudah, "This time odeh I will thank YHVH."[73] Up to this time, Leah has produced four sons for Jacob, while Rachel has not given birth to one. Leah fears, however, that regardless of how many children she bears, Jacob's love for Rachel will always overshadow his love for her. Thus, when Leah gives birth to her sixth and last son she names

---

67. Sarna observes that in Deuteronomy 21:15, where the same term s'nu-ah is paired with ahuvah in reference to a wife and co-wife, s'nu-ah does not mean "hated" as opposed to "beloved." Rather, it refers to a lesser degree of preference. Dt. 21:16 states that if the son of the wife who is s'nu-ah "less preferred" is the first born, the husband may not transfer that son's right to inherit a double portion to a younger son of ha-ahuvah "the preferred wife." (Sarna, JPS Genesis, 206). Abraham, however, does this in regard to Ishmael, by giving his entire estate to Isaac, the second born son who is the child of Sarah, the preferred wife (Gen. 25:5–6).

68. Gen. 29:30.

69. Gen. 29:32. This interpretation derives from the root reish-aleph-hey "to see" which occurs in the first syllable in the name R'uvein as "See a son!"

70. Gen. 29:32. This interpretation sees the syllable vein in R'uvein as a homophone of the last syllable of the word ye'e-havani from the root aleph-hey-beit "to love."

71. Gen. 29:33.

72. Gen. 29:34. This interpretaion of Leivi is based on the root lamed-vav-hey "to attach or accompany."

73. Gen. 29:35. She links Y'hudah to the root yod-dalet-hey "to give thanks."

him *Z'vulun,* a name which she interprets to mean "this time my husband *yizb'leini* will exalt me."[74] To her sorrow, Leah's hope to be number one in Jacob's affections is never realized.

My understanding of Leah's relationship to Jacob is that he loved her, but with nowhere near the intensity of the love he held for Rachel. Surely, he was grateful to her for giving him six sons and a daughter. The most children that any of his other three wives bore him was two. Furthermore, many years later, when Jacob speaks to his sons of his desire to be buried in Canaan, he recalls how he interred Leah in the ancestral burying ground, the cave of Machpelah.[75] That he buried Leah alongside his mother, Rebekah, and his grandmother, Sarah, as well as his father and grandfather, Isaac and Abraham, and that he intends to be buried next to her, are clear indications of his love and esteem for Leah as his wife and as a matriarch.

From a larger biblical and covenantal perspective, Leah takes on crucial importance because she is the mother of Judah, the son from whom the Davidic royal line descends. Leah is also the mother of Levi, the son whose tribe produces the the Levites and the priests (*Kohanim*), the key religious functionaries of the kingdoms of Israel and Judah. Since Moses and Aaron are from the tribe of Levi, they too descend from Leah.

Overview of the Matriarchs and the Covenant

We have observed that all four Matriarchs struggle with infertility at some point in their lives. God's continuing role in facilitating matriarchal conception adds a sense of divine drama to the suspenseful process and underscores the idea that the birth of patriarchal sons is not a random series of events, but part of God's deliberate oversight of the covenant. The Matriarchs, however, are not just child bearing vessels. The leading matriarch in each generation plays a key role in God's overall plan for covenantal succession. Thus, Sarah and Rebekah take active roles in having their favorites, Isaac and Jacob, assume family leadership over Ishmael and Esau, their husbands' favorites. And in the third generation, Jacob's selection of Joseph to be the family leader in Egypt is influenced by the fact that Joseph is the son of Rachel, Jacob's favorite wife.

---

74. Gen. 30:20. She understands *Z'vulun* to be based on the root *zayin-beit-lamed* "to exalt."

75. Gen. 49:31. The Torah does not tell us the circumstances of Leah's death.

The Matriarchs provide support and comfort to their husbands in different ways—Sarah as a risk-taking protector for Abraham in the royal courts of Egypt and Gerar, Rebekah as a comforter to Isaac in mourning for his mother, and Rachel and Leah as Jacob's allies against their devious father Laban. Because they live in a patriarchal society, the Matriarchs do not enter into covenants with God. Nonetheless, their support of their husbands and their individual efforts are crucial to the continuity of the Covenant of Abraham.

CHAPTER 16

My Mother the Matriarch

SARAH, REBEKAH, RACHEL AND Leah are our biblical Matriarchs. Tradition has conferred their revered status upon them by reason of their marriages to the Patriarchs and their importance as the mothers of the first leaders of the Jewish people. They are also deserving of the title matriarch because they displayed courage and leadership as they sought to sustain and influence the role of their husbands and sons in the course of the covenant. Today, this Jewish matriarchal model is to be found among women of our people who are recognized as leaders of their families. My mother, Eleanor Lowenstein Zoob, is an example, for she was a matriarch in her family of origin and in our family as well, where she provided leadership, guidance, and inspiration.

The second of six children, my mother was born June 24, 1902, in Mitau, Latvia,[1] a city twenty-five miles southwest of Riga, where her family on her mother's side were the poor relations of department store moguls in Riga, the capital city. She was almost four years old when she left Europe. She was accompanied by her mother, Helen, her maternal grandmother, Jennie Kahn, her sisters Ida and Evelyn, and her brother Aaron. Two more siblings, Bob and Jean, would be born in America. Her uncles Hugo and Henry Kahn also joined them on their journey to the States. They traveled in the steerage section of the Umbria, a Cunard ship which embarked from

---

1. Mitau is the German name for the city of Jelgava. In the *Encyclopedia Judiaca*, 9:1336, a census from 1897 (9 years prior to my mother's emigration) states that there were 5,879 Jews in the city, which had a total population of about 35,000. I infer that she was born or at least raised in Mitau, because that city is cited as the family's home in my Uncle Aaron's appplication for US citizenship. My thanks to my cousin Janet, Uncle Aaron's daughter, for sending me a copy of her father's citizenship application.

Liverpool, England, arriving in New York on June 10, 1906.[2] Like many immigrant Jewish husbands, my mother's father, Heiman Lowenstein, had come to America a few years before his family arrived. Upon their arrival, he brought his wife and family to a section of Brooklyn known as Brownsville. Soon afterwards, they moved to Newark, New Jersey.

My mother's father was a jeweler, but according to my mother, a very poor businessman. I remember her telling me that when things were difficult, he had to drive a horse-drawn bread delivery wagon to supplement the family income. My grandmother contributed to the family earnings as a milliner, a maker of fine women's hats. They were of very modest means, but my mother and her siblings never thought of themselves as poor.

When she was a young girl, my mother was known as Ella. Later, her family called her El, while my father and her friends referred to her as Eleanor. Growing up, my mother was a voracious reader whose second home was the local public library. She enjoyed telling me how much she looked forward to the arrival at the library of the *St. Nicholas Magazine*, a popular monthly periodical of illustrated stories for boys and girls. She excelled as a student in the Newark public school system. After graduating Central High School in Newark, she found work as a court stenographer. I remember the old stenographic machine which she kept at home. It was like a small typewriter which produced a number of shorthand symbols. I assume that from her experience in the court room, she became interested in the law and applied to and was accepted at Rutgers Law School. In those days, one did not need an undergraduate degree to attend law school. My mother was one of three women in her law school class. She took night classes so that during the day she could earn money to contribute to family expenses.

My mother's first position as an attorney was in the Newark law firm of Lum, Fairlee and Wachenfeld. When she entered the firm in the 1920s, like many female lawyers in those days, she was asked to devote herself exclusively to "family law," that is, cases involving divorce or adoption, because it was thought that women were naturally attuned to family issues. In addition, women were not considered competent or tough enough for the rough and tumble world of corporate or criminal law. My mom, all five feet of her, was very competent and plenty tough, and in time, Mr. Lum, the senior partner, saw that she was capable of handling a wide variety of cases. Her law practice soon expanded to include wills and corporate

---

2. This information was gleaned from my Uncle Aaron's citizenship application which is mentioned in the previous footnote.

clients and she also served as a court arbiter. Quite an accomplishment for an immigrant girl! Her earnings along with those of her sister Evelyn, a primary school teacher, helped defray the tuitions for their younger brothers—Aaron at medical school in Charleston, South Carolina and Bob at Johns Hopkins where he earned a PhD in French Literature.

When my parents married in 1930, they settled in Trenton, New Jersey, midway between Philadelphia and Newark. In the morning they would drive to the Trenton train station. My mother would take a thirty minute train ride north to Newark, while my father would travel about the same distance in the opposite direction to Philadelphia. In the evening they reunited in Trenton and drove home together. In the early days of their marriage, my mother's income was essential for the financial well-being of our family. This was the era of the Depression and her work in a large established Newark law firm made her the major bread winner, while my father was just starting to build his own legal practice in Philadelphia. In the forties when my brother Mike and I were young boys, it was somewhat unusual to have two working parents, but I did not feel neglected in the least. I was well cared for during the day by Laura, an African American nanny, and by dinner time, my parents were always home. I remember being proud of the fact that my mother had a job while all of my friends' mothers were at home during the day. I thought of my mother as remarkable and talented, and in the long run, I think the pride I took in her career contributed to my own self-esteem.

Mom practiced law for about twenty-five years. When we moved to Philadelphia in 1948, she retired to become a full time housewife, but still found time to draw up wills and trusts for my father's law practice. I was nine years old and my brother was thirteen at the time of the move. In addition to running an immaculate house, she was involved in a variety of other activities. When I entered Friends' Central in the tenth grade, she drove me to school every day and helped provide transportation for my soccer team for away games. She took up ice skating and ice dancing at the Philadelphia Skating and Humane Society in Ardmore,[3] an activity which she continued into her eighties. After she gave up ice skating, she swam laps

---

3. The term "Humane" in the club's name refers to volunteer rescue work that the members performed when the club was founded in the middle of the 19th Century. When my mother first began taking lessons at the Ardmore rink in the early 50s, the skating club did not have any Jewish members. I think she was eventually invited to be one of the first Jews to join the club, but she declined. Today, membership at the Ardmore skating club is open to everyone.

at the local YMCA and continued daily walks in the neighborhood well into her nineties. She volunteered with the League of Women Voters and was an active member of the Temple Rodeph Shalom Sisterhood. Of course she never stopped reading and learning. She took French lessons and also helped organize a course in James Joyce's *Ulysses* taught by Ben Schleifer, a family friend and a renown English teacher at Gemantown Friends School. Being knowledgeable about human behavior and very self-confident, she also became a mentor to many younger women. In these relationships, she functioned as an amateur psychologist, a patient listener who knew enough to refrain from telling her young "clients" what to do. She was also a great cook and had impeccable taste in clothing, interior design, and art. She was a very skilled seamstress, a craft she learned from her milliner mother. My father was an exceptional pianist, and Mom enjoyed listening to him play classical, popular, and jazz pieces, on his treasured Steinway. On Saturday afternoons they loved to sit together in our den as they read and listened on the radio to live Metropolitan Opera performances.

Although my parents did not have the resources to be major philanthropists, my mother made many modest donations to a variety of causes as she was imbued with the belief in the importance of *tz'dakah*. One summer day when I was in camp in Maine, one of my bunkmates, who received the daily *New York Times* in order to keep track of the Yankees said, "Hank, your mom's name is in the *Times*." I was surprised, but when I looked, sure enough, she was listed as a contributor to the New York Times Fresh Air Fund which provided summer camp scholarships for inner city children. I'm sure she never imagined that up in Maine I would learn about her gift, but this incident reinforced my appreciation of my mother's belief in the importance of trying to help those in need. It's a value I've tried to follow throughout my life. I also know that from time to time when family members encountered financial difficulties, Mom took the initiative to provide them with funds.

Growing up, I had always believed that my father was the head of our family, the one who made the major decisions. I think I assumed this because our family lifestyle was oriented towards meeting my father's needs and acknowledging his experience and wisdom. When he was ensconced in his favorite barcalounger reading or watching TV in our den, there was a standing order to my brother and me not to disturb him in case he should want to take a nap. My mother also looked to my father for approval of every meal that she prepared and for his definitive word on political or cultural events. It was the kind of home setting which clearly suggested that my father was number one. When I reached adulthood, however, I realized that my perception of my father's dominance in the family was much too simplistic.

Because my father had tremendous respect for my mother's judgment in personal matters, he most often deferred to her opinion in matters that affected my brother and me. When Mike experienced academic problems in high school, my mother was the moving force to get him some counseling and eventually to send him to a boarding school where he thrived academically and socially. She was also the one who strongly supported my request after ninth grade to change from public school to private school. I believe that if I had stayed in public school, I would have done well, but I would not have succeeded as I did at Friends' Central where the smaller number of students and the personal involvement of many of my teachers and coaches gave me more of an opportunity to achieve academically and athletically. My mother instinctively knew that this was the best move for me to make at this stage in my life, and I'm thankful for her insight.

During my freshman year at college, my father began writing letters to me in an attempt to impart his parental wisdom. I was ambivalent about these handwritten fatherly epistles on large yellow legal pad paper which were nearly illegible due to my father's dramatic, scrawling handwriting. On the one hand, the letters kept me connected to him, but like most freshmen I was in the process of "leaving my father's house" so that I bristled at some of his rigid pronouncements. My mother was concerned that his letters were overly preachy, so she convinced him to stop. Although I felt relieved at the time, I think her intervention was a mistake, because I eventually came to realize that I had appreciated those awkward attempts by my father to stay connected.

After the funeral of Grandma Lowenstein, my mother's mother, one of my aunts happened to matter-of-factly refer to my mother as a "tyrant." I was totally surprised. I assume there was some resentment behind my aunt's statement, but I think she was referring to the fact that my mother made most of the important decisions in the extended family. For example, when my grandmother was unable to manage on her own, my mother was often the one who decided how my grandmother would apportion her time at the homes of her six children. If my mother was a tyrant, she was an artful one, because when she made up her mind about what was to be done either among her own siblings or in our family, she did it in a way that seemed benign and inclusive. Her tenacity and powers of persuasion were so effective that there was usually no inclination to thwart her.

I imagine my mother to be somewhat like Sarah who made the major family decisions regarding Hagar, Ishmael, and Isaac. Sarah's matriarchal attributes in Genesis are decisiveness, determination, and loyalty to her husband and son. My mother had all these qualities, but she was not as brusque as the first matriarch. Unlike Sarah, my mother was a uniter. All of the Lowenstein siblings were devoted to each other, but my mother, by means of her natural leadership as well as her familial loyalty and love provided the strongest force for family unity. A key aspect of her role as a family unifier was that she was a prolific and amazing letter writer, a true rarity today. Although Barbara and I spoke to her by phone once a week from New England, she preferred to communicate through beautifully typed or handwritten letters, telling of her personal experiences and her thoughts about books she was reading at the time, such as Ernest Jones's biography of Freud, or her favorite studies on the Bloomsbury group.[4] In her letters, she would also share her latest views on politics. Mom was an ardent liberal. I remember when I was eight years old, she took me to hear Henry Wallace speak at an outdoor rally in Trenton when he ran for President on the Progressive Party ticket in 1948. Sometimes in her letters to us in New England she included clippings from the *New York Times* or the *New Yorker*, some of which were intended to provide me with sermon topics, while others included recipes and household tips for Barbara. She not only wrote several times a week to Barbara and me and to my brother Mike and his wife Rose, she often wrote to her three grandchildren Jessica, Rachel, and Sam. In addition, she kept up a steady correspondence with her five siblings and her many friends, and made a special effort to remember her nieces and nephews and even their children with handwritten notes and small gifts on their birthdays or other special occasions.

My mother and her five siblings were particularly long lived. Mom lived to the age of one hundred two and three quarters (June 24, 1902–February 25, 2005). As family matriarch she was concerned with the health and well being of her brothers and sisters and took it upon herself to advise the entire

---

4. "The Bloomsbury Group was a group of writers, artists, and philosophers living in or associated with Bloomsbury [England] in the early 20th century. Members of the group, which included Virginia Woolf, Lytton Strachey, Vanessa Bell, Duncan Grant, and Roger Fry, were known for their unconventional lifestyles and attitudes, and were a powerful force in the growth of modernism" (*The Oxford Dictionary of Phrase and Fable*. Oxford: Oxford University Press. 2005, 87).

family about the most up-to-date diet and medical information. Her brother Aaron and her youngest sister Jean died in their mid-eighties, while her elder sister Ida died at the age of ninety-nine. According to my mother, Ida died because she didn't take care of herself! Her sister Evelyn died at the age of one hundred and her brother Bob lived to one hundred and five!

My parents were the same age, but when we were younger my mother took some years off her actual age, probably because most Americans of that era thought that a husband should be somewhat older than his wife. When Mom reached her eighties and nineties, however, she used to tell everyone how old she was because she enjoyed surprising people with her vigor and youthful appearance. She and my father were married for fifty-seven years. It was a wonderful marriage built on love and mutual respect. I recall staying with my mother for a week or more after my father died at the age of eighty-eight. I was fearful that she would have a very difficult time without him. I underestimated her strength and self-sufficiency, because soon after the week of mourning, she encouraged me to go home and told me that she was perfectly capable of managing on her own, and she was. She continued to read, exercise, drive, shop, cook, see her friends, and come up to Gloucester for summer vacations. She missed my father, but his death did not diminish her capacity to live life to the fullest.

In her late nineties, Mom began to fail. The first sign of her decline involved her favorite activity, reading. At the time, she became particularly interested in a biography about the great twentieth-century English philosopher and thinker Isaiah Berlin, who like my mother was born in Latvia. We knew something was wrong, however, when over a period of months she kept telling us about this book over and over again and never progressed to her next book of interest. It was a sad time, for it was an indication that her intense intellectual life was coming to an end. At the age of ninety-nine she suffered a serious stoke, but even after her stroke, which diminished her physical and intellectual powers, she continued to display the dignity of spirit that was the hallmark of her role as a modern matriarch. What an indomitable life force!

My mother, Eleanor Lowenstein Zoob was the matriarch of our family, guiding us through many of life's difficult decisions, setting an example of courage, tenacity, love of life, devotion to Judaism and the Jewish people, and most important of all, loving and supporting me, my brother, and father with force and energy. She provided the primary family influence in regard to my appreciation of Jewish tradition. She was a wonderful mother-in-law to my wife Barbara and to Mike's wife Rose. She offered her love to each of them, gave them advice, but never interfered in our marriages. She was actively supportive of her three grandchildren providing them with unconditional love and approval of everything they did. For all of her positive qualities, my mother was not perfect. She was very judgmental of those whom she thought were boorish or ostentatious, and she was overly in awe of doctors or university professors with impressive academic credentials. Despite these minor flaws, I cannot imagine having a better champion than my mother, the matriarch of our family.

Mom sometimes entertained thoughts about writing her memoirs, for she certainly had an interesting and varied life. Born in a poor but educated family in Latvia, emigrating to the United States at the age of four, becoming a proficient lawyer at a time when so few women were practicing law, having a rewarding and loving marriage, raising two sons who have made their way successfully in the world, serving as a mentor and a purveyor of taste to many younger women, and becoming a matriarch in her own family of origin as well as our family, she had quite a century of life. Although she never got around to writing her memoirs, I'm glad that I had the opportunity to compose this small portrait of her. I miss her, but I know her values of hard work, love of family, devotion to God and the Jewish people, and generosity to those in need are with me every day of my life.

CHAPTER 17

Joseph, the Saving Covenantal Link

Why Joseph is not a Patriarch

THE DRAMATIC STORY OF Joseph covers *thirteen chapters* at the end of Genesis.[1] By contrast, the major events in Isaac's life, except for the *Aqeidah*, are recounted in just *three chapters*.[2] Why then is Joseph not accorded patriarchal status like Isaac? I would submit that Joseph is not considered a patriarch because there are three elements common to Abraham, Isaac, and Jacob, that are not present in Joseph's life: God appears to each patriarch, God speaks directly to each of them, and most important of all, God makes a covenant with each of them.[3]

---

1. The thirteen chapters are Genesis 37, 39–50. Robert Alter argues that although some scholars see Genesis 38, the story of Judah and Tamar, as an unrelated interpolation in the Joseph narrative, there are a number of parallels that suggest that the story is meant to be part of the larger Joseph cycle. One such parallel is Jacob's "recognition" (*vayyakkirah* Gen. 37:33) of Joseph's bloodstained coat and Judah's "recognition" (*vayyakkair* Gen. 38:26) of his telltale seal, cord, and staff, which he had given to the cult prostitute (Tamar in disguise) as a pledge for her services (Alter, *Art of Biblical Narrative*, 3–12).

2. The Isaac cycle in Genesis begins at Gen. 25:19 and concludes at Gen. 28:9 a span of about three chapters. Although there is no *Aqeidah* without Isaac, the story of the *Aqeidah* in Genesis 22 is primarily about Abraham.

3. See chapters 3, 5, 7, 9, 11 in this book for examples of God appearing, speaking, and making covenants with the three Patriarchs. Isaac has the fewest references—all three of these divine actions in regard to Isaac (appearing, speaking, and making a covenant) occur in a single passage (Gen. 26:2–5).

Joseph's Love for His Father and Brothers Leads to the Survival of His Family

In Genesis 15, God informs Abraham that before inheriting the land of Canaan, his offspring will be "strangers in a land not theirs, and they shall be enslaved and oppressed four hundred years, but I will execute judgment on the nation they shall serve . . . and they shall return here in the fourth generation . . ."[4] Joseph's descent to Egypt is the first step in the fulfillment of this oracle. Once in Egypt, Joseph goes from being a servant to a prisoner, until by means of his God inspired talent as an interpreter of dreams he rises out of the dungeon to the position of second in command next to Pharaoh. In Pharaoh's court Joseph begins a journey which leads him away from his Hebrew background. Pharaoh gives him an Egyptian name, Zaphenath-paneah,[5] and an Egyptian wife, Asenath, the daughter of the priest of On.[6] What is particularly revealing about Joseph's state of mind is his interpretation of the name he gives his first son *M'nasheh*—"God *nashani* has made me forget completely my hardship and my parental home."[7]

But Joseph cannot forget his "parental home," because when famine strikes Canaan, his brothers come to Egypt to purchase grain and bow down before him, just as his childhood dreams of sheaves and stars had foretold. Joseph maintains his Egyptian masquerade during their first visit, but when his brothers return for the second time to purchase grain, Joseph is overwhelmed with love for them and makes the pivotal decision to turn away from the path of assimilation by tearfully confessing, *ani Yoseph, ha-od avi chai* "I am Joseph. Is my father still alive?"[8] He then invites his father, his brothers, and their families, to live under his protection in Egypt in the region of Goshen.[9]

---

4. Gen. 15:13–16.

5. Gen. 41:45. There are several interpretations of this Egyptian name—"God speaks, lives" or "the creator/sustainer of life" which fits with Joseph's role in Egypt of devising and executing a life-sustaining plan to cope with the seven years of plenty followed by the seven years of famine (Sarna, *JPS Genesis*, 288).

6. Gen. 41:45. Sarna notes that On was the great cultic center of the sun-god Re. The priest of On had the title "Greatest of Seers," so that Joseph was marrying into the circle of the Egyptian elite (Sarna, *JPS Genesis*, 288).

7. Gen. 41:51.

8. Gen. 45:3.

9. Gen. 45:9–11.

Jacob Seeks to Connect Joseph and His Eleven Other Sons to the Covenant

Although as a servant in the home of Potiphar, and subsequently, during his imprisonment, Joseph's faith in God grows stronger, he seems unaware that his rescue of his father and brothers from starvation has anything to do with the covenant. His sole motivation is his love for his family. The Torah does not tell us whether Jacob tries to educate Joseph about the covenant when he comes to live in Egypt, but shortly before his death, Jacob summons Joseph to his bedside to take an oath to inter him in the burial place of his parents and grandparents in Canaan.[10]

Soon after his visit with his father, Joseph learns that Jacob's health has deteriorated, so he returns with his sons, Manasseh and Ephraim, to Jacob's bedside where his dying father speaks of the covenant that God offered him when he returned to Canaan after twenty years in Haran.

> El Shaddai appeared to me at Luz in the land of Canaan,
> and He blessed me, and said to me,
> "I will make you fruitful and numerous;
> making of you a community of peoples,
> and I will give this land to your offspring to come
> for an everlasting possession."
>
> Gen. 48:3–4

After hearing his father's words about God's promise of numerous progeny and the inheritance of Canaan, there can be no doubt that Joseph understands the significance of the covenant.

Jacob then looks at the two boys who have accompanied Joseph and does not seem to know that Manasseh and Ephraim are Joseph's sons, for he says, "Who are these?"[11] His failure to recognize his grandsons may be due to poor eye sight,[12] or more likely, it means that even though Jacob has been living in Egypt for seventeen years, Joseph and his family have not maintained close ties with the boys' grandfather. I assume that Ephraim and Manasseh were being brought up as Egyptians in Pharaoh's court rather than as Hebrews in Goshen with their cousins from Canaan. Indeed, Jacob's remark that he had not expected God to enable him to see Joseph

---

10. Gen. 47:29–31.
11. Gen. 48:8.
12. "Now Israel's eyes were dim with age; he could not see" (Gen. 48:10).

let alone Joseph's children[13] suggests that Jacob may be meeting Manasseh and Ephraim for the first time! At this poignant moment, Jacob makes a spontaneous attempt to shape the future by adopting Joseph's two sons as his own.[14] Jacob concludes his blessing of his grandsons with a reference to the first pillar of the covenant, the promise of progeny: "May they (Ephraim and Manasseh) be teeming multitudes upon the earth."[15] Joseph then notices that his father's right hand is on the head of the younger son, Ephraim, and his left hand is on Manasseh, the elder. Joseph tries to uncross his father's hands so that Jacob may give the preferential blessing to the first-born, but Jacob demurs. And so, just as Jacob's own father, Isaac, did with him and Esau, Jacob elevates the younger over the elder.[16] Jacob ends his bedside testament by reminding Joseph about God's promise for the future—"I am about to die, but God will be with you and bring you back to the land of your fathers."[17]

After focusing his efforts to gain Joseph's commitment to the covenant, Jacob seeks to do the same with Joseph's brothers. He gathers them around his deathbed and speaks to them of his vision of the future in which the land of Canaan will be home to their descendants. While he made Joseph take an oath to inter his remains at Machpelah, he now instructs all of his sons to bury him in the cave where Abraham, Sarah, Isaac, Rebekah, and Leah are interred.[18]

Jacob dies, is embalmed at Joseph's order and "bewailed" by the Egyptians for seventy days.[19] Joseph then sends a request to Pharaoh to let him fulfill the oath he made to his father to bury him in the land of Canaan. And so, with Pharaoh's consent, a large group of Hebrews and Egyptians make the journey with Jacob's embalmed remains to the cave in the field of Machpelah. The Egyptian attendees include all of Pharaoh's officials, the senior members of his court, all of Egypt's dignitaries, along with Egyptian chariots and horsemen. The Hebrews who travel to the Cave of Machpelah for Jacob's burial include Joseph, his brothers, and their households, ev-

---

13. Gen. 48:11.
14. In Gen. 48:5.
15. Gen. 48:16.
16. Gen. 48:19.
17. Gen. 48:21.
18. Jacob's blessing of his sons and request to be buried in Canaan are recounted in Gen. 49.
19. Gen. 50:3.

eryone except the children and flocks who remain hostage in Egypt.[20] As the presence of so many Egyptian dignitaries is an indication of Pharaoh's esteem for Jacob and Joseph, their attendance, especially the presence of the chariots and horsemen, sends a message to Joseph and his brothers that Pharaoh is determined to have them return to Egypt.

In Death, Joseph Demonstrates His Devotion to the Covenant

Joseph lives to the age of 110 and experiences the joy of seeing his great grandchildren.[21] As he approaches his death, it becomes evident that Jacob's last minute attempt to enlist Joseph's allegiance to the covenant has succeeded, for on his deathbed, Joseph, like his father before him, reminds his brothers about God's intent to fulfill the covenant through them.

> I am about to die.
> God will surely take notice of you
> to bring you up from this land
> to the land He promised on oath to Abraham, to Isaac, and to Jacob.
>
> Genesis 50:24

Joseph then makes his brothers swear that when God brings them up to Canaan in fulfillment of the covenant, they will carry his bones with them.[22] Joseph's insistence on his burial in the promised land, like that of his father, is intended to encourage his surviving family members to hold fast to the covenantal vision of a return to Canaan. Joseph may have expected that the return would occur in the lifetime of his brothers, but many generations pass before Moses recalls the brothers' oath to Joseph and takes Joseph's bones with him on the Exodus:

> And Moses took with him the bones of Joseph,[23]

---

20. Gen. 50:7–9.
21. Gen. 50:22–23.
22. Gen. 50:25.
23. Eventually, in the days of Joshua, Joseph's bones that Moses had brought up with the redeemed Israelites from Egypt are interred at Shechem (Joshua 24:32) in the parcel of land that Jacob had purchased from the children of Hamor (Gen. 33:19). Shechem was the first site where Abraham stopped when he entered the land (Gen. 12:6). At Shechem, then, we have come full circle, from the beginning of Abraham's sojourning in the promised land to the burial of Joseph's bones in the days of Joshua.

> who had extracted an oath from the children of Israel saying, "God will be sure to remember you: then you shall carry up my bones from here with you."
>
> Exodus 13:19

The only way that Moses could possibly know about Joseph's oath is that memories of Joseph's efforts to sustain an awareness of the divine covenantal promise of redemption and a return to Canaan were kept alive, initially among his brothers, and eventually, among the generations of Israelites before and during their enslavement in Egypt, a period which the Tanach sets at four hundred years.[24] Although Jacob initiated the effort to instill in his sons a commitment to the covenantal dream of return, it seems that Joseph's devotion to this objective was decisive, for it is not Jacob's bedside blessing of his sons that Moses recalls as he sets out on the Exodus, but Joseph's words to his brothers about their future in Canaan and the oath he extracted from them to bury his bones in the promised land. I imagine that the presence of Joseph's embalmed body in a coffin was also a tangible reminder among the Israelites in Egypt that the future of "Joseph's bones" as well as their own destiny lay in the north. The Torah does not tell us where the Israelites kept Joseph's coffin for all those years, but it must have been a venerated object that was secreted in a special place. And so from the moment that he reveals himself to his astonished brothers until the very last day of his life, Joseph steadily traverses the course of becoming the *decisive link* in the covenantal connection between the Patriarchs and Moses.

Retrospective on Joseph and the Patriarchs as Heroic Figures

I believe that Joseph and his three patriarchal forebearers, Abraham, Isaac, and Jacob, are heroic figures, not only because they prevail over the many

---

24. In Gen. 15:13 the length of the Israelite enslavement in Egypt is mentioned as four hundred years, and three verses later (v. 16), it says that they will return in the fourth generation. This implies that each generation lasts 100 years. The lives of the Patriarchs and Matriarchs averaged over 100 years so that 100 year generations make some sense. Ex. 12:40 says that the length of time the Israelites lived in Egypt was 430 years. Rabbi Ian Silverman argues for a shorter span of years for the Egyptian exile (210 or 86) on the basis of biblical exegesis and traditional midrashim (Ian Silberman, "Hebrew Slavery in Egypt: How Long and How Come? A Traditional Perspective" *CCAR Journal*, Fall 2016, 123–145.) I like Silverman's argument for a shorter period of time for Israel in Egypt, because I find it difficult to imagine how a population that was eventually enslaved maintained a memory of God's promise of a return to Canaan for 400 years.

Joseph, the Saving Covenantal Link

external trials and challenges that confront them, but also because each of them overcomes personal vulnerabilities in order to make a significant contribution to the continuity of the covenant.

In chapter 9 "The Testing of Abraham," we focused on the many difficult external tests that Abraham passes—leaving his father's home, the kidnapping of Sarah in Egypt and Gerar, the War against the Kings, self-circumcision at the age of ninety-nine, and the terrifying divine command to sacrifice Isaac. Abraham is also challenged by internal doubts as to whether God will fulfill the covenantal promises of land and progeny. These doubts persist during the first quarter-century of Abraham's sojourning in the land of Canaan. Finally, God announces to Abraham that he and Sarah will have a son within a year and that the name of that son will be Isaac. With that divine declaration, Abraham puts aside his anxieties concerning God's fulfillment of the covenant, and displays total faith and confidence in God's promises for the remainder of his life.

Isaac evinces heroism by overcoming his tendency towards passivity. As a child he is threatened by Ishmael and probably overprotected by Sarah. Later, he submits without a word of protest to his father's near sacrifice of him at Moriah. As a young adult, he lingers in despair over the death of his mother until Rebekah's love restores him to an active life. And as a father of twins, he is manipulated by Rebekah so that he gives Jacob rather than Esau the blessing of the first born. Nevertheless, Isaac overcomes his inclination to be passive as well the trauma of the *Aqeidah*, by marrying Rebekah, raising a family, responding to God's challenge to stay in the land despite famine and adversaries, and by becoming the only patriarch to farm the land.

Jacob's heroism involves staying the covenantal course in spite of the many obstacles and tragedies of his life: the threat of being killed by his vengeful brother, the machinations of his father-in-law Laban, midnight combat with the angel at the Jabbok, his tense reunion with Esau, the rape of his daughter Dinah, the cruel massacre of the Shechemites by his sons Simeon and Levi, the death of his beloved Rachel in childbirth, Reuben's shocking affair with Bilhah, the assumed loss of Joseph to a wild beast, severe famine in Canaan, and finally, exile in Egypt. But perhaps Jacob's greatest challenge comes from within—his tendency to be cautious, crafty, and self-serving. The calculating side of his personality seems to rule his behavior in his relationships with Esau, Laban, and even God, when in his dream of a stairway at Bethel, Jacob tentatively agrees to be God's covenantal partner but not without some major conditions. Eventually, Jacob overcomes his inclinaton to be overly cautious and self-serving when he fully assents to God's second offer of a covenant at Bethel. And at the end of his life, despite an initial period of depression when he first comes down to Egypt, Jacob devotes himself to preserving the covenant for the future generations by successfully enlisting Joseph in the cause and by encouraging his eleven other sons to do the same.

Joseph begins his life as a self-centered adolescent who as Jacob's favorite is gifted with an ornamented tunic that arouses the jealousy of his ten older brothers. His fascinating life is marked by his egotistical sharing of dreams of leadership with his family, his sale into servitude by his angry brothers, imprisonment in Egypt on false charges, his emergence from prison by means of his God-given ability to interpret dreams, his rise to the position of second in command of all of Egypt, his revelation of his true identity to his atonished brothers, his rescue of his family from famine in Canaan, and ultimately, his taking upon himself his father Jacob's mission to instill a belief in his brothers of the importance of the covenant and a return to Canaan. Joseph's life story, then, can be viewed as the evolution of a narcissistic adolescent into a mature, heroic, family leader, who makes a crucial contribution to the continuity of the Covenant of Abraham.

Today, four thousand years after the Patriarchs, like Abraham, we have doubts about God, like Isaac, we have periods in our lives when we are immobilized by passivity, like Jacob, we struggle to overcome self-serving inclinations, and like Joseph, we are challenged by immaturity and egotism. The crucial question for us is the same as it was for the Patriarchs and Joseph—can we, despite our doubts and vulnerabilities, contribute to the continuity and eventual fulfillment of the covenant, which envisions the establishment of a time when the entire world will be blessed with justice and peace, due in part to the exemplary lives of the Jewish people as individuals and as a nation? I have based my life's work on the belief that we and those who follow us can indeed do it!

CHAPTER 18

My Commitment to Jewish Messianism

JEWISH MESSIANISM IS A belief in a redemptive Jewish future—a better life for the Jewish people, and in many versions, for all humanity. Israel and God play variable roles in the realization of the messianic age—some messianic visions call for a partnership between God and the Jewish people, as in the Covenant of Abraham, while others envision a messianic day in which God acts alone, as in Ezekiel 36:22-28, where the Eternal promises to gather Israel from among the nations, restore them to their land, cleanse them from their iniquities, and give them "a new heart," all for the sake of God's "holy name."

Jewish messianism began with God's covenantal challenge to Abraham to "be a blessing" so that "all the families of the earth might bless themselves by you."[1] Two crucial moments in Joseph's life kept the Covenant of Abraham and its messianic objective alive. The first was Joseph's decision to end his masquerade as an Egyptian by revealing himself to his siblings as their long lost brother, an action which led to the rescue of Jacob and his sons from starvation in Canaan. The second was when Joseph made the decision to adopt his father's covenantal vision of a return to the promised land. Like Jacob his father, Joseph on his death bed assured his brothers that God would surely remember them and bring them to the land which the Eternal promised to the Patriarchs. With this confident assertion about the future, Joseph helped to sustain an allegiance to the Covenant of Abraham among his brothers and their descendants, setting the stage for Moses and

---

1. Gen. 12:3.

the redeemed Israelite slaves to enter into a more comprehensive covenant with God at Sinai centuries later.

When messianic days are envisioned in connection with the Covenant at Sinai, as in Leviticus 26 and Deuteronomy 28, surprisingly, there is no mention of Israel as a moral exemplar for other nations as is the case in the Covenant of Abraham. Instead, we find that at that glorious time, because of their obedience to God and the covenant, Israel will enjoy such abundance that "all the peoples of the earth shall see that the name of YHVH is proclaimed over you, and they shall stand in fear of you."[2] It is not until many centuries later, that Isaiah revives the universal Abrahamic messianic concept of "being a blessing" for the nations, when he prophesies to the exiles in Babylon that God has appointed them to be *livrit am l'or goyim* "a covenant people, a light of the nations."[3]

The Rabbis fixed their hopes for a future of peace and prosperity on a Messiah,[4] a figure from the House of David, who would usher in a messianic age. As a reminder of this goal, the Rabbis infused almost every aspect of Jewish observance with messianic elements. The Passover seder, for example, concludes with the messianic hope *bashanah haba-ah birushalayim* "Next Year in Jerusalem," and every worship service ends with the *Aleinu* and *Kaddish*, two prayers which look forward to the reign of peace when "*Adonai* will be one and God's name will be one." Even something as basic as the blessing recited over the bread, *hamotzi lechem min ha-aretz* praising God "who brings forth bread from the earth" has a messianic interpretation of looking forward to the days of plenty when God will cause bread to miraculously pop out of the ground, perhaps like bread from a toaster.[5] In short, the Rabbis built a pervasive messianic motif into the daily observance of Judaism. When this futuristic Rabbinic view is combined with the many passages from the Tanach which look forward to a final redemption

---

2. Dt. 28:10.

3. Isaiah 42:6.

4. Messiah is the Greek pronunciation of the Hebrew *Mashiach* "Anointed One." Israelite priests and kings were consecrated by means of anointment with sacred oil. Thus, every priest and every king was technically a *mashiach*.

5. In *Genesis Rabbah* 15:7, in regard to the benediction over the bread, the Rabbis say this refers to the future. Eugene Mihaly, my Midrash Professor at HUC-JIR in Cincinnati, suggested in class that this points to the days of the Messiah when bread will come forth from the ground without human labor. See also *Midrash Rabbah*, commentary by Mosheh Aryeh Mirkin, (Tel Aviv: Yavneh, 1985) 1:112.

My Commitment to Jewish Messianism

of Israel, it is not surprising that the belief in a better future comes naturally to the Jewish people, no matter how desperate our situation.

As a child in religious school, I learned that Reform Jews no longer believe in a personal messiah. Rather, it is our obligation to think of ourselves as a "messianic people" dedicated to work for a messianic age as envisioned by the prophets of Israel. Prophetic passages from the Tanach such as "Let justice well up as waters, and righteousness like a mighty stream"[6] were part of the basic vocabulary of Reform youth who held fast to the prophetic dream of a messianic day as envisioned by the prophet Micah:

> And they shall beat their swords into plowshares,
> and their spears into pruning hooks.
> Nation shall not take up sword against nation,
> they shall never again know war.
> But every man shall sit under his grapevine or fig tree
> with no one to make him afraid.
>
>   Micah 4:3b–4a

For approximately the first seventy years of the twentieth century, American Reform Judaism was known as "Prophetic Judaism," because it emphasized social action based on the messianic goals of peace and justice that were proclaimed by the prophets of Israel. The messianism of the prophets helped to inspire many Reform Jews to be in the forefront of the struggle for civil rights that reached its zenith in the 1960s. Today, in the second decade of the twenty-first century, even though Jewish educational enrichment and spirituality have become the top priorities in Reform synagogues, social action is still an important part of our movement. The Union for Reform Judaism continues to maintain the Religious Action Center in Washington, D.C., an organization devoted to the advancement of a Jewish social action agenda through the political process. Its presence is a testament to Reform Judaism's continuing dedication to the messianic concept of *Tikkun Olam*[7] "Repair of the World."

---

6 Amos 5:24.

7. The phrase *Tikkun Olam* "Repair of the World" has been used for the last half century to refer to social action. It has been borrowed from the Kabbalah where the term *tikkun* "repair" refers to the theory of Rabbi Isaac Luria of Safed (the Ari 1534–72 CE). According to Lurianic Kabbalah, at Creation, divine sparks were lodged in *keilim* "vessels" which broke apart because they were not strong enough to contain the concentrated divine energy. The sparks dispersed and became imbedded in the material world. *Tikkun* is the messianic process of "repair" by which the divine sparks are gathered and returned to their original source. See Gershom Scholem, *Major Trends in Jewish Mysticism*, "Isaac

A Lifetime of Genesis

Throughout my life, I have found inspiration in Jewish messianism. When I was a teen, my vision of a better future was reinforced by the social action agenda of my synagogue, Rodeph Shalom, which is located in an African American neighborhood in downtown Philadelphia near Broad and Spring Garden Streets. I recall participating in a number of meetings and activities with African American youth at nearby Fellowship House where we learned about the problems of racism. Subsequently, Rodeph Shalom encouraged its members to serve as tutors in the local schools. Another synagogue project was the Well Baby Clinic designed to share medical knowledge and resources with neighborhood mothers. Looking back, I can see that the social action programs and the teachings about messianism in my synagogue in combination with the progressive influence of my Quaker education at Friends' Central schooled me in the ideal that God's number one priority is social justice.

In the days of my youth, the vision of a better world seemed clearly doable. Full of adolescent energy, I thought that I, along with other idealistic young people, could usher in an era of peace and justice. As I matured, I began to question whether the dream of a messianic age could be taken seriously. I still do. In my lifetime, the world has witnessed the murder of six million Jews and myriads of others whom Hitler and the Nazis viewed as "undesirables." Also, as often happens, we should not overlook the millions who were sent to their death by Joseph Stalin, the paranoid, anti-Semitic dictator of Russia. In the aftermath of the concentration camps and the gulags, shocking acts of genocide continued to take place in the twentieth and twenty-first centuries in Cambodia, Bosnia, Rwanda, Darfur, Syria, and elsewhere. Today, there are millions of people who lack sufficient food, housing, and basic health care. Human slavery and trafficking are global problems. In addition, despite God's challenge to Adam and his descendants to take care of the earth,[8] we are in danger of destroying the air, soil, and water, that make life possible. I also view with dismay the materialism

---

Luria and His School" chapter 7 (New York: Schocken, 1961).

David Widzer notes that the original phrase *mipnei tikkun ha-olam* occurs in the Mishneh and Tosefta, and later in the Talmud. Widzer concludes (42) that in these legal contexts the term "indicates an amendment to, or clarification of, the existing legal system or social order, specifically designed to address an issue of social status, prevent some harm to society, maintain the communal well-being, and/or to best orient the community in service to God." (David Widzer, "The Use of *Mipnei Tikkun Ha'Olam* in the Babylonian Talmud" *CCAR Journal*, Spring 2008, 34–45.)

8. Gen. 2:15.

that dominates the aspirations of many Americans and others throughout the world; it threatens to suffocate the sacred values of love of family and service to God and humanity. There is ample reason, then, to fear that the messianic goal to improve the welfare of humanity that began with the Covenant of Abraham is futile.

Yet, there is also cause for viewing the messianic glass as half full. In the last century, treatment and understanding of mental illness has increased tremendously, and for the first time in history, buildings, sidewalks, and vehicles, have been modified to be handicap accessible. We have also made tremendous progress in women's rights in this country and are beginning to do so in other parts of the world. With the end of apartheid in South Africa and the election of an African American president in the United States, we have demonstrated that major racial barriers can be overcome. We have become more inclusive in regard to civil rights and societal acceptance of homosexuals and transgenders. Effective organizations such as Project Bread, Oxfam America, Mazon, the American Jewish World Service, Habitat for Humanity, and Drs. Without Borders, have been combating the social ills of poverty, hunger, homelessness, and inadequate health services throughout the world. The 1960s which witnessed nationwide protests against the Viet Nam War were a siginificant watershed in the struggle against warfare. I know of no other period in the history of the world when citizens rose up in such great numbers to declare that their country's involvement in a specific war was immoral. We have also initiated vital work on global warming and other environmental problems, and although we have a United Nations organization which is highly politicized, the UN is a significant force in formulating a global strategy in regard to the human rights and problems of all the people on earth.

It is also important to recognize that God's hope for Abraham and his descendants—to become a blessing for all the peoples of the earth—has in some degree already come to pass. Judaism is the religious wellspring from which the two other great religions of the Western world, Christianity and Islam, have emerged. The moral values expressed in the Ten Commandments and throughout the Tanach provide the ethical foundation for these two major religions. It is self-evident, however, that because we are only a tiny percentage of the world's population, we cannot achieve our covenantal goals by ourselves. If there is to be substantial progress in the quest for a better world, Jews, Christians, Muslims, Hindus, Buddhists, and peoples of other faiths and philosophies must work together to improve the lives of individuals in the four corners of the earth and to save the environment for future generations.

Currently, I am a proud contributing member of two rabbinic organizations dedicated to global justice and righteousness. The first is Rabbis for Human Rights, under the leadership of a personal hero of mine, Rabbi Arik Ascherman. RHR is an organization devoted to seeking justice for all the inhabitants of the land of Israel, Israelis and Palestinians alike. The second is Teruah: The Rabbinic Call for Human Rights, directed by Rabbi Jill Jacobs, a group of 1800 rabbis in North America from all walks of Jewish life who seek to implement the highest Jewish moral and ethical values in our modern society.

My Jewish messianism does not envision a perfect world, a world without evil, sin, poverty, and sickness. The Torah reminds us that "there will never cease to be needy ones in your land."[9] The future I have in mind imagines a world where most people have opportunities similar to the ones I have had—food, shelter, and basic health care; freedom of religion, assembly, the press, and speech; safe communities and a clean environment. So many people who share this planet with us lack these basic benefits which are taken for granted by many Americans. To me, a world where most inhabitants have access to these essential opportunities and freedoms would be more awesome than all of the miracles described in the Bible. It can only happen by the sustained work of human beings inspired to pursue the ideals of *tz'daqah umishpat* "righteousness and justice."

Messianism is a choice. Joseph made that choice in two stages. First, he had to ask himself, "Should I devote my energies to become a fully assimilated Egptian, or should I reclaim my Hebrew identity with all of its attendant responsibilities to my father and brothers?" Joseph chose the latter. Second, at the bedside of his dying father, Joseph decided to cast his fate with the Covenant of Abraham by encouraging his brothers to hold fast to a challenging future in Canaan rather than to remain in Egypt, a place which seemed safe and secure at the time. By choosing Canaan over the land of the Nile, Joseph safeguarded the future of Israel. Every American Jew confronts a similar choice. We can chose to become assimilated Americans enjoying the freedoms and blessings of American life, but at the same time risk the possibility of becoming engulfed by the American idols of materialism and shallow chauvinism, or without abandoning the best part of our American heritage, we can affirm our Judaism by committing ourselves to the values,

---

9. Dt. 15:11.

traditions, and covenantal goals of our Jewish faith. To make such a commitment is to make a choice for a life of meaning, as Joseph did when he said "I am Joseph. Is my father still alive?" and as Abraham did when he answered God's call "Go forth," and "Be a blessing."

ADDENDUM 1

Divine Covenants in the Bible

A DIVINE B'RIT IS a covenant or pact that God establishes with a single person, a group of people, an entire nation, or even every living creature.[1] Some divine covenants are unconditional, such as the Covenant of Noah, in which God promises never to destroy the earth again by water.[2] Others are conditional, in that God specifies obligations for the participants in the covenant. If they fulfill their covenantal obligations, God will bestow blessings upon them; if they break or neglect their covenantal obligations, divine punishments or the withdrawal of divine favor will ensue.

Most conditional divine covenants need to be accepted by word or by deed by the human partner. At Sinai, the Israelites exclaim *na-aseh v'nishmah* "we will faithfully hearken" to the words of the covenant. In the case of Abraham, his setting forth for the land of Canaan indicates his acceptance of the Covenant of Abraham. Sometimes, a ritual accompanies the acceptance of the divine covenant, such as the dashing of sacrificial blood upon the Israelites at Sinai or Jacob's pouring of sacred oil on a special pillar.

In addition to the Covenant of Abraham, there are a number of other divine covenants in the Bible. One is God's *unconditional* covenant with King David which is mentioned in David's last words: "Is not my house established before God? For He has granted me *b'rit olam* an eternal covenant, drawn up in full and secured. Will He not cause all my success and

---

1. In the Covenant of Noah, God makes a covenant with every living creature promising to never again destroy the earth by flood (Gen. 9:10).

2. Gen. 9:15.

[my] every desire to blossom?"³ Another *unconditional* divine covenant with an individual is God's contract concerning Phineas the priest, when God says to Moses, "Say therefore, 'I grant him (Phineas) *b'riti shalom* My covenant of friendship. It shall be for him and his descendants after him *b'rit k'hunnat olam* a covenant of priesthood for all time, because he took impassioned action for his God, thus making expiation for the Israelites."⁴

The most significant *conditional* divine covenant outside of the Covenant of Abraham is the Covenant at Sinai between God and the Israelites. The Sinaitic Covenant signals the initiation of a new contract between God and Israel which includes the Ten Commandments as well as many other ritual, ethical, and legal standards. If Israel observes the rites and obligations of the covenant and remains loyal to YHVH, God promises to bless them with bountiful harvests, protection against their enemies, and enduring possession of the land which the Eternal had pledged to Abraham, Isaac, and Jacob. If they fail to observe the laws of the covenant and turn to the worship of other gods, they can expect poor harvests, humiliating defeats on the field of battle, and even exile from their land.

Like many biblical institutions and concepts, the Covenant at Sinai appears to have been influenced by pre-existing ancient Near Eastern models. The closest extant example is the Hittite Suzerain–Vassal treaty in which a suzerain (a major regional ruler) arranges for a vassal (a subject king) to enlist in a treaty that demands total loyalty to the suzerain. Sarna, identifies seven common elements between the Hittite Suzerain–Vassal treaty and the Covenant at Sinai:

1. A preamble identifying the suzerain is paralleled by an introduction identifying the God of Israel.
2. An historical view of what the suzerain did for the vassal is matched by deeds that God did for Israel.
3. Stipulations—the shalls and shall nots of the treaty and the covenant
4. The placing of the treaty and the covenant in a sacred site: the Hittite treaty is put before the idol of a god, while the covenant (the Torah) is kept in the Holy Ark.⁵

---

3. 2 Sam. 23:5.

4. Numbers 25:12–13. Phineas is rewarded for killing an Israelite and a Midianite woman who are having sexual relations as part of a pagan rite.

5. Ex. 25:16.

5. Instructions for periodic public readings of the treaty and the covenant

6. A list of witnesses—Hittite gods serve as witnesses in the treaty; "heaven and earth" are the witnesss at Sinai.[6]

7. Curses and blessings[7]—obedience to the suzerain or God will result in blessings for the vassal and Israel; curses will be the lot of the vassal and Israel if they break the pact.[8]

Sarna comments that despite the notable similarities between the Covenant at Sinai and the Hittite Suzerain–Vassal pact, the Covenant at Sinai is not a mere imitation.[9] There are many innovative aspects of the Covenant at Sinai, the most significant one being that the God of Israel is making a covenant with the people; ancient Near Eastern treaties of non-Israelite nations never feature a diety who establishes a covenant with human beings.[10] As I wrote in chapter 3 of this book, it probably didn't occur to the pagans of the ancient Near East to make a covenant with one of their gods, because for the most part, their gods were capricious and unreliable.

---

6. "I call heaven and earth to witness against you this day (Dt. 30:19)."

7. In the Covenant at Sinai the blessings precede the curses (Lev. 26; Dt. 28), while in the Hittite treaty, the curses come before the blessings (*ANET*, 205–206).

8. Sarna, *Exploring Exodus*, 136-8. Archaeology has uncovered a number of Hittite treaties between suzerain and vassal kings that date from the middle of the second millennium BCE. Two examples of Hittite Suzerain–Vassal treaties translated into English can be found in *ANET*, 203–206.

9. *ANET*, 136.

10. Ibid., 140.

ADDENDUM 2

Sh'mini Atzeret—Simchat Torah in Reform Judaism

LEVITICUS 23:33 STATES THAT Sukkot, the Festival of Booths, continues for *seven days*. The first day is a *miqra kodesh* "a sacred occasion" on which no work may be done. The next six days of Sukkot, when work may be done, are known as *chol hamo-eid* the secular (non-holy) days of the festival.[1] The last day of *chol hamo-eid*, the seventh day of Sukkot, is Hoshanah Rabbah, a day on which there are seven *haqaphot* (circlings) with the Torahs in the synagogue, and leafy willow branches are beaten against the pulpit, a custom which Theodore Gaster posits has to do with inducing fertility.[2] I think it may have to do with the induction of rain, similar to the waving of the lulav.

Despite the identification of Sukkot as a seven day festival in Leviticus 23:33, the Torah mentions an *eighth* day, which is also designated as a *miqra kodesh* "a sacred occasion."

> *Bayyom hash'mini* On the eighth day you shall observe
> *miqra kodesh* a sacred occasion and bring an offering by fire to YHVH,
> it is *atzeret;* you shall not work at your occupations.
>
> Leviticus 23:36

Because of the association of the word *atzeret* with the eighth day of Sukkot in this verse and in Numbers 29:30, the Rabbis named this festival Sh'mini

---

1. The five days between the first day of Pesach and the seventh day of Pesach are also known as *chol hamo-eid* the secular days of the festival.
2. T.H. Gaster, *Festivals of the Jewish Year* (New York: William Sloane, 1953), 95.

Sh'mini Atzeret—Simchat Torah in Reform Judaism

Atzeret. The meaning of the word *atzeret* is unclear; it is most commonly understood to mean "assembly" which renders Sh'mini Atzeret as "The Eighth Day of Assembly." The word *atzeret* comes from the Hebrew root *ayin-tzadi-reish*, which means "to close up." This suggests another understanding of Sh'mini Atzeret as "The Concluding Eighth [Day of Sukkot]."

In Orthodox and Conservative synagogues, the beginning of the festival of Sukkot is celebrated on two days—the first and the second days of Sukkot. Similarly, the conclusion of Sukkot, Sh'mini Atzeret, is celebrated on two days, the eighth and ninth days of Sukkot. The second day of Sh'mini Azeret which is the ninth day of the festival is known among traditional Jews as Simchat Torah, "Rejoicing with the Torah," the day on which there is a celebration in honor of the completion and beginning of the annual cycle of Torah reading. Reform Judaism differs in that we follow the biblical tradition of celebrating both the beginning of Sukkot and the conclusion of the festival for one day. Thus, in Reform, the first day of Sukkot is celebrated as a holy festival, and Sh'mini Atzeret and Simchat Torah are celebrated together on the eighth day of Sukkot as a holy festival. What, then, accounts for the disparity between the one day observance of the festivals in Reform and the two day observance by Conservative and Orthodox Jews?

The two day celebration of the festivals originates from the time of the Second Temple in Jerusalem, when the beginning of each month was determined by a visual report of witnesses who testified before a rabbinic court in Jerusalem to having seen the first crescent of the new moon. A month could be either twenty-nine or thirty days, depending on when the witnesses observed the first crescent moon. The distances from Jerusalem to the communities *outside* of the land of Israel were so great that news of the sighting of the new moon could not be received until several weeks had passed. Therefore, Jews outside of Israel, who were unsure as to when the previous month ended and the new month began, celebrated two days of the festivals in order to make sure that at least one of the days corresponded to the festival observance in Jerusalem. Today, even though there is no doubt as to the end of a month and the first day of a new month because the Jewish calendar has been standardized,[3] the observance of the second days of the festivals by Orthodox and Conservative Jews living outside of Israel has been retained as an intentional reminder that we are in exile. Reform

---

3. The calendar is no longer determined by visual sightings of the moon in Jerusalem. It is done by a complex fixed system that is said to have originated by Hai Gaon, the head of the Talmudic academy in Pumbedita, Babylonia, in the early eleventh century CE.

Addendum 2

Judaism does not see the need to make this kind of distinction between Jewish life in the Diaspora and in Israel. Thus, Reform Jews and Israelis follow the observance of the festivals as they are described in the Bible: the beginning of the festivals of Pesach, Sukkot and Shavuot are observed on one day. Similarly, the last days of the festivals of Sukkot and Pesach, Sh'mini Atzeret and the Seventh day of Pesach are observed for one day.

In Israel and in some Reform congregations, there are two days of Rosh Hashanah. This is because Rosh Hashanah comes at the beginning of the month. So even though in Temple times the beginning of the month of Tishre was determined by two witnesses who saw the new crescent moon, there was not sufficient time to let people in the outlying districts of Israel know that the new month had begun, despite the tradition of relaying the information by lighting bonfires on the mountain tops. Thus, even in Israel, Rosh Hashanah was celebrated for two days. That custom has survived to this day. The Reform congregations who observe Rosh Hashanah for two days, such as my congregation in Westwood, MA., tend to have many members who were raised in traditional homes where the observance of two days of Rosh Hashanah was standard.

ADDENDUM 3

The Documentary Hypothesis

IN THE LAST QUARTER of the nineteenth century, a German school of biblical criticism, headed by Julius Wellhausen and Karl Graf, proposed that the Torah is a compilation of human literary strata. Their theory became known as the Documentary Hypothesis. They posited that there are at least three documents or codes in the first four books of the Torah that are identifiable on the basis of vocabulary, style, content, and ideology. The first is J—a document whose author preferred to use YHVH as God's name. The second document is known as E—a document whose author tended to use *Elohim* as a name for God, and the third is P—a document that reflects the agenda of the Israelite *priesthood*. According to the proponents of the Documentary Hypothesis, the J, E, and P documents were interwoven throughout the first four books of the Torah (Genesis, Exodus, Leviticus, and Numbers) by a Redactor (R). The fourth document, which includes the entire book of Deuteronomy, is known as D.

The majority of contemporary biblical scholars view the Documentary Hypothesis as the most accurate lens for the study of the Torah. In the last century, however, several Jewish scholars such as Umberto Cassuto, Chanan Brichto, and Benno Jacob, argued against the validity of the Documentary Hypothesis from a literary and ideational perspective.[1] They saw the books of the Torah as more homogeneous texts. I would also point to the work of Nahum Sarna in *Understanding Genesis* who, in sharp contrast

---

1. See U. Cassuto, *The Documentary Hypothesis and the Composition of the Pentateuch*, a book which includes eight lectures devoted to pointing out the weaknesses and fallacies which Cassuto finds in the Documentary Hypothesis. In the same vein, see H. Chanan Brichto, *Names of God: Poetic Readings in Biblical Beginnings*, 3–34; and Benno Jacob, *The First Book of the Bible, Genesis*, 14.

Addendum 3

to Ephraim Speiser's *Genesis* in the Anchor Bible series, limits references to the "documents" to a few pages and seven footnotes. Robert Alter is a contemporary academic who expresses doubts about the Documentary Hypothesis. In his book *The Art of Biblical Narrative*, Alter challenges the significance of viewing the text of the Torah as disparate documents which have been stitched together. He emphasizes the key role of biblical authors and editors who "make use of composite materials to achieve a comprehensiveness of vision that is distinctively biblical."[2] In general, I am inclined to agree with those scholars who de-emphasize the importance of the Documentary Hypothesis, even though I sometimes find that knowing a certain passage has been identified as belonging to the Priestly code provides significant insights. An example is my discussion of the ritual of the Covenant of Circumcision where I concur with biblical scholarship that the priestly authors were interested in emphasizing the importance of circumcision as a sign of the covenant because it is a ritual,[3] their sphere of expertise. Other than that particular topic, I have chosen not to bring the findings of the Documentary Hypothesis to bear on my study. Instead, I have concentrated my analysis on trying to determine the overall covenantal themes in Genesis, because I think that a comprehensive approach leads to the most significant understanding of the Covenant of Abraham in Genesis.

---

2. Alter, *The Art of Biblical Narrative*, 133. See chapter 7, "Composite Artistry," in the same book, for a thorough discussion of Alter's literary approach to biblical narrative.

3. See chapter 7 in this book.

Bibliography

Aharoni, Yohanan, and Michael Avi Yonah. *The Macmillan Bible Atlas, Revised Third Edition*. New York: Macmillan, 1993.
Albright, William Foxwell. *From Stone Age to Christianity*. 2nd ed. Garden City: Doubleday Anchor Books, 1957.
———. *Yahweh and the Gods of Canaan*. London: Athlone, 1968.
Alter, Robert. *The Art of Biblical Narrative*. New York: Basic Books, 1981.
———. *Genesis, Translation and Commentary*. New York: W W Norton, 1996.
Barth, Lewis M., ed. *Berit Milah in the Reform Context*. USA: Berit Milah Board of Reform Judaism, 1990.
———. "Sermon For the Second Day of Rosh Hashanah: The Ten Trials of Abraham." *Hebrew Union College Annual* 58 (1987) 1-31.
Bernat, David A. *Sign of the Covenant Circumcision in the Priestly Tradition*. Atlanta: Society of Biblical Literature, 2009.
Blank, Sheldon. *Jeremiah, Man and Prophet*. Cincinnati: Hebrew Union College Press, 1961.
Brichto, Herbert Chanan. *The Names of God: Poetic Readings in Biblical Beginnings*. New York: Oxford University Press, 1998.
———. *The Problem of "Curse" in the Hebrew Bible*. Journal of Biblical Literature, Monograph Series, XIII. Philadelphia: Society of Biblical Literature and Exegesis, 1963.
———. *Toward a Grammar of Biblical Poetics: Tales of the Prophets*. Oxford: Oxford University Press, 1992.
Buber, Martin. *Tales of the Hasidim, Early Masters*. New York: Schocken, 1961.
Cassuto, Umberto. *Biblical and Oriental Studies*, Vol. 1: Bible, translated by Israel Abrahams. Jerusalem: Magnes, Hebrew University, 1973.
———. *A Commentary On the Book of Genesis, 1 From Adam to Noah*, translated by Israel Abrahams. 2nd edition. Jerusalem: Magnes, Hebrew University, 1972.
———. *A Commentary On the Book of Genesis, 2 From Noah to Abraham*, translated by Israel Abrahams. Jerusalem: Magnes, Hebrew University, 1964.
———. *The Documentary Hypothesis and the Composition of the Pentateuch*. Jerusalem: Magnes, Hebrew University, 1961.

Bibliography

Cohen, Norman. *Self, Struggle & Change: Family Conflict Stories in Genesis and Their Healing Insights for Our Lives.* Woodstock, Vermont: Jewish Lights, 1995.

———. *Voices From Genesis, Guiding Us Through The Stages Of Life.* Woodstock, Vermont: Jewish Lights, 1998.

Cohen, Shaye J. D. *Why Aren't Jewish Women Circumcised: Gender and Covenant in Judaism.* Berkely: University of California Press, 2006.

Diamant, Anita. *The Jewish Baby Book.* New York: Summit, 1988.

Eichler, Barry. "On Reading Genesis 12:10-20." In *Tehillah LeMoshe: Biblical and Judaic Studies in Honor of Moshe Greenberg,* 23-38. Winona Lake, Indiana: Eisenbrauns, 1997.

Eilberg-Schwartz, Howard. *The Savage in Judaism: An Anthropology of Israelite Religion and Ancient Judaism.* Bloomington: Indiana University Press, 1990.

Eshkenazi, Tamara Cohn, and Andrea L. Weiss. *The Torah, A Women's Commentary.* New York: Women of Reform Judaism, 2008.

Fishbane, Michael. *Biblical Interpretation in Ancient Israel.* Oxford: Clarendon, 1985.

———. *Text and Texture: Close Readings of Selected Biblical Texts.* New York: Schocken, 1979.

Fox, Everett. *The Five Books of Moses.* New York: Schocken, 1995.

Frankl, Victor E. *Man's Search for Meaning.* Boston: Beacon Press, 2006.

Friedlander, Gerald, trans. *Pirkei De Rabbi Eliezer.* 2nd ed. New York: Hermon, 1965.

Friedmann, Meir, ed. *Seder Eliahu Rabba,* second edition. Jerusalem: Bamberger and Wahrman, 1960.

Friedman, Richard Elliott. *Commentary on the Torah.* San Francisco: Harper, 2001.

———. *The Hidden Face of God.* San Francisco: Harper, 1995.

Frymer-Kensky, Tikva. *Reading the Women of the Bible.* New York: Schocken, 2002.

Ginzberg, Louis. *The Legends of the Jews, From the Creation to Jacob* 1. Translated by Henrietta Szold. Philadelphia: Jewish Publication Society, 1961.

———. *The Legends of the Jews, From Joseph to the Exodus* 2. Translated by Henrietta Szold. Philadelphia: Jewish Publication Society, 1964.

———. *The Legends of the Jews, Moses in the Wilderness, From the Exodus to the Death of Moses* 3. Translated by Paul Radin. Philadelphia: Jewish Publication Society, 1954.

———. *The Legends of the Jews, From Joshua to Esther* 4. Philadelphia: Jewish Publication Society, 1954.

———. *The Legends of the Jews, Notes to Volumes I and II* 5. Philadelphia: Jewish Publication Society, 1955.

———. *The Legends of the Jews, Notes to Volumes, III and IV* 6. Philadelphia: Jewish Publication Society, 1959.

Gold, Michael. *and Hannah wept: Infertility, Adoption, and the Jewish Couple.* Philadelphia: Jewish Publication Society, 1988.

Held, Moshe. "Philological Notes on Mari Covenant Rituals." *Bulletin of the American Schools of Oriental Research* 200 (1970): 32-40.

Heschel, Abraham Joshua. *God in Search of Man: A Philosophy of Judaism.* New York: Farrar, Straus and Giroux, 1981.

———. *Heavenly Torah, As Refracted through the Generations,* edited and translated with commentary by Leonard Levine and Gordon Tucker. New York: Continuum, 2006.

Hoffman, Lawrence A. *Covenant of Blood: Circumcision and Gender in Rabbinic Judaism.* Chicago: University Press, 1996.

Bibliography

Jacob, Benno. *The First Book of the Bible, Genesis,* abridged, edited, and translated by Ernest I. Jacob and Walter Jacob. New York: KTAV, 1974.

Kaufman, Yehezkel. *The Religion of Israel,* translated and abridged by Moshe Greenberg. Chicago: University of Chicago Press, 1960.

Levenson, Alan T. *The Story of Joseph: A Journey of Jewish Interpretation,* ed. Marc Lee Raphael. Williamsburg, VA: Department of Religious Studies, The College of William and Mary, 2004.

Levenson, Jon D. Commentary on Genesis in *The Jewish Study Bible,* edited by Adele Berlin and Marc Zvi Brettler, 8–101. New York: Oxford University Press, 2004.

———. *Creation and the Persistence of Evil: The Jewish Drama of Divine Omnipotence.* Princeton: Princeton University Press, 1994.

Levine, Baruch. *The JPS Torah Commentary Leviticus.* Philadelphia: Jewish Publication Society, 1989.

Lieber, David L., Chaim Potok, Harold Kushner and Jules Harlow, eds. *Etz Hayim, Torah and Commentary.* New York: The Rabbinical Assembly, 2001.

Pitzele, Peter. *Our Fathers' Wells: A Personal Encounter with the Myths of Genesis.* San Francisco: Harper, 1995.

Plaut, W. Gunther, ed. *The Torah: A Modern Commentary,* revised and edited by David E. S. Stein. New York: Union for Reform Judaism, 2005.

Pritchard, James B., ed. *Ancient Near Eastern Texts: Related to the Old Testament.* Princeton: Princeton University, 1969.

Sarna, Nahum M. *Exploring Exodus: The Heritage of Biblical Israel.* New York: Schocken, 1987.

———. *The JPS Torah Commentary Genesis.* Philadelphia: Jewish Publication Society, 1989.

———. *Understanding Genesis: The World of the Bible in the Light of History.* New York: Schocken, 1996.

Shanks, Hershel, ed. *Ancient Israel, Revised and Expanded.* Washington: Biblical Archaeology Society, 1999.

Segal, Alan F. *Sinning in the Hebrew Bible: How the Worst Stories Speak for Its Truth.* New York: Columbia University Press, 2012.

Speiser, Ephraim A. *The Anchor Bible Genesis.* Garden City: Doubleday, 1964.

Wiesel, Elie. *Messengers of God: Biblical Portraits & Legends.* New York: Random, 1976.

Zornberg, Avivah Gottlieb. *Genesis: The Beginning of Desire.* Philadelphia: Jewish Publication Society, 1995.

———. *The Murmuring Deep: Reflections on the Biblical Unconscious.* New York: Schocken, 2009.

www.ingramcontent.com/pod-product-compliance
Lightning Source LLC
Chambersburg PA
CBHW051737230426
43670CB00012B/2060